BEHIND THE MAN

KEVIN BORG

*The Trials and Triumphs
of a Soldier, Cop and Man of God*

Behind The Man

Copyright © 2024 Kevin Borg.
All rights reserved.

No part of this book may be used or reproduced in any manner without the written permission of the author. This book may not be reprinted without permission from the author.

Holy Bible, New Living Translation, copyright © 1996 Tyndale Charitable Trust. All rights reserved.

Book designed and formatted by Laura Murray at Peanut Designs www.pnutd.co.uk

Contents

1. The early years and joining the army
2. My first army posting abroad
3. God, me and the army
4. Meeting Emma and Jesus
5. Marriage and living out my newfound faith
6. Early days as a married couple
7. The calling
8. Operation Granby – The Gulf War
9. The real thing
10. My war diary extracts
11. Liberation
12. Transition
13. War and peace – RIP Michael Derry
14. From green to blue
15. My first shift and beyond
16. Isn't she lovely
17. On the beat
18. Onwards and upwards
19. Number 2
20. Promotion
21. Number 3
22. Acacia – The vision is born
23. Serious and Organised Crime
24. Working for the top floor – strategic!
25. Back to my roots
26. 2011 – And so it begins
27. The riots – Summer 2011
28. Chemo and all that jazz
29. Love, hope and charity
30. The moment of truth
31. On the home straight – retirement
32. The new normal family life
33. Losing my precious Emma

Dedicated to my late wife Emma,
who always saw the best in me.

26.9.1967 – 7.9.2018

Foreword
David Carr

When Kev asked me to review his book, I thought like other books, I would skip through it and give my approval. I was wrong! I needed to read all the story.

This lifetime journey was so gripping that I felt part of the story... from youth, born in a different culture, to a career in the British Army and then the police, the reader will enter the world of this man's life. The pain of war, riots, the struggle of early marriage – for all these issues Kev opens up his thoughts and actions to the reader's scrutiny.

It's difficult to explain one's personal faith in every day life. Kev deals with this in a range of topics including being mobilised for war and the sickness and death of his wife. These events allow us to capture his heart.

I have only recently become the minister of the church that Kev attends. I've already grown to love this man for his transparency of character.

This a must read. Be warned, he tells the story in the language his life was lived in – and that's what makes it real!

Rt Revd David E Carr OBE OSL KCHC

1.
The early years & joining the army

1975, Luqa, Malta. I was seven years old walking gingerly along a narrow 15-foot-high wall. My older sister was following me encouraging me to keep moving. I started to waver and wobble and as I plummeted over the edge my sister let out a yelp and tried to catch hold of me. I fell headfirst and landed on the marble flooring with a dull thud. My sister feared the worst but to her surprise I jumped up, checked myself over and ran away embarrassed!

Wise choice? I don't think so. Youthful and adventurous? Yes!

I always looked up to my dad, wanting to be like him. He was my hero. A man who was proud to have served with the SAS. Dad was a confident man that was fearless and believed he could do anything. He always drummed into us the importance of will power and not giving up.

Dad was old school and saw his role in the family as being our protector, provider and punisher for bad behaviour. If we crossed dad, he would get angry very quickly and it didn't go well for you if you crossed him. That said the majority of the time he was like a lion; the majority of the time when he was at home, he was sedentary because he had been at work all day. Mealtimes and confrontation meant there could be only one winner. Dad always had the steak and if I was lucky, he would cut a bit off and offer it to me on his fork. I would gratefully bite it off the fork before one of my siblings got there first.

I learnt to swim when I was six at a rocky beach in Malta. We used to go to Birzebbuga most weekends as a family. When I say family, I mean brothers, sisters, cousins, uncles, aunties and family friends. So, it was a tribal occasion! On one visit to the beach my dad decided that it was time for me to learn to swim without my armbands, so he caught hold of me and tossed me into the sea, despite my screaming and shouting not to. So that day I learnt to swim and swallow copious amounts of the Mediterranean Sea.

As a young boy although I had some friends, I was always quite lonely inside. Arriving in the UK, aged eight, I looked different to English boys and spoke differently, as I didn't have a brummy accent. I'd never thought of myself as different until other kids pointed out to me that I was a different colour to them. As far as I was concerned I was just brown because my parents came from Malta. I was no darker than someone with a good suntan. But in the 70s I stood out and it caused me a lot of challenges.

I can remember being at a primary school in Hay Mills, Birmingham, and taking my shoes off in the playground to prove to the other children that the bottom of my feet were white like theirs. Other lads wanted to fight me because I was different, and I can remember the worry I felt throughout the school day because a kid called Carl was going to fight me after school and all the other kids were spreading the word so there would be an audience. I felt so alone and just wanted to return to that little island called Malta where I was loved and accepted.

As I endured trying to fit in to my first school in England, St Bernadette's, things didn't get easier. One day I arrived at the school gates to be met by three lads, the ringleader was called Jerry. He was an Irish lad with a large nose. When he was taunting me, I could remember looking at it thinking how big and red it looked. He approached me and said: 'Your mum is a fat pig'. I instinctively punched him on that big, fat, red nose of his and it started to bleed profusely. I was pumped with adrenalin and incensed that he had been so rude about my mum, who I loved very much. To slander someone's mother is massively disrespectful and it had to be addressed. A teacher was soon alerted to the incident, and I was marched into the headteacher's office with the other boys.

We were all lined up and I sensed something bad was going to happen, and I was right. The headteacher reached for his cane and flexed it between his hands bending it to a place where I thought it would snap. He'd obviously done this before, and the cane was his weapon of choice. I had heard that on occasions he preferred to use the slipper, but this situation seemed to warrant a heavier weapon.
He walked to the end of the line where Jerry was standing and said: 'Were you involved?' to which Jerry replied with his bloody nose: 'Yes, sir'. Whack! Then a burbling, murmuring noise escaped from Jerry's mouth. The headteacher continued down the line of boys, caning each one of them. Burbling noise turned into blubbing and sniffing as all the culprits tried to control their reaction to the pain and humiliation.

Finally, he came to me flexing his cane as he did with all the others, he said: 'Were you involved?'.
I replied: 'What would you do sir if someone called your mum a fat pig?'

He paused and looked down at me intently. This could go one of two ways; an extra whack for being cheeky or an extra whack and sent home.

He must have been able to see the frustration in my eyes as this incident finally tipped me over the edge, resorting to violence, that had brought me to this point.

All the other boys were dismissed, and I was alone with the headteacher. I wasn't sure what was going to happen next. He closed the door behind the exiting boys and took a deep sigh as he looked at me. He walked towards me and then stooped down so we were eye to eye. His face was kind and he softened when he said to me: 'Kevin. you can't go round punching people on the nose. I know you're upset and that you love your mum very much, but this must never happen again'.

I was very grateful for what my headteacher did that day. I didn't get into any more bother whilst at school and, funnily enough, I started to make friends but it took a long time and there was pain and isolation along the way, at such an early age. Regretfully, Jerry and I never became friends.

Looking back, I was a hot-tempered little boy. As one of six siblings I often struggled to get my voice heard as the youngest. I felt that I always had to get my words out quickly before someone told me to be quiet, or lost interest in what I was saying. I guess that built up an attitude of frustration and I began to become intolerant of others as a way of getting back at them. So, a behaviour started to take root that would revisit me as I continued along life's journey. I'm told by my eldest sister that as a baby I was sometimes placed in a drawer to sleep and my sister would often watch over me whilst mum was busy with the others. She reminisced how she would stick her little finger in my mouth to watch me suckle. Lilian is 10 years older than me so I'm sure she was a great help to mum at that time.

Our home was always noisy as we are an opinionated family that argued a lot. I can remember that mum was often screaming out of frustration. Mum and dad argued constantly, and we probably didn't help. Looking back, it must have been tough for my parents to provide for us all. They always tried to give us their best and when mum was allowed to relax, I would snuggle up to her just grateful to have some of her precious time to feel comforted.

My mother wasn't educated but she had a purity of heart that was very rare. She was compassionate and always had time to listen. She would connect with your eyes and be able to read you. She was very insightful and could read people well. She was my dad's rear guard and safety net. She was a faithful and loving mother and wife.

There were some very happy family times in our home, and I was often the spectator watching my brothers and sisters talk about things I had no idea about, being the youngest sibling. At family gatherings though they would fuss me and get me to stand on a chair and sing, a bit like a performing seal! Dad would also make me stand on a chair and say: 'Red on Green on, jump!', simulating a parachute jump and roll onto the ground. Then he'd get up from his chair and show me how it was done.

Dad was my hero and I really looked up to him. He was a chilled guy and he was cool. He was a handsome young man and only had the best. Whenever he bought a camera or car he'd go for quality. Even when he bought me my first bike, he made sure it had all the bells and whistles. Dad was a tough guy too and wasn't afraid of confrontation if he felt he was right. He was a small guy, probably 5'7" with a wiry build. He smoked most of his life and learnt to drink whiskey whilst serving with the Special Air Service (SAS) in the 1960s. I was born in Hereford so have bragging rights on my birth certificate when it comes to occupation of father, Trooper: Special Air Service.

Dad's relationship with drink would prove to be volatile throughout his life. Mum was often on the receiving end. Many times, my brother and I would lie in bed listening to the arguing and would fear for mum. Throughout my early childhood I wet the bed up until I was 10. I just wanted mum and dad to be happy.

Dad was a product of his childhood as many of us are. His father was quite remote, and I gather from dad that he had to find his own way and got very little in the way of fatherly guidance. What he did do is provide for his family and, if needed, he would protect us as well. I always felt safe with dad as if he were invincible but once he had a drink the dynamics changed from felling secure to uncertainty. As a parent now I know that the perspective of a child is different. They are oblivious to the challenges that adult life brings. Pressures of life make us behave differently often in a way that we regret later.
Dad would have a last dance with alcohol when later in his life it had lasting consequences and seriously affected his health.

I was constantly trying to figure out during my lonely moments how to get people to like me. I wanted to fast track friendships so that they could just get on with me without the obligatory 12-18 months of trying to figure me out, looking past their prejudices.
Other kids used to find me quite funny, so I started to use that to try and build relationships. I desperately wanted friends I could trust. I tried too hard and became a bit of a school clown, which had the downside of people not taking you

seriously but turning to you when they wanted to be entertained.

Thankfully, when I went to secondary school, I met some great lads that were to become lifelong friends and loved me for who I was. I found that being around others that were genuine and kind, brought out the best in me. The feeling of having nothing to prove recalibrated me so that my behaviour was balanced, being able to have a serious conversation as well as lark around at the right moment.

Wisdom/Reflection
- *Above everything provide quality time to listen to your children, and really focus on hearing what they are saying*
- *Take time out from your kids when possible, remembering that your relationship as husband and wife is very important*
- *Stay connected, have family time where everyone has a voice*
- *Create time for laughter and fun, it's a great medicine*
- *Be aware of your actions even if you think the kids are in bed, you are responsible for maintaining a safe and peaceful environment for the family*

Many important lessons were learnt at an early age. I acquired the art of knowing when to speak and when to keep my mouth shut. This lesson was galvanised and deeply embedded in me when I first joined the army at 16 as a boy soldier, in the early 80s. Once again, I had to endure the prejudice due to the colour of my skin and only a couple of lads were willing to be associated with me to begin with. Isolation and being misunderstood was horrid. It knocked my confidence so that the real me was rarely seen to begin with.

Being away from home and not having someone to encourage me or listen to me was like being starved emotionally.

One evening I was sticking up for myself about some issue and the lad I was arguing with was getting visibly frustrated and red-faced. I laughed at him in a mocking way, and I think I advised him to 'do one', in other words, go away. The next thing I knew a guy called Steve entered the room. I knew Steve to be quite handy with his fists and I knew he didn't like me. He approached me and we came nose to nose, which was a big mistake on my part. With a lighting jolt of his head, his forehead met the bridge of my nose that cracked and started bleeding profusely. He walked off coolly as I nursed a broken nose.

Wisdom/Reflection
1. *Disagree by all means but don't try and humiliate the other party*
2. *Don't allow someone to invade your body space, especially in a confrontational situation*
3. *Don't be afraid to back off even if it looks like you've lost*

What disappointed me most was my instructors at that time that brushed the incident under the carpet and didn't address the situation. If they had I would have gleaned some learning as well as the other two guys. As a result, the resolution may have improved relationships. Instead, a barrage of racial abuse followed, and I just had to persevere because I was going to finish my training and be a soldier, whatever it took.

As it happened, I became very good friends further down the line with Jock, but, unfortunately, not with Steve, who became famous for skewering a litter of kittens he found with a mine prodder. Sick behaviour I hear you say. I agree. I learned some years later that Steve died in a car crash as he became trapped in his car that burst into flames. A sad ending to a life that seemed very troubled. Thankfully, although Steve and I weren't friends we did acknowledge each other, and I learned to forgive him.

As I got older, things seemed to getter better for me. Being accepted by people was very important to me. Perhaps because this didn't happen most of my life until people got to know me, getting past their own prejudices.

After completing my basic training and combat engineer training, I applied for selection to become a paratrooper within the Royal Engineers. This meant being posted to Aldershot where the training and selection took place. I had trained and thought I was fit enough. What I hadn't envisaged was the toll this would take on my 17-and-a-half-year-old body. I wanted to follow in my dad's footsteps and become an airborne soldier. I was light, could run fast and was full of enthusiasm. I had marched with weight on my back and was advised that I would have to get the hang of 'tabbing' which is marching at a very quick pace but not running.

I want to make it clear that I have the utmost admiration for those that partake in pre para and P Company (the selection training and testing to become a paratrooper). For those that give it a go and fail, and for those that give it a go and pass. Our airborne troops are second to none as a corporate fighting force. I also know that the camaraderie is very special, and friendships are made for life. That said, I was later to discover that those admirable qualities could be found in non-airborne units too.

The first week was just a blur of beasting. When I look back now it was comical. Every day out on the hills running and tabbing with 36lbs on your back. Maximum respect for the men that pass pre para and P company. I was just too young and inexperienced. My body wasn't strong enough and I don't think I was resilient enough with my mindset. Soon I was to develop a festering sore on the inside of my foot on the arch. Day after day we would run through water and mud with weight on our back that put extra pressure on my injury. Despite using neat iodine and plastic skin patches to try and cover the sore, it didn't heal. Clean dressings would be rubbed off within the first few minutes of setting off on a pain session.

I think the lack of support and encouragement played a big part in me deciding not to finish the course. One of the men referred to me as a sand-blasted nigger and I can't remember one positive conversation or friendship whilst I was there. I could have stayed and waited for my foot to get better but in that time, I would have been used as a skivvy and felt desperately alone and unhappy.

I was the only one that went to Aldershot from my intake so all the friends I had made in training were now posted across the world. The vast majority in BAOR (British Army Over the Rhine), West Germany. Perhaps they were the wise ones!

Despite feeling gutted about having failed the course, I decided that I was done. Once I had made the decision I had to go and see a corporal called Jugsy. He was a mountain of a man, and I wasn't looking forward to telling him that I wanted to leave. I went into his accommodation block and approached his room. He wasn't in and I thought great, an excuse to perhaps approach someone else. Then I heard a deep grunt and someone said: 'I'm in here'. The voice was coming from the toilets.

How he knew that I was outside his room I'll never know. I approached the cubicle where the voice had come from and immediately, I could see that the door was open and Jugsy was sitting on the toilet having a shit. The smell was overwhelming. He said: 'What do you want?'. I said that I needed to discuss how I was getting on. He said: 'Can't you see I'm having a shit?'. I awkwardly apologised and hurried away.

So, I'd have to look for another opportunity that came the next day when I attended the staff office. There were three staff members there that all looked me up and down and one of them said: 'What do you want?'. I said I no longer want to stay on the course as my foot was not getting better and I didn't think I was mentally or physically fit enough at this point in my career. In my mind I was thinking, and I hate the ethos of this place and the unfriendliness. The lack of encouragement and support. You may be thinking what did you expect Kevin? Well, now that I know what I know about getting the best out of people, you can get the desired performance with a more supportive approach. I have no issue with banter and tough love, believe me, but this was on another level. Fine if that's what you want, but it wasn't for me.

After notifying them that I wanted out, they sneered and said: 'Go to Crap Hat land then you waster…. get out of our sight'. What a relief, I was getting out of that hellhole. I packed my kit and was out of there posted to Nienburg, West Germany just before Christmas 1985.

Wisdom/Reflection
- *Know when to quit because that can be your victory*
- *No matter how isolated you feel do not tolerate abuse of whatever kind*
- *If there are no allies or friends in your environment, consider changing your circumstances. You are in control*
- *Remember your worth and seek out a critical friend who will support you*

Dad posing on a ship off the shores of Malta

Me aged 4 next to my dad's beloved Wolseley car

Mum and Dad as a young couple in Cyprus

2.
My first army posting abroad

I arrived in Nienburg on a dark night having landed at RAF Guttersloh then onto a train to Nienburg. I can remember getting a taxi from Nienberg Train Station in a Mercedes 190 to 21 Engineer Regiment Camp. I can remember being impressed with how plush the Mercedes was. In England you'd only drive a Mercedes if you were well off.

When I arrived, I reported to the guardroom where I was told where my accommodation was. I was to share a room with three other guys who I hadn't met yet. As I entered the accommodation block some lads were coming down the stairs and greeted me. I nodded and mumbled hello back. I wasn't sure who was who, so I kept my head down and shuffled to my room balancing my kit on my shoulders.

I felt alone and isolated not knowing anyone. Having to start again building friendships was emotionally exhausting for me. Having left 9 Para Sqn I was extremely fit despite having failed the course. This was going to stand me in good stead, as 21 Engr Regt was well thought of in the Corps of Royal Engineers. Fitness levels were high, and we were renowned for having a very good rugby team.

I soon settled into life in Support Troop, 1st Field Squadron. We prided ourselves on being 1st and were envied by 4 and 7 Squadrons, where competition was high whenever there were regimental competitions.

Not long after arriving I was told that I would be going to watch the regimental rugby team. I was only 18 when I joined 1st Fd Sqn, so was quite young compared to most who were in their 20s and 30s. I was certainly the youngest in my troop. Standard dress for such events was jeans, t-shirt and desert wellies. Desert wellies were sandy-coloured suede lace-up boots that were mandatory footwear.

The old sweats scared me because they were quite ruthless, particularly with sproggs, (newly-posted recruits). We were like slaves. If they wanted something, you were expected to get it for them. If there were any dirty jobs that needed doing, then as a sprogg you were expected to volunteer and do it. You didn't speak until you were spoken to. It was always risky knowing when to join in and laugh and when to stay quiet. It was horrible but you had to endure it, until a new sprogg came along then, if all was going well for you, you'd move up a notch in the pecking order.

I was up bright and early and made my way to the rugby pitch. On arrival I could see that there were groups of old sweats laughing loudly and they already seemed to be drunk. I scanned the groups to see where best I would fit in. I desperately wanted to see a familiar face, but I couldn't find one. I stood on the edge of the pitch trying to look interested in the game when two guys from my squadron approached me. They said: 'Stand there!' Where else was I going to go? They laughed and took out their dicks and started to piss all over my desert wellies, laughing and swaying as they relieved themselves onto me. I just had to stand there and take it. I smiled as they did it. They shook themselves off and sauntered away laughing and tottering as they went.

I soon became desensitised by the thuggish behaviour. I'm sure that it started to change me as my swearing and drinking increased. That said, I was never a big drinker and considered myself a lightweight compared to most.

Christmas leave was approaching, and I had been told that I could return to the UK for Christmas.

Friday nights were 'happy hour' in the Squadron Bar. I dreaded happy hour because you were expected to drink copious amounts of beer. The preferred weapon of choice was Herforder (known by squaddies as Herfy), or Grolsch beer ... by the crate loads. By now I was joined in the troop by another sprogg who would turn out to be a great friend, who I will always remember fondly as we navigated through this hell minefield together.

I stood nervously at the bar with a bottle of Herforder and tried not to make eye contact with anyone in particular as this could be construed as wanting to fight them or be seen as an act of defiance. I was stood with all the old sweats from my troop when some drunken lout from another troop shouted out: 'haircut time!'. He was brandishing a set of hair clippers, waving them from side to side menacingly. Others started to cheer, and I heard another shout, 'Sproggs line up'. I really didn't want a number 1 shaved head before going on Christmas leave. Loud shouting and chanting of Sprogg! Sprogg! filled the room that was dimly lit and stinking of beer. I was stood next to Sam who was a big Yorkshire rugby player who wore glasses. It was a well-known sign that if Sam took his glasses off, it was a pre-cursor to him taking a swing for you.

As the posse moved closer to me, I had resigned myself to having my head shaved. There was no way I was going to resist as this may be seen as failing the attitude test. Pathetic I know, perhaps I should have stood up for myself and made a stand. You had to be there to know that that wasn't a viable option. As one of the barbers went to grab hold of me Sam turned to me and said: 'Do you want your hair cut?'. Was this a trick question? Should I say yes? I found myself saying: 'No, I don't want my hair cut'. Sam took a step forward and removed his glasses and placed them on the bar and shouted in a broad Yorkshire accent: 'The lad doesn't want his haircut, alright!'. The henchmen dressed back and walked slowly backwards away from me, Sam and the others from support Troop. Even though I was a sprogg, I was a Support Troop sprogg and that offered me some protection from the other troop bullies. Sam nodded and winked at me and put his glasses back on. I waited until everyone was suitably well-oiled and slinked away out of the bar and back down to my room to bed.

The Squadron Bar was often a place of drinking games and competitions. Sproggs were often used as objects of fun and entertainment. Prior to attending the bar there would usually be drinks that you would share as a troop. So once you had knocked off on a Friday afternoon you would all sit in the troop office and have a beer or two together. In reality, it was more like six-10 beers. There were crates of the stuff that cost next to nothing so there was always lots to go round. So, this was viewed as pre-drinks prior to attending the bar.

Going to the bar was always an anxious time as you didn't know whether you were going to be a victim. One night, during happy hour, some bright spark had the idea of putting pillowcases on the heads of unwilling volunteers and then getting them to dance on the dancefloor whilst swinging and punching the other contestants on the floor! I watched in horror as bodies fell to the floor after being punched or hay baled by other hooded thugs. It was madness and it wasn't unusual for some to be concussed or lose teeth in the process.

Recently I met with a lifelong friend who served with me in 1st Fd Sqn. He reminded me over lunch about some of the other antics that went on that I wasn't aware of. He stared into space as he remembered being asked by his Staff Sgt to headbutt him. My friend, Jack, flatly refused to head butt his Staff Sgt, who became imposingly insistent and wasn't going to take no for an answer. This particular Staff Sgt was well respected and a man mountain, a tough guy by all accounts. Jack felt that he had no option but to comply but knew that either way he was going to be in a world of pain but perhaps with some kudos for taking part. Jack played his part and delivered the headbutt. He recalls that he wasn't sure if he put his heart and soul into it because he didn't really want to hurt his Staff Sgt. Maybe it would afford him some mercy when it came to his turn to receive the butt. No such mercy came after Jack had delivered his blow – there was a pause and then raucous laughter for Staff Sgt. As Jack prepared himself the anticipation of a sharp pain to his forehead followed. He was fortunate as his nose didn't break as the well-placed butt was just for play, but still caused Jack to see stars and have a reddening to his forehead for a day or two after.

Although I haven't witnessed it myself, I understand from a number of sources that another forfeit was to be chucked out of a window surrounded by a mattress for protection. To my knowledge there were no fatalities or serious injury. Oh, what fun we had. Note to the reader; I don't share these accounts for sympathy or to create shock and horror. It's just how it was and looking back now I'm just glad I survived. Did all of this damage me emotionally? Probably. It made you adjust and learn how to cope and respond or not as the case may be. I just held it all in and didn't show how things were impacting me. My fear was that one day it would play a part in how I would behave in the future. I had certainly become desensitised to violence and abuse and tried to use it to my advantage to be a better soldier. But in time to come would it have shaped me to be a better husband, father, friend?

During my time with 1st Fd Sqn a new Sergeant Major (SSM) was posted in and took over our squadron. He was a northerner; a Geordie I think, by the name of Wilkinson. He was immensely proud to be the SSM of 1st Fd Sqn, so much so that if you said 1 Sqn rather than 1st, you would get extra duties which in essence were a punishment, such as extra guard duty. I liked him. He did things that only he could do with the power he had. Thankfully, I was never on the receiving end but watching the misfortune often got us howling with laughter.

On one occasion a new lad was posted to 1st Fd from the UK, I'll call him Barry. This chap was overweight, and it was only a matter of time before the SSM addressed the issue. That time came on a Sqn parade. As the SSM inspected each rank he would pick various people up for different things like, collars not being straight or a twisted lanyard. Then he came to Barry and stepped back as if to act surprised by his weight. He then placed the brass end of his pace stick onto Barry's nose. He paused and there was silence that seemed to last an age and then the SSM said: 'You're too fat to fight'. In a loud voice he shouted: 'No one is to feed this man chocolate. You're going on a diet fat lad!'. Later that day I noticed posters all around camp, with Barry's face then the caption: 'Do not feed this man chocolate!'. Alas, within a week Barry was caught with a chocolate bar and was speedily returned to the UK. You may be horrified how individuals were singled out and then humiliated. Looking back, it was horrendous but it was acceptable at that time and as long as it wasn't you, you didn't give it much thought.

Whilst on parade the SSM wanted to know where a certain individual was. My policy was just to keep my mouth shut even if I knew the answer as often you ended up becoming a victim even though you were trying to be helpful. Jock shouted out from the ranks: 'He's just left camp in a Land Rover sir'. The SSM shouted back: 'Then get after him and bring him back to me you idiot!'. So, Jock turned to the right and ran off the square and out of camp knowing full well that he would never catch the Land Rover. It was madness but you just had to do as you were told even if there seemed to be no point.

Wisdom/Reflection
- *Remember sometimes you just have to do as you are told at the time but look for an opportunity to gain better understanding after the event*
- *If you're in a forced environment it doesn't have to dictate your behaviour, you can still behave with dignity despite your surroundings*
- *Be the best you can and if your environment has negatively influenced you, remember tomorrow is another day*

Without question, the most challenging experience of my time in the army was my Regimental Cadre. Essentially, it's a six-week course to test you to see if you have the skills and abilities to be a non-commissioned officer (NCO). For me, this was the first rung on the ladder, to earn the rank of Lance Corporal.

I can only describe the experience as brutal. Most of the cadre staff were either commando or paratrooper qualified, (59 Cdo and 9 Para). They were all highly-skilled soldiers that could teach us a lot. But with that came a high threshold to pain and suffering. Fifty-six of us started the course and at the conclusion only 22 of us would successfully complete the course. The first week was shock and awe, kit inspections, very early morning beastings that included all our kit being thrown everywhere. At the first inspection I was told that my boots were 'shit state' and I was told to flush them down the loo. Knowing that they wouldn't get past the U-bend I still had to try and get them down the pipe. My boots weren't up to standard because Staff Nixon AKA 'Harry the Bastard' wanted them to gleam like black diamonds as he called them. To be fair though, his boots were immaculate. During kit inspection it was just chaos as stuff was thrown around and staff were shouting so close to your face that their spittle peppered your face.

One particular entrepreneurial individual called Varley, discovered a gloss paint that transformed your boots into black diamonds. He started taking orders for the magic liquid and I must say I was sorely tempted. My better judgement said no and I passed by the short cut to heaven and persevered with spit and polish. The next day having completed our morning beasting of a very fast run we returned to our billet to see Varley's boots cut perfectly in two including the thick rubber soles. His bed space was empty, and he was off the course, presumably because of his Alan Sugar aspirations and trying to outwit Harry.

Nights were interrupted by being woken to banging and shouting as the staff got us out of our beds to deprive us of sleep. All the time shouting how crap we were and how more of us were going to be thrown off the course if we didn't shape up. We'd then be put in stress positions and hosed down with a fire hose and freezing cold water. How long would this go on for? Six weeks, no let-up. In fact, rumour has it that at one point the Commanding Officer told the cadre staff to ease up. For them breaking as many of us as possible was their performance indicator.

Early one morning we were all punished for something like potatoes growing in the gas chamber of our weapon. We were doubled (run not walk) around the parade square with our weapons above our heads. I was asked: 'Is that heavy Borg?'. Now how do you answer that question? If I say no, then I sound cocky and sure as eggs are eggs I'll be given another one to raise above my head. If I say yes then I appear weak, so I'll probably get another one to build me up, to make me stronger! The one thing you didn't want to do is get the rest of the lads punished for a wrong answer or action. I went for the 'no staff give me another please'. Weakness wasn't an option.

As we progressed through the course more and more bed spaces became vacant as candidates were removed for underperforming. I was hanging in there by the skin of my teeth but determined to pass.

Next lesson, section attacks. Essentially, this is where you learn the different formations and tactics to take an enemy position. This occurred well into the course and was the bit where we got to fire lots of ammunition and make lots of loud bangs. This is where my ethnicity put me in a position of disadvantage. Whilst standing in three ranks being briefed by the staff, one of the instructors turned to me and said: 'Borg, haven't I seen you somewhere before?'. I knew that a punchline was coming, and I felt very uncomfortable because I had a feeling that I knew where this little charade was going. I didn't answer because I sensed that the question was rhetorical. 'Because I'm sure I saw you at Goose Green'.

Some started to snigger because the instructor was intimating that I was an enemy Argentinian soldier that were defeated at the battle of Goose Green in the Falklands War. Now looking back, it seems just like banter that was harmless. I'm all for banter even when it may be at my expense, but the tone and the intention is worth paying attention to. 'Borg, fall out and double away to the enemy trenches because that's where you belong'. So, I had to double away to the trenches that were intended to be the trenches of the enemy that the rest of the course would attack. I couldn't help thinking I'm on the same side as you and I joined the army to be part of a team that would protect our country and its interests. I was willing to give my life for my country, but not to be treated like this. It saddened me inside and I pitied my instructors because of their prejudice and their inability to get the best out of people without fear and humiliation. I know that quite a few of my buddies on the course felt it was unfair but had to keep their heads down or it could spell trouble for them.

Wisdom/Reflection
- *Knowing when and how to stand up for what is right and challenge injustice is important to our character. Timing and delivery are key*
- *You can still hold true to your values despite others imposing hardship and pressure*
- *Hold short accounts with others particularly those who have wronged you. The power of forgiveness is immense*
- *If at all possible, find a confidant that you can share your feelings with.*

Harry the Bastard was the Drill King. I recall him doing the Drill Instructors course at Pirbright, where the Guards are based. It's the mecca of all things drill. We spent hours and hours of time on the drill square practicing drill in preparation for our passing out parade that was now in sight. It wasn't unusual for us to have to stand perfectly still for over an hour until the next command was given. By now my boots were starting to look like black diamonds and it had been some time since they had seen the U-bend of the toilet. Our numbers had shrunk, and it felt like a real achievement to still be in the mix. As we stood perfectly still, I remember Harry, who was immaculately dressed and a fine figure of a man, look at me and say:

'Borg, black is beautiful but white is right!'. I was slightly puzzled but looked straight ahead with no emotion. Puzzled because I wasn't black, and I didn't think I was beautiful either. If I was black, I would be proud of it. The only thing I could relate to is that the tone of my skin attracted discriminatory comments.

Six weeks later I was done. Along with 21 other successful candidates I passed the Regimental Cadre. Not bad for a scrawny 21-year-old with brown skin.
During the course my weight dropped to 10 stones, and I was probably the fittest I've ever been. What did I learn?

Wisdom/Reflection
- *Despite adversity I learned to persevere*
- *Even when it's personal, press on*
- *Even if you are misunderstood or wrongly treated, stay humble and gracious. It will pay off and stand the test of time*

I don't feel any ill towards the cadre staff and, despite their methods, I did take away some learning and it taught me to be more empathetic to how people may feel on the receiving end of injustice. It's taught me how to be a better soldier and I learnt some great tips from my peers and staff alike. So, for that I thank you.

Interestingly, over 30 years later I bumped into Harry the Bastard, literally when on holiday in Lanzarote. I was walking to the gents and as I approached the door, three or four men exited together. I stopped in my tracks and looked at the lead man and hissed: 'Harry the Bastard!'. There was a moment of silence and then a roar of laughter as the other men with him patted him on the back and one said: 'He is indeed'. We exchanged pleasantries and I gave him some context around how I knew him. Harry was an old man and no doubt had mellowed as he would have retired from the army many years ago. I wished him well and continued to enjoy my holiday with my daughters.

If I had looked at the course as a whole, I wouldn't been able to cope with the thought of no sleep and tortured body and mind. *I just focused on getting through the next minute, the next hour and sometimes when it was really intense, the next second.*

Even as I write this book it's emotionally draining as I relive some things that I'd rather forget. But if I think of how long this may take me to finish, I may be tempted to pause or stop. So, I apply the same principle as I did back in 1988 on my cadre course.

Wisdom/reflection
- *The incremental approach of breaking things down now forms the way I stay fit, manage my relationships and make life decisions*
- *Pain often promotes growth, it's uncomfortable at the time but the benefits come later*
- *Sometimes 7/10 will do. Consider where you are putting your energy*
- *Allow others to help you and use your strengths to help others*

The cadre course was an extreme example of not quitting. I have since learned that sometimes it is better to gracefully withdraw. Looking back perhaps I should have withdrawn from the cadre course. In a funny sort of way, I felt deep inside that I had to push through no matter what. Conversely, withdrawing from para selection was totally the right move in the circumstances. Knowing when to push through would be a recurring theme in my journey as I experienced greater challenges that would push me to the edge.

Me cradling the light machine gun on a very cold night in West Germany

3.
God, Me and the army

I was never really one for religion but would never disrespect those that were religious. Being raised as a Maltese catholic meant I had completed my Holy Communion and Confirmation ceremonies. I can remember praying as a child if I had a nightmare or if I needed to pass an exam at school. Basically, I used God as a bit of a good luck charm.

When I was about seven and living in Malta, I attended a state school there in Luqa. It was very strict, and it didn't help that I didn't speak Maltese. Every morning we would have to form in neat rows in the school quadrangle where the Maltese national anthem music would play over really crackly speakers and we were expected to sing with enthusiasm. The chosen one would have the honour of raising the national flag. Then we would file into class for handkerchief inspection. On this occasion I only had a tissue so I was made to write I must bring a clean handkerchief to school ... in Maltese! This was the 70s after all and hankies were still an essential for young boys with snotty noses.

A priest would regularly come to our school and on one occasion I can remember him talking to me. He was a kind man and I felt that he really cared and was interested in talking to me. He seemed very old to me but what he said captivated me. He was talking about the importance of prayer and then he gave me a leather-bound small book. On the front it said, 'Small Missal' and at the bottom of the cover 1947. I can't imagine that he gave everyone one of these books. It wasn't new so I presumed it was his and was honoured that he was giving it to me. When I got home, I looked through the book and could see that it was very old, and each page contained prayers and the rituals of mass. I spent a lot of time reading it as I recall. I'm amazed that I still have the book to this day. How it remained safe and not lost is a mystery as we were to move country and home several times as a family.

When preparing for my Holy Communion I can remember not taking things too seriously when being instructed by the nuns. Me and my brother would find most things funny apart from when the nuns looked sternly at us and informed us that if we didn't recite our prayers correctly, we would go to hell! That focused our minds and there was no more playing around in that session.

So, although I had a grounding in the catholic faith, my lifestyle certainly was not God fearing. That said I wasn't a murderer but some of my attitudes and behaviours were less than honourable.

Wisdom/Reflection
- *What you think something is, isn't, religion isn't God*
- *What is cultural doesn't always amount to faith*
- *There is power in ritual if it doesn't become routine and bears good fruit*

As a soldier you were required to go to church. It was mandatory and for some an experience to be endured rather than embraced. Whilst serving as a Junior Leader boy soldier in old park Barracks, Dover, we were issued with small red bibles by the padre at the end of one of the church services. Everyone had to take one and most hid them in their suitcase on top of their locker, including me. I can't remember what the padre said in that particular service, but I do know that I'm writing about it now because I think it was a significant moment that got me thinking about spiritual things. That said the Gideon little red New Testament and psalms didn't come out of my suitcase for a long time.

It was late in 1985 when I had been posted to 21 Engr Regt in West Germany when the most significant event in my life occurred.

Leading up to that time, looking back, a narrative was building. I was now going steady with a girl that would later become my wife. Whilst on leave in the UK I would visit the local catholic church near to where mum and dad lived. In those days church doors were left unlocked so people could go to pray or just be quiet. I would go secretly during the day and stand at the back of the empty church. I would gaze at the sullen white figure on the cross at the front of the church and whisper to myself, you are either the son of God or a liar that has deceived many. Then I used to look into the face of that man hoping that he would answer me. I did this on more than one occasion and would lie to my girlfriend Emma, about where I had been.

So, something was stirring inside of me, something had been ignited at that church service in Dover when I received my little red book. But I couldn't put my finger on what it was. It certainly wasn't the religion I had been brought up with. This was something mysterious that I couldn't see but sensed was around me and real.

You often read about those that have a spiritual or conversion experience, being in a low place. Some are chronically addicted to drink, drugs or something else that steals away their quality of life. There seemed to be a point in most people's life when they consider the eternal even if it's for a brief moment. The death of a loved one or a near death experience can focus the mind on all things spiritual.

As a young boy I was very scared of the dark and I have memories of my brother scaring me about the dark, ghouls and the devil. I have to say that at about the age of five I was terrified of the dark and often had nightmares. Looking back, it was quite an extreme response and my nightmares were frequent. Mum would always answer my call in the middle of the night as I lay frozen, scared to move in case whatever was in my dreams materialised into the reality of my bedroom. Mum would come into my room and often I would need a wee at the same time so I would hold onto the back of her nighty, as she led me down to the loo.

I guess being aware of evil cultivated a longing to be protected by good. My mum would encourage me to pray to Jesus when I was scared. I did wonder at times why He didn't stop the nightmares or at least appear in them and rescue me. I believed Jesus was good but saw Him more as a figure that was almost stone-like, a statue with power, but not as a personable God that loved me. Just like my prayers they were a ritual or procedure that came from the head and not the heart.

I don't think I had much of a conscience of doing wrong really. From stealing things from shops to looking at porn mags that one of my mates stole from the paper shop he worked at. These were all things that you could put down to being young and growing up. Being male and red blooded? Behaviours would soon form habits that I would have to address as an older man.

My parents didn't talk to me about 'the birds and the bees' but from an early age I knew I really liked girls. At the age of five I can remember saying to a girl of the same age as me: 'Quick pull your pants down because a foxy is coming!'. My real intention was to see her private parts. What the foxy had to do with it I'm at a loss to explain. How I remember the incident so clearly and what I said is another mystery. I know it sounds quite comical and trivial, perhaps, but, at that age, I think it was an unhealthy interest in things that should have been explored in more appropriate circumstances.

Walking to school on a cold winter's day at the age of eight I was to see my first pornographic image in the form of a magazine page that was laid waste on the pavement. I can remember seeing it and picking it up and being intoxicated by the imagery. An unhealthy appetite was growing that would need to be fed more and more as I was exposed to stuff that exploited men and women, illustrating a distorted view of relationships and intimacy.

Porn was so prevalent among my circle of friends in secondary school. I'll never forget that one of my inner circle brought a porn mag to school. We all gathered round to gaze at the pages. Frequent shouts of: 'Slow down! Slow down' as the pages were swiftly turned. Simon foolishly took the magazine into our next class, Religious Education. I looked back to where Simon was sitting and could see his bag under the wooden desk. He had a menacing look on his face and I knew he was a risk taker, but I didn't know he was as reckless to do what he did next. Whilst Mr Drake was turned towards the blackboard, Simon reached for his bag and took out the mag. I could see him turning the pages whilst he balanced the mag on his lap. To this day I'll never understand why Mr Drake suddenly turned around and looked intently at Simon and said to him: 'What do you have under your desk Simon?'. 'Nothing sir,' Simon replied. The tension in the classroom was electric because we all knew he was doomed. Simon's pallor had turned from rosy cheeked to ashen grey.

'Come to the front Simon and bring the nothing that you have under the desk with you!' – I felt sick for him and wanted to help but there was nothing I could do as Simon was already out of his seat walking towards the front of the class. There were low murmurings from others in class and then gasps as the porn mag became visible. Mr Drake's head visibly changed colour to a deepening purple, and I could see the veins protruding on the side of his head.

Simon was now stood in front of Mr Drake who snatched the magazine violently from him and shouted: 'Filth!'. Spittle sprayed from his lips that were pursed tight as he tried to contain his anger and disappointment.

Mr Drake was one of my favourite teachers and was well liked by most students. He liked Simon too and that day I think we experienced the sorrow of him knowing the potential negative influence that would seep into our attitudes and behaviours. The eyes truly are the windows to your soul and what goes in I would learn affects how we view the world and everything in it.

I would learn as I continued in my time in the army that porn would be a recurring theme, in a male dominated environment that indulged in many vices. At the time it seemed normal to watch porn on an evening with a room full of lads. It was just like watching a box office film. We'd bring crisps, sweets and beer and often would pee into the empty bottles because we didn't want to lose our place on the sofa or were just too bone idle to walk to the toilets. I'm embarrassed to say that I was one such person.

Although I wouldn't have classed myself as a big drinker, I certainly did drink. At the time it wasn't necessarily for enjoyment, it was more about fitting in. The normal routine was to get the 3S's out of the way (shit, shave and shower) and then get ready for the night out. Drinking usually commenced with your troop in what would be our work offices, but they weren't offices, more like big garages that housed all our vehicles. The rest room had old sofas that we used to sit on to have a brew or indeed to drink at the end of the working day. Then we'd be off to the NAAFI bar all spruced up prior to going out on the town, to a German club or bar. If we were really adventurous, we would venture out as far as Hanover.

One of my very good friends, who was a small Welshman, had bought an Austin Allegro. They were nicknamed the 'All Agro' because they were so unreliable. The car needed to be tested, pretty much like an MOT prior to it receiving its British Forces Germany (BFG) number plates. The Allegro hadn't yet been tested but we were desperate to go out and cruise the streets in our 'All Agro'. So, what did we do? We 'borrowed' some BFG plates from another parked car and off we went.

Just a few months into my posting to Nienburg I had a small friendship group. Some of the old sweats had started to talk to me but I still felt like I was on probation. The trauma of the first few weeks had subsided and either I had become desensitised to the culture, or I was still in shock.

One evening we were in the NAAFI bar drinking and I was well on the way to being quite drunk. I can remember being part of a conversation with some old sweats who were talking about a guy from another troop who they didn't like. I saw this an opportunity to impress and show my loyalty to them by showing my irritation with the guy too, even though I didn't even know him. Clearly the drink was talking as, before I knew it, I was vowing to smash his face in. Arrangements were swiftly made to locate the guy so I could fulfil my threat. What had I got myself into. I could hardly stand, and the room was spinning, but I knew I had to follow through on my slurred promise to smash his face in.

We left the NAAFI bar to return to our troop office for some reason and there I was faced with this guy who I had vowed to fight. I made an aggressive stance and in so many words told him I was going to sort him out and then I lunged at him throwing a punch that missed and, unbalanced, I slipped and fell to the floor. I was not a pretty sight as he sat on top of me punching my head. In the wrestling I was now on my stomach, and he was grinding my face into the painted concrete floor. When I stopped moving, he stood up and walked away. At the time I could hear some of my troop shouting and encouraging me to get some punches in. I might as well have been a punchbag as I had no co-ordination and my strength had sapped away. What on earth was I doing. Some of the guys helped me up and dusted me off, giving me their commiserations for getting battered and not keeping my promise to smash his face in. I felt humiliated and silly for even entertaining the idea of fighting someone in such unwise circumstances.

The next day I woke up with my face covered in vomit on my pillowcase. My head hurt and when I looked in the mirror, I could see that I had friction burns on my face. I so wanted to apologise to the guy for my actions, but it wasn't the done thing and it may have even made matters worse, so I put this one down to experience and vowed that if ever I had the inclination to fight someone, it would be when I'm stone cold sober.

During my time in the army, I had the pleasure of serving with some high-quality people. It's amazing the difference it makes when you have a good boss, that is fair and compassionate, as well as being a decisive leader. Spence came to our troop as our Staff Sergeant. He was a breath of fresh air and had a knack of making you feel valued and treating us all fairly no matter where you were from or how long you had served. He was the ray of sunshine during my remaining time in Nienburg and I have a lot of funny and happy memories as a result of his leadership. What came through very strongly with Spence was that he loved his family above all else. He honoured his wife and girls and seemed content with life. He was a fixer and could get hold of anything kit-wise which was always a bonus. Our reputation as a troop in the Squadron improved too, under his leadership. There was far more laughter heard when he was around but conversely when a job needed to get done, we focused.

It wasn't so for all the troops. Bullying was accepted and/or overlooked as 'character building' by some. One particular sprogg in one of the field troops, was an extreme example of bullying that made as a story in The Sun newspaper. This poor chap became a target and although he looked very thin and very miserable, very few of us had any idea what he had had to endure. It transpired later that he was tied to the fire escape and left in his underwear for long periods of time. There was also evidence that the soles of his feet had cigarette burn injuries. I seem to recall that there were rumours of sexual abuse as well. When the extent of the bullying came to light it transpired that a small number of soldiers were responsible. The vast majority condemned the behaviour and even in those times it was viewed as being absolutely unacceptable.

Despite the very macho culture, there was a strong sense of loyalty, and I had no doubt that we were a brotherhood and would back each other up. As I became more established in the troop life became a little easier for me, this coincided with the way that Spence led our troop.

Wisdom/Reflection
- *Words spoken that seem insignificant at the time can become significant on the future*
- *Your eyes are the windows to your soul and what you see and think about will influence your actions*
- *Fear can breed negative behaviours in an attempt to compensate for how you feel*
- *Religion and ritual won't protect you but a relationship with Christ will*
- *Being drunk will loosen your tongue and your inhibitions and usually ends in tears*

4.
Meeting Emma and Jesus

I had a girlfriend that I had met whilst on leave from my basic training. I met Emma in a Birmingham nightclub. I was captivated by her as I looked down onto the dancefloor watching her dance. I was with a good friend of mine who was a school friend and was on leave following basic training too. I said to Dougie: 'Look at her, she's beautiful!'. I waited for the next song to be played by the DJ then I took the place on the dance floor.

I fancied myself as a bit of a mover so manoeuvred in so that she could see me. Emma smiled shyly at me, and I smiled back adding a wink for good measure. I was pleased with my performance on the dance floor (note: tongue in cheek moment), so I asked her if I could buy her a drink. She accepted so I led her to a quiet place in the club, where we still had a panoramic view of the dancefloor. I left Emma to go to fetch her drink, which was lager and black (blackcurrant). I returned with the drinks and sat down. I paused and held her chin and said: 'You're a pretty little thing aren't you?'. Reading it back now I'm cringing but at the time it was the precursor to me making the next move, as I leaned forward for our first kiss. I was in! I couldn't believe I had just kissed the most beautiful girl in the club.

I didn't want the night to end, but end it must, so we arranged to meet the next day. Venue: The Lickey Hills where we could go for a lovely walk to get to know more about each other. After walking for about half an hour I scanned the ground and found a great spot where I could have another one of those captivating kisses from Em. I suggested the spot to sit, and she lowered herself onto this semi-flat piece of grass. From the very beginning of our relationship Emma knew I was a cheeky chappy and even whilst getting to know each other the night before in the club, we laughed a lot together. I didn't know it at the time, but I was probably light relief for Em as her mum was quite poorly with breast cancer, and the prognosis was not good.

So, I moved closer as we sat together and enjoyed looking at Emma's features, particularly her eyes, that were a hazel green colour. I gently pushed her back in an assertive manly fashion as I lay beside her. I recall the weather being nice, so the grass was dry and the temperature was comfortable. Perfect conditions for another kiss. As I was preparing my move, I was quietly confident that I wouldn't be denied a kiss. As I brought my face close to hers, ensuring that my lips were in alignment I noticed some dried rabbit droppings on a little mound not too far from her head. The next bit is hard to comprehend, but I found myself plucking one of them from the cluster and as Emma closed her eyes in expectation of a sweet tender kiss, I plopped the dropping straight into her mouth. Immature, foolish, inconsiderate, stupid. All justified descriptions of me at that moment. The dropping hit the back of her throat; her eyes shot open as her gag reflex spat the poop straight back out into the atmosphere. I can remember being impressed how far it projected. Emma leapt up and started slapping me with both hands and shouting how stupid I had been. Very quickly her shouting turned into laughter, and I seized the moment to embrace her and then we kissed whilst laughing at the same time. Youthful exuberance. It was a high-risk strategy mixed with special needs on my part. Despite my gross immaturity Emma agreed to see me again.

That year (1984), Emma had attended the Billy Graham Crusade, that was being held at Villa Park, I think. I didn't know this at the time, but Em was to share her experience with me later.
As worldly youngsters we lived out secular values, so intimacy was an important part of our relationship, certainly for me as a red-blooded male that selfishly wanted his needs met. I looked forward to returning to the UK on leave to see my sweetheart, who I was growing closer to through the letters, telephone conversations and closeness when we were together.

Whilst on leave I found myself thinking about what that church service when I received my little red book, New Testament and Psalms. I would lie to Emma about where I was as I visited a catholic church near to where my parents lived. Something was happening but I didn't know what. I was thinking a lot more about God and I had a curiosity about if it was all true.

Getting ready one evening to go out on the town. There was going to be a group of us so there was a hustle and bustle in the rooms as some ironed their glad rags and others got showered. Music was playing and the different aftershave fragrances trailed through the corridors as most hoped to find a mate for the night in the form of a pretty German girl.

I was last to go for a shower as I inhaled the concoction of fused fragrance aromas that were heavy in the air. The ablutions block was empty, so I had a choice of any of the three shower cubicles. I chose the far right one because the shower seemed more powerful than the other two. I turned the shower on and waited for the water to warm up. As I got into the shower, I wondered what the night would bring. I'm quite methodical when showering so I start with washing my hair and work my way down my body. Once all the suds have been rinsed off, I usually stand and just look up into the shower head, letting the water refresh my face and head. Tonight was no different and as I allowed the water to cascade over my head, the strangest thing happened. Out of the shower head came a man's voice that said: 'Don't forget about me Kev'. I couldn't believe what I had just heard! An audible voice but no body. How could this be. I wasn't drunk and I don't take drugs. I've never heard voices before and to my knowledge didn't have any significant mental health issues. I say significant because I believe most of us have a degree of poor mental health at one time or another.

So what would you do if you heard a man's voice in the same shower cubicle as you with the absence of a body that the voice came from. The first thing I did was raise my fists as an automatic reflex. My eyes scanned the small space I was in and I can confirm that I was definitely alone. This all happened within a couple of seconds of hearing the voice. So what did the voice sound like? Did it have an accent? Did it shout or whisper? Even though it was over 35 years ago I still remember it vividly. The volume of the voice was that of a normal conversational volume but loud enough to hear over the patter of the water. There was no accent but the voice was English and neutral. It wasn't a threatening voice but was calm with a sense of familiarity. It was as if the voice was appealing to me. Whoever it was seemed to think he knew me well enough to call me Kev.

Whose voice was it? All these questions were racing through my mind as I tried to evaluate what was happening, quick time. Adrenalin was rushing around my body and my senses felt electrified. With my fists raised I backed out of the shower and scanned left and right still expecting to see someone appear. I snatched the next cubicle curtain aside to find it empty. I did the same with the cubicle curtain furthest away. Empty. I forcefully pushed open the toilet doors, all empty, as was the room with the bath in it. I was alone with this voice. Could the owner of the voice see me? Would he reveal himself? I now came to the conclusion, standing naked in the middle of the ablutions that there was something supernatural going on. Crazy I know but what other explanation was there? I wrapped the towel around my waist and as I reached out to open the door to head for my room, one of the guys told me to hurry up as they were ready to hit the town. I said that I wouldn't be going with them. 'What's wrong?' he said, 'You look like you've seen a ghost', 'I may have,' I said. The rooms soon emptied to excited laughter and banter, and I was alone in my room.

I shared a room with three other guys, who had all gone out that night. I flicked my light on above my bed and sat on the end of my bed. I just stared down at the floor wondering what had just happened. My mind then thought about the little red book the padre had given me. I felt prompted to retrieve it from my suitcase on top of my locker. As I flicked through the pages, I started to read one of the gospels. As I read the words of Jesus speaking, I could hear his voice in my head as I read the words. It was the same voice as I had heard in the shower! It was like having had a conversation with someone on the phone and then meeting them in person and putting the voice to the person. That's what was happening here. The words I was reading were the words of the same one that I had heard in the shower. As this reality dawned on me, I bowed my head. I paused and then said: 'Lord if that was you in the shower then I'm in'. At the time I didn't feel any strange sensations and there were no bright lights. I just felt very peaceful, and I had a deep sense that I had found the truth. So, this Jesus wasn't a liar that had deceived many. That night I believed that he was the Son of God, who loved me and had made himself known to me. This encounter with Jesus would change the rest of my life. This wasn't an outside in change, it seemed to be an inside to out transformation. I felt free and I felt accepted. I felt honoured that God cared enough to break into my life and speak to me, this little Maltese lad.

I slept well that night and had placed my little red book on my shelf. Although it shared a place on the shelf with other bits and pieces, it didn't take long for it to be noticed. I saw it as a small act of faith, as if to say to God, I'm willing to be known as one of your followers. Almost immediately a couple of the guys commented on why I didn't seem to swear any more. My mouth was a bit of a sewer when I was in the army and swearing was just seen as an accepted form of vocabulary. I didn't make a conscious effort not to swear, I just found myself not swearing. I started to notice that some of the guys had started to distance themselves from me. They had a curious look in their eye, not quite being able to put their finger on what had changed. Clearly, since I had talked to God and experienced him calling me, something had changed, and it was starting to get noticed. One of the guys in my room had tentatively asked what the little red book was on my shelf. When I told him it was a bible, he asked whether I believed and for the first time in my life I had counted myself a believer in Jesus.

I started to feel concerned that my newfound faith was going to affect the way I was treated by the others. It had taken me a long time to be sort of accepted and I had a feeling that this was all going to change.

All the rooms that branched off the main corridor were where the 'singlies' (single soldiers), lived on camp. Married personnel lived in quarters that weren't too far away from the barracks. The most senior rank in the accommodation was in charge of 'the lines' which was a floor of rooms. Stokesey was a corporal and was a big Yorkshireman that drank a lot. He owned a Ford Capri 2.8i in metallic blue, I think. I always used to look at his car enviously as it was an iconic car even back then.

Stokesey had got wind that I had started reading the bible. He saw me in the corridor and told me that if he saw me reading the bible, he'd sort me out. He was quite aggressive when he said it, so I took him seriously and nodded respectfully, to acknowledge that I had heard what he had said. What had made him so anti? This was going to be tricky for me because if I disobeyed him, I was quite sure it would end in violence and further isolation for me. What was I going to do because I had this feeling of fulfilment in me and I wanted to learn more about the one I had given my life to. How could the words in this little red book have such an impact on my behaviour and give me such hope. It was like I'd made a new friend that already knew everything about me and loved me no matter what. Oh, and he could do the impossible and was accessible 24/7. I was later to read that all the words in the bible are spirit breathed and inspired. So, they weren't just words, they held power and when you put your faith in them good things happened.

Although I took Stokesey's threat seriously, I wasn't going to stop reading my bible, in fact I was going to read it more. I feared God more than man, I just had to be careful when I read it. Stokesey had his spies who would report to him, so I resorted to reading the bible in the toilet cubicle.

Within a very short time things changed for me. I wasn't invited out to go drinking and I was left out of a lot of the social activities. So, I was often left in the room alone as all the others had gone out drinking. This gave me an opportunity to read my bible. The words came alive to me and seemed to give me wisdom in how to deal with the situations I found myself in. The Holy Spirit would warn me about people and their motives and, increasingly, I would get questioned about what I thought about this situation. On one occasion one guy asked me about divorce. I think he wanted me to say that it was evil and from the devil and every divorced person was going to burn in hell. Obviously, I didn't say this and gave him a more diplomatic answer that aligned with how the bible viewed it. He was a particularly venomous bloke that responded to me after I gave the answer by saying: 'Good job you answered that way otherwise I would have kicked your head in!'. I was constantly praying that God would protect me and give me the answers to help others see the truth. But I was operating in quite a dark and hostile environment, and I felt quite alone. I wasn't aware of any other Christians in my squadron or any of the squadrons for that matter.

I woke up one morning from a dream and I had a sense that in the dream God had asked me what gift I would like from him. I instantly asked for wisdom. I didn't have to pause and think about it. Wisdom was my weapon of choice to refute and confound the arguments and hostility I endured for my faith.

I figured as I was now a Christian I should start going to church. There was a small chapel just off the barracks that I started going to. I went alone and when there I didn't see any other singlies there. I can remember seeing some married couples and families there, and I think they were officers. There weren't many people there, so I sat near to the back fumbling with the hymn book and the service sheet.

The padre seemed like a nice guy, and I could tell he was thinking, what on earth are you doing here on a Sunday morning? Why aren't you hung over with all your mates. That said we exchanged pleasantries and I made my way back to camp.

Despite praying and trusting in God's promises in the bible, things weren't getting any easier. Remember the grief was 24/7 and it wasn't as if I was working 9-5 then going home. I lived with some of these guys that were making life difficult for me. In addition to that I was in a foreign country so couldn't pop round to my brother's house or to a friend for support.

I started to see and experience how my life didn't really line up with how God wanted me to live. Just my thought, life alone was a challenge. Now that I was a Christian, I shouldn't be looking at porn or lying, gossiping or having destructive thoughts about those that were making life hard for me.

I was pleased that my mouth was a bit cleaner in terms of not swearing but I was conscious of areas of my life that I was unhappy with. I didn't feel guilty, it was more conviction that the behaviours were at polar opposites with the best that God had in mind for me. I wanted to change not because it was a set of requirements, but because I loved God and was very grateful for the pit, he rescued me from. I was honoured to be his son and wanted him to be pleased with me.

Emma wasn't yet aware that I had become a Christian because I was worried that she would dump me because things would have to change. I didn't want to explain over the phone, this needed to be conveyed face to face so she could feel and see my passion about what had happened to me. I wanted her to know that I still wanted to be with her, but I couldn't neglect or compromise my relationship with Jesus. Hopefully, she would understand.

As I travelled back to the UK for Christmas leave, my mind was filled with scenarios about how Emma would respond and wondered whether my family would notice if anything had changed about me. I had an inner excitement because no matter what the world threw at me, I knew without a shadow of a doubt that God was for me. It was an unusual, quiet confidence that apart from the benefits of knowing him in this life, there was the promise of being with him forever once this life was done. Amazing!

Before meeting Em, on arriving in the UK I had a job to do driving someone to Manchester as a favour. I was given £25 for my troubles, which was a nice earner in the mid 80s. In the week leading up to Christmas I shared with Em my shower room experience and how I now believed and followed Jesus. I can remember saying to Emma: 'I've seen the light!'. I laughingly cringe now at the use of that cliché. But, at the time, it was absolutely true. It was like I had seen a light, that would be visible and lead me for the rest of my life.

Emma listened carefully and her countenance was glowing as she smiled, almost as if she already knew. I was so relieved that Emma was so understanding and wanted to know more, and then she shared how she had attended the Billy Graham meetings where she too made a commitment to follow Jesus. Em shared that she had started to go to a church too that was really supportive as she tried to cope with her mum's terminal diagnosis of breast cancer.

So, it appeared that God had plans for both of us and had met with us at different times. I was later to discover that Emma's sister prayed for us both every day. A good friend of mine from my school days, Michelle, I discovered was also praying for me. She was full on at school and had a real experience with God that changed her life. She used to talk about Jesus as if he was alive. I remember admiring her because she was so passionate and evangelical about it all.

Back then I used to respond by saying I'm catholic and all Catholics go to heaven. How wrong I was. I now knew from my newfound faith that it was about choices and conscious decisions to leave stuff behind and move in a different direction, in terms of lifestyle choices. Emma and I visited Michelle and told her about how we now followed Jesus. She was overjoyed and as we shared our story, she said that she would like to pray for us both to receive the baptism of the Holy Spirit. I hadn't heard of this and was curious to know more. Mandy a good friend of Michelle's was there too at the time.

There's a bit in the bible where the disciples are in the upper room after Jesus had been crucified and Jesus instructed them to wait there because the Holy Spirit would come. Well, he did, spectacularly, with a violent rushing wind and then tongues of fire above the heads of the disciples could be seen. The disciples starting speaking in other tongues. The church was born as many in Jerusalem heard the good news about Jesus in their native tongue. Some said that the disciples were drunk, and others were convinced and believed. Peter told the scoffers that they weren't drunk as it was only 9 o'clock in the morning. So, the baptism of the Holy Spirit seemed to be for the empowering of believers as well as the giving of supernatural gifts. Well, I was up for that.

We moved into the kitchen area, and I had a sense that something was going to happen but I didn't know what. Michelle started to pray and then as my eyes were closed, I felt a hand on my head. As Michelle prayed for the Holy Spirit to come, she began to pray in a strange tongue. I had read about the gift of tongues but had never prayed that way myself. I felt a strong sense of peace and that The Holy Spirit was present. It was a lovely feeling. There were no strong rushing winds or blinding lights, but I knew something significant had happened deep inside me. I felt empowered and as if I had been given God's blessing and authority to go out and do stuff in His name. We reflected on what had happened over a cup of tea, (Michelle drank a lot of tea!) and then Em and I walked back to my parents' house that was just a minute or so away. Some of my brothers were home and as we walked into the kitchen, with beaming smiles one of my sister's said: 'What's wrong with you two, have you been drinking?'. I laughed saying how could we be drunk it's only 9 in the morning! I realised what I had said and burst into laughter as I recalled the words of Peter in the bible.

We were carrying an inexplicable joy and confidence that this was real, and

God was very close.

Wisdom and Reflection
- *Enjoy the vitality of youth and remember your first love, living out your values to protect you from actions you may regret later*
- *When Jesus knocks at the door, be quick to answer and open it!*
- *Being different can cost you your popularity and friends*
- *Being forgiven by God and starting to live differently brings hope and energy*

Emma and me aged 18

Emma at one of her many modeling shoots

5.
Marriage and living out my newfound faith

I returned to Germany and Stokesey had gone, having been posted somewhere else. There appeared to be a shift in how I was viewed as a Christian. The atmosphere changed from isolation to curiosity. I was fervently praying for another Christian to join me because although things had plateaued in terms of hostility, I needed someone to pray with, so that we could encourage one another. I had read in the bible that the apostle Paul had a helper called Timothy. 'Right!' I said to God, 'I need a Timothy!'

I didn't have to wait too long for the cavalry to arrive. One evening I was just leaving my room when I was approached in the corridor by a guy who I recognised from 2 Troop. He was also one of the regimental PTIs (physical training instructor). I didn't know him to speak to, so I assumed he was in our lines to speak with someone else. As I turned to walk out, he asked if he could have a word with me. I was suspicious of him as I thought this could be yet another snipe at me for being a Christian. He asked me whether I went to church, and I told him I did but wasn't in the mood for any grief. I had become defensive because I couldn't cope with any more rejection. He reassured me that he wasn't trying to be funny and asked if he could come with me to church the next Sunday. I told him that if he was serious and not winding me up then yes, we could go together.

That Sunday, he met me outside the block, and we walked to church. After the service he had many questions and God seemed to be in this. For the next few days, he would come to my room and ask more questions. One evening I suggested that he become a Christian so that he could be forgiven for his sins and accept Jesus who would cleanse him and give him a fresh start. He went away that evening with a lot to think about. The next morning, he came to me and excitedly told me that he had given his life to Jesus as he said the prayer in his room. I was overjoyed. This man's name was Timothy! God had given me my Timothy, and what a great friend he was.

Tim was 'on fire' from the word go. He was bold in his faith and wasn't afraid of showing it. When it came to meals, he would get his food and sit on a table with others and bow his head and say grace. I can remember seeing this happen on one occasion and watched as the others on his table respectfully waited until he had finished grace.

So now there were two of us. I had my prayer partner and I didn't feel as alone anymore. Tim and I started to venture further afield and we started to attend Christian meetings in Hohne where a missionary couple from The Soldiers and Airmen's Scripture Reading Association, (SASRA) had us over for Sunday dinner. Ivor and May were heaven sent as their knowledge of the bible was comprehensive and May's cooking was delicious.

I had a real hunger for knowledge and understanding from the bible. Most of my spare time was spent reading the bible, even when I was on leave with Emma. She would joke about how my head was always in the bible. It was like Jesus was putting me on a crash course to embed his ways for what I would face in the future.

I had since been promoted having passed my Regimental Cadre course so one of the privileges I received was having a room of my own. This provided a bit more privacy for guys who wanted to talk to me about spiritual things. Next came a time where, on a nightly basis, I was having deep conversations with men about Jesus and the need to accept and follow him in order to live life to the full. Men started to accept Jesus and I had the privilege to pray with them as they trusted Jesus and accepted his love and guidance. We soon got known as the God Squad and some weren't happy with this mini revival of soldiers turning to Christ.

Despite having my own room, the persecution still came and one day I came back to my room to find my bed defecated in and my Christian books burnt. Part of me rejoiced because I was being persecuted because of my belief in Jesus, but part of me was saddened because of their inability to see the goodness of God. What was it that made them behave this way? Did they feel threatened? Was it one individual or many that felt this way? Often, they would carry out their deeds when they were drunk and, on this occasion, while I was out.

I cast my mind back to when Michelle and Mandy were praying in tongues when I received the baptism of the Holy Spirit. I hadn't yet spoken in tongues but believed that the gift from God was for everyone, not just a select few. At around this time I went to bed thinking about tongues and I remember asking God for the gift. Now the bible says that it's for self-edification, for building you up in your private prayer time. It also says in the bible that when heard in public, say in church, there can be an interpretation, so it's for the building and encouragement of the church corporately too. Sometimes I didn't know what to pray because I was either weary or lost for words about a given situation. The burning of my books was one such occasion. So, I decided to ask God for this gift to help me.

As I stirred the next morning, in my slumber my mind was filled with a face of a man with eyes like fire and hair as white as pure wool. He just looked at me and I had a strong sense that this was Jesus. Nothing was said, I just saw his face. I was conscious as I started to wake that my lips were moving, uttering unrecognisable words. As I opened my eyes, I could hear myself uttering these words that I believed was a tongue or heavenly language given to me by the Holy Spirit. I wasn't going bonkers because this happened to the apostles on the day of Pentecost when they were baptised in the Holy Spirit. I was so excited and shared with Tim what had happened. As I recall it wasn't long after that Tim and I prayed, and he too received the gift of tongues. In fact, some time later, Tim and I were praying with some other believers in our house group and I began to pray in tongues. Tim opened his eyes and looked at me with a quizzical look and then he whispered to me that he could hear what I was saying in English! We were all amazed as he shared that he could hear me praising God in English despite the tongue sounding sort of Arabic.

I took great strength from praying in tongues and was reminded from the bible that it was the Holy Spirit praying through me. I figured that at times when I didn't know what to pray that he did. So, it worked.

In April 1989, Em and I got married and I moved out from the barracks to a married person's quarter not far from the camp. This was to bring some relief as once work was done, I could go home to my lovely wife who encouraged and supported me.

Em and I had been engaged for around five years. We wanted to get married earlier but Em's dad, Mike, wanted my prospects to improve before getting married. I was the lowest rank in the army at the time and if I progressed, I think this would mean that my prospects had improved! Mike would have been forgiven for thinking that this young soldier will be travelling all over the world and possibly wouldn't want to be tied to one girl. I think the extended time of engagement would serve as a cooling off period if things didn't work out. Mike was quite formal in the early days and insisted that I called him Mr Hale. I thought that this was quite odd at the time and disappointed me as I thought that this did very little to grow our relationship, especially as I was probably going to be his son-in-law one day. When I got promoted to Lance Corporal, Mike's attitude changed, and he visibly showed his approval, but I still had to call him Mr Hale. Mike suffered from depression and had been on medication all his adult life. Losing his wife as well meant that he had a lot on his plate. I was playing the long game and wanted him to value me and to be proud of me as he gave me the hand of his daughter. As the years went by Mike and I would become very good friends, sharing a love for photography.

Leading up to getting married I got the wobbles and although I knew Em was the right one for me, I started wondering, quite selfishly if she was in fact THE one? Could there be another girl out there that I'm supposed to marry? Would she get depression like her dad, or cancer like her mum? Would she be able to cope with me being in the army and living in another country?
A week before getting married I rose early each morning and attended a prayer meeting where I really sensed the presence of God and all my concerns melted away. I was ready and committed to love and cherish this beautiful woman for the rest of her life.

Our wedding day was a sunny day that was a tremendous and moving celebration of our union. Emma was a stunning bride, and some termed it as a fairytale wedding. I was dressed in my number 1 uniform, otherwise known as Blues, complete with the gold braid lanyard and number 2 headdress. Emma had bought her dress from a Spanish designer, complete with headdress but not a veil. She took my breath away when I turned to see her walking up the aisle. I'm sure her mum was whooping from heaven as she witnessed her daughter, now as this beautiful young woman full of hope and promise.

We were fortunate to have a guard of honour that consisted of all my close friends that were also serving in the Royal Engineers at the time. We sang Shine Jesus Shine that was a very popular song at the time written by Graham Kendrick. Revd. Barry Harper married us and over time became a valued friend and mentor. Barry was renowned for his pastoral care and his no nonsense approach to the gospel message. Emma and I would see more of Barry and his wife Val on our return to the UK.

Following our honeymoon to Rhodes we returned to Emma's home to pack up her belongings in the issued army MFO removal boxes.

It was great to see how God was growing Em and I together as a Christian couple. I found that things got easier for me in terms of my witness as I wasn't in amongst the resistance 24/7. It provided an opportunity for the lads to come to ours for a meal and have a civilised conversation about God, without a drunken interruption or heckling from others.
We prayed together and always made lots of time to talk and listen to one another. We had so many aspirations and were excited about being married and expectant about what God was going to do through us. Emma loved being a home maker and, although the place we were given to live in by the army, wasn't the Ritz, it was our first home, and we were very grateful for it.

When we moved in, we were surprised to find that the living carpet was bright orange with psychedelic lime-coloured circles. It was awful. Emma's eyes filled up and she looked at me and said: 'I can't live with this carpet!'. The flat was quite basic but not a bad size. We were fortunate to receive some inheritance money from Emma's grandfather passing, so next stop would be the furniture and carpet shop as we had no furniture at all.

Married life was good. I was well taken care of by Em, receiving three lovely meals a day and lots of love and cuddles. What was there not to like. At this time several of the guys had become Christians so Em and I started a home group, that provided a welcoming environment for people to meet and encourage one another. We often had a living room full of soldiers but also the wives of soldiers too. We even had a couple of locals as well as two teachers that taught at the school where army children attended. It was a special time in our journey where we saw Jesus move powerfully in people's lives. We took the bible literally and believed that all the great things Jesus did, we could do too. We expected miracles and to see The Holy Spirit move in power, and we did.

On one occasion, a woman that attended brought her daughter who was about 16. My attention was drawn to the woman's daughter as I felt The Holy Spirit was going to touch her that evening. As the guitar started to play and we began to sing and worship, the girl put her fingers in her ears and started to shake her head from side to side. I can assure you that although we weren't the best singers, we certainly weren't the worst! I noticed this immediately and as I walked across the room to where she was sitting on the floor, she literally slid away from me into the corner of the room. How could she slide on carpet I hear you say? I don't know either, but she did. She was now cowering in the corner, still with her fingers in her ears. By now everyone in the room knew that something extraordinary was going on.

I sensed that this was a spirit, not the Holy kind that was causing this reaction. I had read about some of the stuff that Jesus did to cast evil spirits out of people, setting them free from their torment. As I said earlier, I have no problem in taking Jesus at his word. All this defied logic but I was reminded that faith is activated by the heart not the head.

So, what do I do now? I knew I had to do something, so I just told the spirit to leave her, and it did, but with a little shaking and then the girl started to cry. I glanced over at her mum, and she fidgeted awkwardly and started to make excuses for her daughter's behaviour. As her mum was talking the girl had her knees drawn up to her chin, with her face buried into her arms, that were pulling her knees up to her chest.

I sensed that the Holy Spirit was giving me a 'word of knowledge' about the mother/daughter relationship. I'd read about words of knowledge in the bible. They were given to believers to reveal things only known to the person that it was given to. So here I am in Germany in the 20th century living out biblical principles that Christ commanded us to do. Doing the stuff was what made it more real to me and those in the room that evening. I looked at the mother intently and sensed that there was an unhealthy strand of parental domination in their relationship so much so that the mother was living her faith through her daughter. I turned to the daughter and asked her whether she had made a personal decision to follow Jesus. She replied saying no but her mum had for her. Amazing! The Holy Spirit had revealed this information that otherwise I would have had no clue about. The scripture came to mind where it says that the Holy Spirit will reveal things to you that are not yet known. I loved the fact that our 'all knowing' God is interested in the intricacies of our lives and relationships, because, after all, Jesus was all about relationships.

I asked the girl to raise her head and look at me. She found this incredibly hard, but I encouraged her to do so. As she looked up her mum interrupted and started to make excuses for her behaviour. I gently asked her to allow her daughter to have a moment. Red-faced she agreed. I asked the girl if she would like to accept Jesus into her life for herself and not on behalf of her mum. She nodded and I could see the beginning of a smile and relief. We prayed with her, and she made a conscious decision to follow Jesus for herself that night. Her mum could feel the power of the moment and prayed herself saying sorry, for all be it, well meaning, she had smothered her daughter unintentionally creating spiritual consequences that had trapped her daughter. Years later when I became a parent, I would remember this occasion and sympathise with the mum who thought she was doing the best for her daughter. Parenting is complex and at times when we think we're saving our kids, we're smothering them.

As the God squad grew, these fine soldiers, who had decided to follow Jesus, started to ask questions about baptism. They had started to read their bibles and wanted to take that step. One said if Jesus needed baptising, then so do I. I agreed to speak with the Padre to see if he could arrange something. I was sure that there must have been planned baptism services. Perhaps the guys could be part of that service. I was also aware of protocol and how, if possible, it should be done through the correct channels.

I visited the Padre's office and explained how pleased I was that men were believing in Jesus and now wanted to be baptised. Naturally I expected the Padre to be as excited as I was, but I was detecting passive reluctance. He was smiling politely at me, but in a way that he wanted to call security to take this mad man away. I was a bit puzzled by his response which was, 'How nice'. I left it with him with a view to him getting back to me with a date and other details.

The Padre came from the Church of Wales tradition and seemed to be a nice guy but during another conversation I'd had with him he told me the pay and rank was good as an army padre and you got a big house too. I was disappointed not to hear how he could support the men and tell them about the good news of Jesus.

Several weeks passed and still I heard nothing from the Padre. The lads were getting impatient and suggested that we go ahead without him. I know that they wanted to get baptised by full immersion and in a lake or river. The padre had talked about if he could do it, it would be like babies are christened at a font in the chapel. I knew this wouldn't be acceptable to the guys. Finally, the lads said that if the Padre wasn't going to baptise them would I do it. I'd never baptised anyone before and felt like this would get me in a spot of trouble. But on the other hand, I knew it was biblical and Jesus commanded us to baptise. I said I'd pray about it and would make the decision once I felt I'd heard from God.

Em and I prayed about what the way forward should be. I felt strongly that we needed to proceed as it had been at least a couple of months since I had spoken to the padre. I felt disappointed that we didn't have his support and I detected that he had started to avoid me.
Emma had decided to get baptised too, so a friend called Mary, in our home group, was a local and they had a property by a lake, so she offered it as the venue to conduct the baptisms.

I let the guys know that I was happy to baptise them, so we started to plan. Dez, Troy and Emma were to get baptised. Others were invited to come and see and witness their declaration of faith. It was a lovely warm evening. The lake was calm, (but still freezing!). There was a grass bank that looked onto the lake where we decided to baptise them. On the bank sat around 12 friends and supporters, most being single soldiers without a faith. Bless them, they sang the songs that we chose out of respect for the three that were getting baptised. Tim and I conducted the service and had the privilege of dunking all three. It was particularly special baptising my wife. It was a truly special evening as all three gave their testimony of why they had decided to follow Jesus. Tim and I looked at each other with a look that said: 'This is the stuff we should be doing!'. We all went home on a high thanking God for his goodness.

The next morning, I was told that the OC (Office Commanding) wanted me to report to him. What on earth could this be about? You were usually only summoned if you had done something very good or very bad. I couldn't think that I had done either recently. Our OC was a nice guy and seemed to me to be a fair but firm guy. I started to get an inkling of what this could be about when I heard a soldier call over: 'Hey, John the Baptist!'. I smartened myself by adjusting my beret and pulling my lightweight trousers down straight, to exaggerate the creases. I entered Squadron HQ and waited outside the OC's office door until I heard a muffled voice say: 'Come in Corporal Borg'. I marched in smartly, threw up a salute and then stood perfectly still. He said: 'At ease Corporal Borg'. He leaned back in his chair looking at me quizzically. Then he leaned forward with his hands resting on his desk with his fingers interlocked: 'So what's this I hear about you baptising soldiers'. I started to panic in my mind thinking is this going to wreck the little bit of career I had. Who grassed me up? Would I receive a punishment posting? I knew I couldn't bottle it and play it down. Despite this stressful situation I found myself in, I knew I had to be faithful to my Commander in Chief, The Lord of Heaven's Armies, Jesus Christ. I quickly remembered the bit in the bible when the Holy Spirit said I will give you the words to speak in front of the authorities.

I responded to the OC by confirming that I had baptised soldiers and my wife the night before. He motioned for me to go on, so I continued to explain that they had become Christians, having chosen to follow Jesus and that Jesus commanded us to get baptised. He sat there listening intently. I sensed that he was intrigued by this working-class soldier that had such a conviction for Jesus. This was a rarity amongst the rank and file. I explained to him that I had initially approached the Padre and that it seemed to take a long time to get back to me. The OC let me finish, paused and then said: 'The Head Chaplain for BAOR (armed forces Germany) has contacted me wanting to know if it was true and what was going on'. I was speechless that it had gone so far up the chain and so quickly. I just wished the Padre could have organised the baptisms that quickly! I sensed now that the Padre was involved and not necessarily in a supportive way. I apologised to the OC if I had brought any disrepute to the Squadron but defended my actions by explaining that these men will be even better soldiers than before they were baptised because they would be working to standards that pleased God, that would also benefit the Squadron. He looked at me pensively, leaned forward and looked me straight in the eye and said: 'No more baptisms! That will be all Corporal Borg'. I saluted smartly, turned to the left and marched out of his office.

The John the Baptist jokes soon subsided, and I felt that I had honoured the Lord and he had honoured me. Don't get me wrong I am not one for breaking rules or acting subversively. I fear God more than I fear man and it was just something I had to do. It felt right despite being mildly reprimanded for it. I think it's right to obey and submit to the authorities apart from when it contravenes what God says in His word, the bible. I was reminded of an incident in the bible when Peter was taken before the authorities, and he was ordered not to speak any more about this Jesus. Peter was respectful but said that he could not stop speaking about his Lord and Saviour. Would I have baptised more men if the need arose? Of course, I would. Sometimes it's better to seek forgiveness than permission. It was ironic that it was the religious leaders that were stirring the pot, pretty much like in the times of Jesus and the apostles. No change there then.

Wisdom/Reflection
- *Be consistent in your lifestyle and others will see that what you have is real*
- *Get adopted by older wiser people, that can help you navigate life*
- *A time of persecution or difficulty will be followed by a time of blessing if you persevere in doing good*

Our wedding day Aprill 22 1989

Royal School of Military Education on my A1 Planter operator mechanic course

6.
Early days as a married couple

Emma and I were about to spend our first Christmas together as a married couple. We were so excited and had started to plan to have family come to visit from the UK. Em was determined to get the flat looking nice first. We were now the proud owner of some dark wood furniture, consisting of a dining toom table, an ornament stand, coffee table and a small lamp table. We'd also bought a three-piece suite that had blues and browns in the fabric. Looking back, it was a bit of an odd colour combination, but it worked at the time. Em's touch started to transform the flat into a welcoming homely place that I looked forward to returning to each day.

Periodically I would be deployed on exercise and could be a way for a couple of weeks. Often 'Active Edge' was initiated in the early hours of the morning. Active Edge was a simulation of an attack or imminent attack from Soviet forces. Most of the time it was a relatively short exercise to test our readiness to deploy with all our vehicles and equipment to a designated area.

On one occasion I left Emma in the early hours of the morning to respond to a deployment. I leant over and gave Emma a kiss and told her I would see her soon. How soon was soon? I did not know. No mobile phones in those days so calls on the move or texts or emails were not an option. I returned from the exercise in the hours of darkness, laden with my bergen and other bits of kit. Feeling slightly grubby but relieved to be home I crept lightly into the lounge area without putting the lights on so as not to disturb Emma who was nicely tucked up in bed. I sat on the sofa and took off my boots and then made my way to the bedroom. I was quite tired so got straight into bed and was soon in the land of slumber.

On waking up a few hours later Emma was sat on the end of the bed, and she looked agitated almost as if she had waited for me to wake before she shared her annoyance. She smiled at me through pained lips and then said: 'Come with me!'. She led me into the lounge where I could clearly see a trail of my oily boot prints……. on our lovely new cream carpet that Emma had fitted whilst I was away. I looked at Emma with a contorted face as I tried to wish the footprints away, knowing they were there to stay at least until I got some carpet stain remover. A hug and a heartfelt apology were my only available offering to console Em as she blubbed into my neck saying: 'It was meant to be a nice surprise having nice new carpet'. Oh, how I loved my wife who showed patience and love against all the odds!

Christmas was upon us, and we spent it alone as a couple. Christmas Eve was spent sipping a glass of sherry sat on the floor next to the Christmas tree. Emma and I made prayer a regular habit and as we prayed together this night, we had a time of quiet and reflection as we thought with gratitude about how blessed we felt with life and the fact that we had each other.

Whilst meditating on God's goodness I felt an inner voice in my head say: 'I'm calling you to the police'. Now when I talk about an inner voice in my head, that might be difficult for you to grasp or imagine. The only way I can describe it is that it's a silent voice in your head space. Any clearer?! I know unless you've had the same experience you would be forgiven for thinking I have mental health issues. It made me pay attention and I heard it very clearly. Over time I have learnt to recognise this as the still small voice of the Holy Spirit. If my mind was crowded or thinking of a hundred other things or plagued with worry, I may have missed it. I opened my eyes and repeated what I had heard to Emma. She looked up and said: 'What?!'. I repeated it again and Em just looked at me open mouthed. It provoked this reaction because my intention was to be a career soldier completing a full career in the army; and Em knew this. I only had one relative that had served in the Police and that was my cousin Silvio, in Malta. To my knowledge we had never had a conversation about the police, and, to be quite frank, I had no interest in the police. I had no friends in the police and my stereotype of police officers were power happy individuals that persecuted the public. Clearly my appraisal of the police was biased and unfair but at the time that was my blinkered view.

Emma and I pondered on what we felt God was saying and where He was leading us. Would that mean I would have to apply immediately? What would the army have to say about my potential career change? What about if I failed the entry tests? How would I go through the application process living out in Germany? What a Christmas present this was going to be. Emma had only just joined me in Germany and potentially we would be moving again.

I was intrigued at where this was going as I had learnt to trust God, but every new challenge was a test of our relationship and whether I was willing to trust again and more importantly obey and follow His leading. In my relatively short journey with God, I had learnt that God tests you with small things in terms of how you trust and obey and then he increases the stakes, often when there are more implications if you choose to trust or not. This seemed to be next level trust involving a major life decision not only for me but for my wife, Emma too.

I so didn't expect this, and I started to get flashes of doubt and thoughts of what if I was wrong and it was just some random thought that had popped in my head. Maybe I had watched a programme involving the police and subconsciously a thought was sown in my mind. But then what if it was The Holy Spirit. That would mean that he had something for me to do, presumably in the UK. Where would we live in the UK? Where would I be posted? How on earth would I pass the entrance exams that involved a maths test! I hated maths and to this day am not a numbers' person.

Emma and I had a lovely Christmas that was very special just being the two of us. We talked about where our life could be heading and I was always aware that there was a sadness in her for the loss of her mum, Gill. I suspected that Emma was still grieving from when her mum passed away from breast cancer in 1985. Emma was 17 at the time and it was a particularly traumatic time as she lost several members of her extended family, in a relatively short period of time. This left Emma with a degree of anxiety that loss was always around the corner, which understandably made her a bit of a worrier at that time in her life. I probably wasn't the most empathetic young man, always trying to find a solution rather than listening more carefully to understand and hear the cries from the heart.

I had only met Emma's mum, Gill, a handful of times, mainly when I was on leave visiting Emma's home in Great Barr. I used to tease Emma because her address was more in the Perry Barr area, but there was a bit of postcode snobbery going on so I agreed to go with Great Barr. No offence if you're from Perry Barr, but it was a bit of a dump back then, but I'm sure the people were lovely!

Gill was a nursery schoolteacher, so by her very nature she was kind and attentive. She always had a smile for me and was interested in what I was doing at the time. I remember that although always well presented, Gill was very poorly as the cancer had spread to her bones, which made her look quite frail, despite only being in her mid 40s. I remember Emma's dad having an underlying tension in his expressions and sometimes he appeared on edge, understandably so.

As a 17-year-old I knew very little about cancer. My Aunty Jane, in Malta, was the only person I knew in my family at that time that had died from the disease. So, I'd never really got up close and personal with cancer, but I knew that it was serious and, in some cases, it was a killer disease. Little did I know that decades later I would become well acquainted with the disease.

I called Emma most evenings whilst courting, when I was posted to Gibraltar Barracks, which was the Royal Engineers training camp, in Camberley, Surrey. Emma would give me updates on her mum's health. One evening in May 1985 Emma told me that her mum was hospitalised and very poorly, not having long left to live. Em left a silence, and I could sense that she was deeply upset and felt helpless. As a family, they had reached the point where their mum's journey was coming to an end and both Emma and her sister Jo were so young to lose their mother. I filled the silence by reassuring Em that I would speak to my Corporal in the morning to get some time off to be with her at this very sad and challenging time.

The next morning, I approached my corporal and explained the situation and how important it was that I get home because of the deterioration in Gill's health. I was disappointed with his response, not only was he cold but he was lacking in empathy too. He said that I could take some time out but at the expense of being back coursed. This was a real blow as I couldn't bear the thought of having to go through all the training again and even worse with a group of guys I didn't know.

I was dreading giving Emma the news that I wouldn't be able to be with her in her time of need. She was so gracious when I told her, and I sensed that she was emotionally numb. Unusually, there were no tears or sobbing just an acceptance. I wanted to hold her and console her. I felt helpless and trapped by my circumstances. Today I think about my decision back then and in hindsight feel that I should have taken the leave to be with Emma. It was a significant and heavy moment in Emma's life, and I probably didn't appreciate the depth of her pain. From an early age I had learned to box off my emotions for fear of rejection and hurt. As I grew older, I became adept at compartmentalising experiences and starving the emotion out of situations, so I protected myself. I would later learn that this is false economy and eventually there would be leakage from those boxes of emotions, that wanted to be heard. When you are like that you feel that you are being strong and in control. My experience found that usually you were delaying the inevitable and robbing the moment of the response and emotions it deserved.

Gill died a short time later and I continued with my training, putting the situation aside so I could concentrate on passing my training course.

I was fortunate to have a mum who was in good health and as strong as an ox. She was this small Mediterranean matriarch that was passionate about family and food. Mum loved Emma and used to try to get Emma to put some weight on by loading her plate with pasta. She always worried that Em was too slim. She was a model after all, and I wasn't complaining!

Emma's education was shadowed by her mum's poor health particularly in her senior school days. Despite that she passed her exams but wouldn't have described herself as an academic. Emma was very creative so loved fashion and makeup. She attended the College of Food and Domestic Art and took a course in hair and makeup. In between she worked as a Promotions girl, often working at the motor show and other corporate events, usually hosted at the NEC in Birmingham. Em had an infectious personality, always looking for the good and the eternal optimist. People tended to gravitate towards her, and she had the ability to understand where people were at.

She was a hope giver.

Wisdom/Reflection
- *Set your boundaries wide as newlyweds. Give yourselves time to talk and listen to one another. Communication is key*
- *Weigh up what's most important then make a decision to act. It may cost you though*
- *You may not understand how someone else is feeling or what to say, just be present for them*
- *Be mindful of making memories that gladden the heart, you may need to draw on them later*

7.
The Calling

Christmas had come and gone, and I had returned to work. I knew I had to progress God's plan for me to join the police. My fail safe was that if the army didn't release me or some other detail didn't fit, then I would take it that this was some random thought I had sipping sherry under the Christmas tree. To me that would be a closed door and I'd put it down to experience. Not an exact science I know but give me a break, I was new at this hearing God's voice lark.

I waited until Spence, my troop Staff Sgt was on his own and then I approached him, asking if I could chat about a potential move. He was very attentive to what I was saying and shared that he had come to a similar crossroads in his career when he had considered leaving to join the police too, but without the God voice thing. He said that now was the time to make the switch before I progressed any further in the army. Although Spence was willing to support me, he didn't hold out much hope for my chances with the OC who was reluctant to let staff be released in light of future deployments.

The OC had changed since the last time I was summonsed to his office for the baptism telling off. I made an appointment with his clerk, and I think it was the next day that I got to meet with him.

I marched into his office and saluted him. He stood me at ease and asked me what this was all about. Major Heron reminded me of one of the British Army officers from Black Adder, a satire series, set in the first World War, starring Rowan Atkinson. He had an old-fashioned looking face and struck me as more of an administrator than a soldier. That may be an unfair assessment but that was my impression at the time. I'm sure he worked very hard to attain the rank of Major, so no offence, Mr Heron!

I explained to him that I felt that now was the time to change my career and that I wanted to apply for the Police Force. I didn't have the bottle to tell him that I felt God had spoken to me, as he would have probably had me sectioned and admitted to a psychiatric ward. Whilst I was explaining my plan, he didn't make eye contact but just stared at his desk. When I'd finished, he said: 'Very well, get out'. I took it that it was time for me to leave so I saluted him and marched out smartly. Well, what could I make of that? The 'get out' at the end made me think that he was annoyed and bottom line is he had the power to grant my request for a posting to the UK to make the application process more straightforward logistically.

Our house group were praying faithfully that the Lord would make a way and grant me favour. For me, it was simple, the bible says: 'If God is for us who can be against us'. So Major Heron would just have to get in line with God's plan. During the time of waiting for the decision to be made I was to-ing and fro-ing with doubt. If he doesn't release me that means it was all in my head, and now I won't get any opportunities for promotion or development, as a punishment for wanting to leave the squadron.

I think it was within a week and I was called in by Spence. He looked at me with a wry grin and said: 'I don't know how you managed to pull it off, but you did'. Major Heron had agreed to release me. So maybe, just maybe, this was a move of God. From that sense after praying that The Holy Spirit was calling me out of the army and into the police, the process had now started. It was actually happening. I now started to believe that I was going to get into the police. This was a real faith builder, but it only came as a result of me choosing to trust and obey.

My final days with 1st Fd Sqn, 21 Engineer Regt. were special times. I felt the pressure was off me because I was leaving for pastures new. I used this time to create good endings, in terms of friendships and trying to put right things that had been left undone. People that had wronged me I forgave and although that didn't mean I became best mates with them, I had released myself from that pain that they had caused me.

During my last couple of months, I volunteered for a March and Shoot competition. A small team of us would be representing the regiment. The competition involved a march/run for several miles carrying your webbing (pouches, belt and yoke) and weapon. The march would end at a shooting range where you would have to hit targets at various distances. You were required to shoot in various positions, either the prone position, (lying down), kneeling, standing and sometimes running towards the target. Added to this some of the shooting had to be done wearing your respirator, which is a nightmare, making aiming and breathing a lot more challenging. The team consisted of three of us. One of the other guys I knew and the other was a corporal from a different squadron. The other two guys would be carrying the SLR, (Self Loading Rifle) and I would be carrying the LMG, (Light Machine Gun). I was looking forward to the competition as I had volunteered to go knowing I was fit enough and not a bad shot. When we got to the location, we had a bit of time to prepare which also gave me an opportunity to get to know the other two a bit better. One of the guys was also in my 1st Fd Sqn, I think he was in MT (military transport) as a driver of four-tonner trucks. They were the most common form of transport for moving troops at the time. I was surprised to see Suddsy but I learnt that he was a really good shot. A year or so earlier he was involved in a very serious car accident where two of the guys in his car died at the scene. Suddsy struggled terribly with the guilt as, at the time, I think he was over the alcohol limit. He was very fortunate to only have sustained minor injuries.

The competition began and each team set off with an interval time in between. We were ready to go, and I could feel the adrenalin building. As we started off at a quick march, I started to develop some tummy pain. I gritted my teeth and put it to the back of my mind and started to get into the rhythm of the pace that was set. We were all aware of each other and periodically looked at each other giving a nod to signify that the pace was ok and we were good. I could now feel an earthy deep pulsating feeling in my abdominal area. There was no way I was going to stop. The embarrassment and humiliation would be unbearable. I could feel the discomfort and suffering that took me back to my cadre course days. I just had to put my head down and crack on. I'd made it to the end of the march, and we had made good time. We made towards the range and prepared our weapons for firing. Whenever possible I used to carry the LMG. Firing it was a dream. I loved the noise it made especially on automatic and the smell of cordite. For a machine gun it was quite accurate and about 25lb in weight loaded. It was easy to clean and reliable. The LMG was based on the Bren Gun that was used in the Second World War, so it had been around for a long time.

As I got into the prone position, I could feel my webbing belt buckle sticking into my tummy right on where I'd experienced the pain. I had to lift my body up slightly that wasn't ideal whilst trying to hit the target. In this type of competition, they always create conditions that put you under pressure. So, for example, the target will show for three seconds then disappear and in that time you have to hit the target three times, then you'll have to get up and run to a given point, fit your respirator and then wait for the command: 'Watch and shoot, watch and shoot!' As I was firing the LMG all of my shots were taken in the prone position, which was probably the worst one for me with my stomach ache. I could tell that I wasn't hitting the target. Ideally, I should have put my hand up to be withdrawn because at this stage I was very uncomfortable. I continued to the end and very quickly it became apparent that my shooting was dreadful, and I hardly contributed any marks to our team score. The other two guys did really well and were in the running for a prize. I could tell that the other corporal on the team was really annoyed with me as all that he knew was that I was a crap shot, that was now complaining of having a poorly tummy.

It looked like I was making excuses and I felt terribly responsible for letting them down and the regiment. I'm not that much of a wimp, something must be wrong to make me feel in so much pain. The other smiled awkwardly at me and said: 'Never mind'. We walked back to the billet where we were stopping overnight and after getting showered and changed, I sat down where Suddsy also was and told him that I was in some real pain. He suggested that I go to the medical centre and get myself seen. I did just that. I was really hoping they would find something to justify my pathetic performance.

I find it hard to recover from situations where I feel that I've let people down. It was even harder as a soldier because there was such a dependence on each other playing their part. Reputation was important especially as we were representing the regiment. I could just imagine the other competitors returning back to their regiments laughing about our performance. The Royal Engineers is a corps containing many units known as regiments so potentially stories of my poor shooting could travel far and wide.

I entered the medical centre, and I was seen almost immediately. I was told by the army doctor to strip down to my underwear and lie on the examination table. He started to press with his hands around my abdominal area and asked me to say when he touched the area where the pain was emanating from. 'Here, here, here' he said as he pressed along my lower abdomen. Then as he started to press around close to my tummy button, I arched my back and said through gritted teeth: 'There, the pain's there'. He looked at me and said: 'Ok let's get you in'. 'Get me in where Sir?' I said. I was off to theatre and not the singing kind. I was wheeled up to theatre in one of those white, starched robes that you tie around the back. The next thing I knew I was being asked to count to 10 and then I was out for the count.

I awoke some time later feeling groggy and disorientated. My mouth was dry and I was gagging for a drink of water. A short time later a nurse came to my bedside and told me that I had been operated on to repair an umbilical hernia. She smiled sweetly and told me that I no longer had a tummy button! Not long after the nurse had left me, I needed to answer a call of nature. As I stood, I could feel a tight pulling sensation around the area where my tummy button had been. I lifted my gown to see the extent of the damage. Jeeps! There was a two-inch-long scar that had neatly been stitched. So, the pain wasn't psychosomatic, I really did have something wrong with me. I was so relieved that I now had a reason for my sloppy shooting. When I returned to the regiment, all was forgiven and the corporal that was on my team apologised and commended me for completing the march and not quitting. The silver lining to the ordeal was that I was granted convalescence leave back to the UK for a couple of weeks. So, Em and I travelled back to the UK, and I started to ponder on how the mysterious hand of Jesus had worked through this ordeal.

Whilst in the UK Em and I visited family and caught up on all the news. Meeting with friends and new friends that we had made as a result of Emma going to St John's Church in Walmley. It was nice to meet other Christians and I felt at home with other believers, who loved the Lord and were interested in this soldier and model's life. What a combination, a model and a soldier. St John's was a vibrant church where people were made to feel welcome. It was typically white, middle-class though and to begin with this council house kid did feel a bit out of place. The attraction and common ground were our faith and before long we would make some lifelong friendships.

As people heard my testimony about how I became a Christian there was a real sense of awe as I shared that I had heard the audible voice of Jesus. People were captivated and it seemed to excite them that this Jesus they follow does actually speak. I carried an excitement and passion about Jesus and what the Holy Spirit was doing. By this time, I had witnessed many things that I shared with others that had a more traditional experience. I realised that at times I was full on, and perhaps a little overwhelming, but I just couldn't stay quiet about how God had worked in my life.

Nigel and Angie were a lovely couple that we met early on in St John's. They were very kind to us and invited us around for meal when we were home. Angie at the time was working for the police in a finance/admin role. When she heard about my calling to the police, she said she would speak to her friend in recruitment to see if they were recruiting at that time. Angie suggested that I visit Lloyd House, the police headquarters of West Midlands Police to get an application form and maybe chat about the process with someone.

It sounded like a good suggestion, but I was concerned that I needed to study for the entrance exam and the assessment that would follow later. The army actually provided a resettlement course that prepared you for the police recruitment procedure so I was thinking of enrolling onto it so I had a better chance of passing. That said there would be no harm in paying a visit to take an application form and perhaps have a chat with someone.

The next day I got ready to visit Lloyd House. My trousers were freshly pressed and I starched my shirt and wore my Corps tie with my blazer complete with Corps badge. As my stitches were still in I had to leave my trouser button undone and kept my blazer buttoned up to disguise my current state.

When I arrived at Lloyd House I felt quite daunted and was reminded by that still small voice within me, that this was all in His plan and to just go with it. That's easy for you to say Father. You know the beginning from the end! I dutifully entered through the glass doors and made my way to the reception desk. It was all very civilised and I remember feeling like I had a right to be there whereas often in the army you felt under the pecking order all the time.

I was met by a smiley policewoman who had an air of authority. You could tell that she was quietly confident but polite with it. Not a sniff of arrogance or power trip as I had pigeon-holed police officers. I was put at ease and my prejudices started to melt away. I politely asked her for an application form and any other literature she could give me. My plan was to then go away and digest what the requirements were and come up with a plan of action. She looked at me and said: 'No time like the present'. Then she ushered me to a door that led me to an area behind reception where there was a corridor with rooms going off it left and right. My heart was racing, and my words came out muddled as I tried to explain to her that I wasn't ready to take any tests. If I failed, the test I would have to wait 12 months I think it was, so I wanted to be prepared to give it my best shot.

I could feel my wound site where my stitches were, twitching. It must have been the stress. We stopped in the corridor where a door was open, and I could see desks and chairs. She asked me to sit at a desk and she would be with me shortly with the first paper. 'I'm really sorry but I don't think I'm ready to take this test. I'd rather come back when I'm more prepared'. She smiled at me and said: 'Don't be silly you'll be fine'. So now we were entering the surreal. Why on earth was this very assertive policewoman so intent on me taking the entrance exam. Did she have a quota that she had to reach? Or was this God giving me a push? It's not like the police were desperate. At this time, it was seen as a respectable profession, that paid reasonably well too. I got a sense that the mysterious hand of the Holy Spirit was guiding this situation, so in my mind I resigned myself to going with it.

I sat at the first desk I came to, wondering whether there would be other candidates joining me. As I sat down, I had to rearrange my shirt and trousers as my stitches were starting to ache and I realised when looking down that there had been some seepage from the wound. I felt a little queasy so took some deep breaths and then it was time. She put the first paper on the desk and gave me a list of examination rules and told me the amount of time I had to complete the paper. As I recall there were three separate papers and then she led me to a room where I had an eye test. We then went through the application form, and I submitted there at the time.

She left me for a few minutes and then came back and said: 'I'm pleased to report Kevin, that you've passed your entrance test for West Midlands Police, congratulations!'. I looked at her in disbelief and said: 'Really?'. She nodded and shook my hand. At that moment I was extremely humbled and grateful that I had passed. God obviously had a schedule for me to keep. I sat with the policewoman who I think was called Alison. She took me through what I could expect next, including an extended assessment with more scenario-based tests and a home visit by a sergeant. Then, if I passed all of that, I would have a final interview before a panel who would decide whether I was a suitable candidate or not. I thanked Alison and made my way back home to share with Emma what had happened.

We were both now convinced that what we sensed God had said was becoming a reality. How mad is that. In faith you follow what you think you heard God say and it starts to happen. Amazing!

My convalescence leave at an end we returned to Germany to see out the remaining time of my posting. On our return our home group had organised a bit of a get together for Em and me. They presented me with a lovely cake that was of a torso without a tummy button, with the caption saying 'the way we were' around where it should have been. I had grown very close to this band of believers that had faithfully supported each other for several years. I loved them all dearly and counted them as special friends.

Prior to leaving Germany I was asked to jointly lead a Combat Engineer Tractor (CET), Crew Man's Course. Paul Golding and I would be the lead instructors, with about 10 students on the course.

The CET was an 18-tonne tracked vehicle made of aluminium alloy. It had a large earth moving bucket at one end of the machine and was amphibious and was commonly known as the Frog. Its primary role was to dig in main battle tanks into their defensive positions, so basically digging big holes in the ground with a bund of earth around them for added protection. This allowed the tank or other armoured vehicle to be at ground level but still able to fire its weapon systems.

The course was going very well and the students seemed to be enjoying mine and Paul's friendly and practical approach. The final module of the course was training the students how to 'swim' the CET. This involved preparing the vehicle by ensuring that all of the seals on the various hatches were in good working order. Floats had to be fitted into the heaviest side of the vehicle in the bucket, to balance the weight. With the flip of a few levers the vehicle can then be steered like a boat as the propellers engage.

All of the students were doing really well on the course and providing they passed this phase of the course they would become fully fledged 'Frog Ops". All swimming of the Frogs was conducted on the River Weser, that wasn't far away from camp. I remember it being a clear but chilly day and Paul and I had arrived ahead of the students to prepare the Frog for the swimming demo. As instructors we would demonstrate how it should be done. In the army you followed the EDIP pneumonic when instructing. First you explained the technique, then you demonstrated it, then they would impersonate what they had been shown, and finally practice, practice, practice.

Paul and I had a discussion to decide what vehicle we should use to demonstrate the swim. I was all for using a vehicle that we had that was almost new, so the seals and other working parts should be in good order. Paul was really insistent that we used one of his squadron vehicles. I had my doubts as it was working ok but it was old and as Frogs weren't often used for swimming, I had my doubts about the condition of the seals. It was a friendly debate and I could see that Paul cared about this more than me, so I conceded and left him with the words: 'On your head be it' with a bit of a cheeky laugh as I walked away. After all what's the worst that could happen ...

With all the students assembled adjacent to the river on an area of concrete hardstanding, we briefed them on the events of the day. This was an exciting day for them because it was quite a dynamic procedure driving 18 tonnes of metal down a ramp at full pelt, hitting the water hard enough to create a wave of water that curled over the front of the splashboard, crashing onto the front deck. Then navigating this lump of metal across the river was quite impressive.

Paul and I readied the Frog and we tested our communications as we adjusted our helmets, nicknamed, 'bone domes'. Everything seemed to be working well so we started to move towards the launch area. We decided to have a good run up to the entrance to the river so that the students could judge the speed and line that we entered the river at. The river was fast flowing and quite wide, around 100 metres where we were crossing.

My role within the Frog was to pilot it across the river whilst Paul was sat behind me keeping a watch for any risks in the river, so, in effect, he was sitting higher than me. I felt quite relaxed about the procedure as I had swam the Frog on a number of occasions. I was confident in mine and Paul's abilities and was looking forward to hitting the water at full pelt.

I looked down at my instrument gauges and everything seemed to be as it should be. I turned and glanced at Paul and he gave me the thumbs up. I looked to my left and could see all of the students lined along the riverbank watching expectantly.

I revved the engine and went through the gears to gain speed. I loved the sound of the Rolls Royce engine roaring and the clattering of the tracks below us. As we reached top speed and started to descend down the concrete ramp and into the water I dipped my head slightly as the water crashed into the washboard at the front sending a massive surf wave of water over our heads. I noticed that Paul had ducked down too, wise move. I engaged the props and hey presto we were started to make our way across the river. As I settled in to steering the Frog and monitoring the gauges, something didn't feel quite right. The freeboard which is the level at which the water should come up to was higher than usual. Normally, you can see the water level from where you were sitting as you looked down the vehicle. But, at this time, it was starting to lap over the open hatch where I was sitting. When we were about a third of the way across, I spoke to Paul over the intercom telling him that I was concerned about the water level that was now lapping over my hatch creating a puddle in the footwell.

Paul made light of it and said it would be ok, so I looked up at him and smiled nervously, then looked to my front again to navigate the Frog towards the exit point on the opposite bank. By the time we were three quarters of the way across the river the water level was to my knees. I was started to feel quite cold now despite being dressed suitably for the occasion. This was due to the temperature of the water that was now slopping around in my compartment. As we approached the exit point, I breathed a sigh of relief as I knew that we were going to make it. As we climbed up the bank and out of the water, I looked back at Paul with a look that said, that was close. I took the vehicle out of gear and let it idle whilst I took my helmet off to talk with Paul about the swim over. I had my concerns about taking the Frog back into the water to swim back to the other bank. I pointed to the water that was filling the compartment and suggested that we give the return swim a miss. Clearly the seals were compromised, and the age of the vehicle didn't help either. Paul was really keen to finish the job off and was sure we could make it. Reluctantly I agreed to swim it back so positioned the Frog for the return trip. My mind was seriously considering my options in the event of the vehicle sinking. I wasn't a bad swimmer, but neither was I the strongest. I was aware that the river was fast flowing, and we were quite near to a weir.

As model instructors we would, of course, carry out the correct drill in the event of the Frog sinking. This would mean battening down the hatches to seal the compartment and then waiting until you felt the vehicle hit the riverbed and then push out the emergency side hatch and swim to safety. Job done! In theory that seemed easy peasy lemon squeezy, but in reality, there was a strong possibility that in the panic your intercom cable could get caught on a lever or your clothing could get snagged as you tried to exit through the small hatch. As there were two of you it was imperative that the first exited quickly in order to give the second crewman a fighting chance. All of these thoughts were rushing through my mind as I approached the water, this time not as fast and furious as our first entry. We entered the water and immediately water started to lap over into the compartment again. At about halfway across the river I could fell a rumble below my feet and then to my right I could hear a spluttering noise coming from the exhaust stack. I could see that the exhaust fumes were black, weaving a black plume of smoke up into the sky. This was not good, and

I sensed the end was nigh. Despite all of the signs of doom around me I pressed on. Although I couldn't see Paul, I could feel his panic. The image in my mind of his panic-stricken face caused me to let out a short burst of hilarious madman like laughter. Why I did this I don't know. I put it down to a personal coping mechanism.

The lapping of water had now turned into a constant pouring of water that was now up to my chest. It was a bit like a dam that had burst. It was all over. I now feared for our safety. As I took a brief look down at the gauges, I could see that the dashboard was lit up like a Christmas tree. There was only one way this Frog was going and that was down, and I certainly wasn't planning to go down with it.

Paul was unusually silent. I think he was saying his prayers. I shouted over the intercom that we needed to prepare to get out and leave this sinking hulk. Paul pleaded with me to stay and carry out the proper drills. I gave him a look that let him know that I wasn't hanging around. This was a dangerous situation. There was no safety boat or other contingency plan. It was just us. I quickly unclipped my helmet and threw it down into the compartment. I shouted to Paul to get out quick. He started to unclip himself too. As I went to put my foot onto the front deck it had already started to sink. At the same time, I heard a boom and remember seeing black smoke. I'm ashamed to admit that as I hit the water I shouted: 'Fuck!'. I'm not sure if it was the shock of the water temperature or the disbelief that the Frog had sunk. Probably a combination of the two. I started to swim faster than usual. I couldn't see Paul but hoped that he was close behind me. I glanced over to the bank and could see the students quietly watching and could sense their anxiety as something serious had happened and our fate was in the balance.

I could remember gasping for breath as I swam against the fast current, desperately trying to swim the shortest route as the current pushed against me. The adrenalin flowing through my body got me to the other side. I was so relieved when my feet touched the bottom and I started to walk to the bank. Paul was close behind me, thankfully, and when we were both out of the water, we gave each other a relieved bear hug. We were both very cold, dripping wet like two drowned rats. As soon as we made it to the hard standing, we heard whoops and raucous laughter from the students. They gathered round us and started ribbing us and back slapping asking what had gone wrong. We were hastily given dry clothing and arrangements were made to recover the drowned Frog.

As we were transported back to camp one of the guards on the gate shouted: 'Kev Borg swearing, naughty, naughty!'. Can you believe it? I got ribbed for having a dirty mouth, particularly for a Christian, for a few days. Something that I wasn't proud of, but I was glad that they picked up on it as it showed that they were aware that I didn't normally swear. I think in the circumstances God may have smiled too.

The following day I had to report to the OC of 7 Sqn to give him an account of what had occurred. He was a friendly man as I remember and, as I entered his office, I sensed that this wasn't going to be a rollocking type of meeting. He asked me how the course had gone and thanked me for my efforts. Then he asked me what had happened on the river. It seemed to me that the reason for this meeting was for him to get all the juicy detail first hand. He waited eagerly with a smile of anticipation on his face. As I knew I had a friendly audience I took my time and dramatised it a little which I know he appreciated. It was hard to depict us as courageous rather than foolish, but I tried my best. He appreciated the storytelling and finished by thanking me and saying: 'I bet you were glad it was one of ours rather than one of yours!'. I was indeed. I wasn't so sure Paul would get the same response from his OC, after all I did say on his head be it. All was well and the Frog was recovered, and Paul and I remained friends until I left for the UK, where we caught up with each other many years later.

I had received my posting to the UK. I was joining 39 Engr Regt, 34 Fd Sqn, in Waterbeach, Cambridge.

Wisdom/Reflection
- *When God calls his plan into being it will be completed if we agree to trust and obey*
- *You don't always have to understand to believe*
- *Pride comes before a fall. Do the right thing even if it means you don't get the credit*

- *Best made plans can be interrupted with a disappointing outcome. Look for the learning from the situation*

Emma was delighted to be moving to the UK, especially beautiful Cambridgeshire. Although Em made living in Germany work, having friends and family nearer was a real comfort and support for her.

Looking back, living in Germany as a 21-year-old newly-married woman must have been a challenge. The language barrier alone created another layer of complexity when doing routine tasks like food shopping. Emma made friends with the other army wives and was intrigued by the pecking order that existed among the wives too. It was almost as if they adopted the rank of their husband. So, officers' wives often led groups or would be responsible for communication and organising a lot of the time. There were exceptions and, thankfully, that wasn't as prevalent in the troop I was in.

Emma soon settled into our lovely home in Waterbeach. Our back garden backed onto a field where we would often see the farmer with his tractor or combine harvester. Soon Emma was employed and worked at Debenhams on the Clinique cosmetics counter, in the centre of Cambridge. Having a job did wonders for her as she felt that she was now contributing and providing a service and having daily interactions with customers. Em thrived on chit-chat about the small things and had a knack of putting people at ease and making them feel special.

I joined my new troop in the UK and was amazed at the slowness of pace compared to Germany. They rarely went on exercise and usually had every weekend off. Wednesday afternoons were known as recce afternoons where you were allowed to play a sport or go for a run, basically physical activity.

All of the guys were friendly and there was a general respect for those that had served in Germany as we were usually more 'switched on' in terms of soldiering skills. By now I had qualified as a Plant operator (Plant Op) class 1 so at the top of my trade, which essentially meant I got paid more and could operate a wide range of construction vehicles, diggers to most people. I noticed straight away that there didn't seem to be the same team spirit that I'd experienced towards the end of my tour in Germany. Perhaps I just needed to give it time for relationships to grow. A plus about UK postings is that there were often tours to far flung countries like Kenya, The Falkland Islands and Belize.

During the summer of 1990 as a squadron, we were the Spearhead squadron. That meant that essentially, we were on call for duties anywhere in the world. This placed certain restrictions on being contactable and able to return to camp within 24 hours or sooner.

Em and I took our summer holiday on the Isle of Wight, camping. Life was very simple and uncomplicated, and we were enjoying times of just having each other. Laughing and full of youthful exuberance. We loved camping because we were close to nature and fresh air was on tap. It was a first visit for us and we were impressed by the cleanliness and the friendliness of the people.

Wisdom/Reflection
- *Enjoy the moment because you don't know what's around the corner*
- *Don't plan too far ahead and too specifically, because there are too many variables in between*
- *Be mindful of what those closest to you may be going through. Transition from one thing to the next can be more challenging for others*
- *When going through transition be sure to communicate checking in on how each other is feeling*

8.
Operation Granby – The Gulf War 1991
The build up

On August 2, 1990, we awoke in our tent to the news that Saddam Hussein had invaded Kuwait. This provoked different reactions in both of us. For me it meant a potential deployment and for Em it meant potentially, sleepless nights and stricken with worry, awaiting my return. For the rest of our holiday, we kept our portable radio tuned in to the world service. It soon became apparent that this was a major world event that a Spearhead Squadron wasn't going to help solve.

On our return home there was a buzz around camp as people speculated whether we would go to war and whether we, as a regiment, would be deployed.

21 Engr Regt had been put on notice as part of an armoured battle group that would most likely be deployed. For them, preparations started as the situation in the Middle East developed. Despite the pollical process that was underway, the military started to train and plan for imminent war.

For every soldier this was a time of expectancy and, although I can't speak for every soldier, there was a real desire to be in the mix and be part of it. To put all that training into practice and to be able to say you saw action, having the medal to prove it. To those that have been in combat previously, the view may have been very different compared to us green soldiers that really didn't have a clue of how active service could impact you, physically, emotionally and spiritually.

As a community in Waterbeach there was a real sense of togetherness, and it was far less formal than in Germany. Our neighbours were very supportive and helped us settle in easily. We often had meals at each other's homes, where there was usually lots of laughter and storytelling.

There were rumours that 34 Fd Sqn would play a part in the mobilisation, dependent on your skill set. As tensions mounted and it could be seen that Saddam Hussein was not going to leave Kuwait, the likelihood of a large coalition force responding was becoming a reality. As an experienced CET operator there was a likelihood that those skills would be needed. Usually, where the battle group went, so did the CETs.

One of my neighbours was a veteran from the Falklands War. He was also Commando trained so a fit and able soldier. As we discussed current world events, I expressed how much I was up for the fight and getting involved. I was aware that I was talking with passion in my tone as I shared my views and what should happen. I wasn't getting the same passionate response back from him, in fact, I detected a drawing back. He actually looked fearful, which I found strange considering his experience and stature. He paused and then expressed how, if at all possible, he didn't want to be deployed. He clearly knew something I didn't, and his response was far more cautious and probably wiser than mine. He was a few years older than me and had two small children too. I recovered my overzealous comments by recognising that his experience spoke for a lot and that there were still many unknowns that could and would change my outlook. What did he know that I didn't? I had a fleeting thought that he could be cowardly and despite him having seen action before maybe he was just of that disposition. This was a fleeting thought, and outrageous in some ways, and most probably untrue.

Later in 1990 it became clearer that war was the most likely outcome. British troops had already deployed to Saudi Arabia, including my old regiment, 21. They were busy training in desert conditions and doing a lot of waiting.

Back in Blighty individuals were warned that they would also be deployed. Doc Holiday, (not his real first name), my next-door neighbour and I would be going. There weren't many of us notified from my squadron. Those that were going were soon looked upon with envy by some and relief by others I'm sure, particularly those with children.

The end of 1990 would be a fraught time for Em and I as I was put on notice to leave and then cancelled. This happened a number of times, so false starts became a feature that we had to adapt to. It was taking its toll on Emma as the news constantly reported and debated on the projected casualty numbers of allied forces. Emma had dealt with enough loss to last a lifetime in a relatively short period of time. Her mindset was resigned to losing me too and she couldn't see a happy ending in sight. This was understandable and, thankfully, being part of a local church, provided us with spiritual nourishment and fellowship. Histon Baptist Church would prove to be a critical element of our time in Cambridge. It was here that we made many deep friendships.

Peter and Sue would prove to be lifelong friends that we would see grow in faith as they too found faith in Jesus, that transformed the way they would live their lives. We shared many evenings eating together and talking about God. They hadn't been Christians long but very quickly grew in their knowledge of the bible and prayer.

Now what I'm going to describe will either cause you to put this book down or entice you to read more. Thankfully, the events that follow are the experience of Pete and Sue and not mine. They reported it to Em and I shortly after it happened.

The first evening we invited Pete and Sue for a meal, we wanted to make it special, with delicious food and a welcoming ambience. Em had made our married quarter look lovely and homely. By now we had learned about how to create nice lighting when positioning our lamps and bulb lighting. Fresh flowers were always a feature in our home as well as pot pourri. So, there was always a pleasant fragrance scent in our home. Em had planned the meal we were going to have and we had bought in some nice wine and Schloer too, a favourite soft drink for Christians!

Pete and Sue arrived on time and there were hugs and kisses on the doorstep and a feeling of happiness because we all got on so well. Sue is a Geordie so her accent along with a high pitched shrill was a pleasure to hear. Peter was born and bred around Cambridge and has a very relaxed demeanour, so between them a great combination.
I would describe Pete and Sue as a safe pair of hands, totally trustworthy, with a great sense of humour and loyal. I sensed these qualities early on in our relationship, that have proved to be correct over 30 years later.

I took their coats and Em ushered them into the living room. I took the drinks order, Pete and Sue were having the obligatory Schloer and Em and I had wine. The evening went well, and everyone enjoyed the meal Em had cooked. After dessert we relaxed back in the living room with a hot drink and our conversation continued about Jesus and our experiences. We also discussed things that were written in the bible that were particularly relevant for life application for where we were at, at that time. For most of the evening there was lots of story telling and sharing life detail.

Towards the end of the evening Pete and Sue seemed agitated but I wasn't sure why. Perhaps it was tiredness or perhaps they'd reached saturation point with our company. I glanced over to Emma who I could see was puzzled but masking her curiosity well. I got their coats and a moment of awkwardness occurred as we stood in the hallway allowing Pete and Sue to shuffle by as if they couldn't wait to get out!

I closed the door behind them and exhaled looking over at Emma. "That was a bit of a strange ending!" she said. We climbed the stairs to bed, agreeing to face the kitchen in the morning.
A few days went by until we heard from Pete and Sue again. They called us to thank us for having them around but also wanted to share with us what happened that night. What happened that night? We had a meal and some time together, that's what happened. What else could have happened?

Peter started to tell me his account of what happened towards the end of the evening. I was astounded at what he shared next. At a point in the evening whilst we were discussing spiritual matters, Peter saw what he described as demonic faces that had transposed over mine and Emma's faces. He explained how at the time he was perplexed and scared at the same time. He wondered whether Sue could see what he saw and by her body language knew that she was sensing something too. Our voices were normal, it was just our faces that shocked them into leaving earlier than expected. Both Pete and Sue were fearful and couldn't make sense of why this would or could happen to people that loved God and were talking about wholesome things.

Theologically, I couldn't put their experience into any box, but one thing was for sure, Em and I believed them. Peter went on to tell us that he and Sue both had to take the next day off work due to the effect the experience had on them both. My only explanation of why this happened could have been that the devil didn't want our friendship to form and perhaps wanted to scare Pete and Sue away from the Christian faith as they were quite new believers. In fact, it had the opposite effect as they went on to serve faithfully as part of a church community and still do to this day.

In December 1990 I went from being on standby to being deployed to Sennelager, Germany for supplementary training prior to being deployed to Saudi Arabia. Emma and I were very sad to be parting and despite the support we were receiving from our church, the pain of separation was palpable. Just prior to being deployed Em and I had taken a short break up north to a Christian retreat centre, called Scargill House. We met lots of lovely people there and felt comforted and supported by prayers and times of reflection. We managed to go out on group walks too, enjoying the wintery northern weather.

I believed that The Holy Spirit had given me Psalm 91 to hold on to. It brought both of us great comfort and confidence that God had my back and that I would return. My thinking was quite simple. If God had called me to serve in the police sometime in the future, then I had to come back in one piece. Emma was a worrier, and my concern was more for her than for me. When she was anxious, she would stop eating and lose weight and her sleep would be affected too. I was far more mechanical in my thinking and found that I responded by boxing things off in my mind. I was very task orientated and could disconnect from my emotions quite easily. Probably not always the best approach but it's the only way I knew how as a soldier in his 20s.

I have to say I was so excited to be going on my first active deployment. The media at the time was speculating on casualty rates and strategies from both sides. As a soldier I longed to see combat, to get involved and experience war. I was keen to try out my kit and put all those years of training into practice. Reading this back I realise how much my attitudes and views have changed, but I can only be honest about how I felt at the time. I didn't have a political view of the impending war; I just knew that we needed to kick Saddam's proverbial ass. I hadn't considered the carnage, death, emotional and psychological damage. I hadn't considered the impact my deployment would have on my family. The worry and toll on their mental health.

What I did know is that this was going to be a significant event in world history, and I was going to be part of it. I wanted to have stories to tell my grandchildren and I wanted my country to be proud of me for my part in it. I wanted a medal too, a visible representation of achievement. All these things as a young man were important to me, it was a mark of accomplishment for a soldier to have gone to war.

On arrival at Sennelager we were ushered off the coach to our accommodation that was pretty basic but liveable, the dormitories having rows of bunkbeds with very little room in-between. There were only a few of us deployed from 24 Fd. Sqn and that was due to our skill set. Doc Holiday, my next-door neighbour, was a combat engineer (class 1) as well as a chippy (carpenter). I was a combat engineer (class 2), Plant Operator Mechanic (class 1), as well as a CET operator.

At the time Doc had a young daughter, I think she was about three years old. Doc had kissed her goodnight and told her daddy would be back soon. Although aspirational, none of us could make that promise because we just didn't know whether we would survive or come back in one piece. We knew that the Iraqi army at the time was the fourth largest in the world and that it was going to be no walk in the park.

I soon made some new friends and there was a real feeling of camaraderie. Doc and I stuck together and soon a group of us formed and became good friends, despite coming from different regiments. I had a keen interest in modern military history and in military hardware. I scored highly on enemy vehicle and weapon recognition and looked forward to our training that would include the firing of different weapons.
We would also receive advanced training for navigation and survival in the desert as well as first aid that included administering intravenous drips. There was a big emphasis on nuclear, biological and chemical (NBC) warfare drills too. It was believed that the Iraqi forces had the ability to deliver

such agents and the threat of this happening was believed to be high. The thought of dying from an NBC attack sowed fear into the hearts of most of us, that's why everyone paid close attention to NBC training. We rehearsed our drills relentlessly, from using the Chemical Agent Monitor (CAM) to detect any chemical threat, to donning our masks, exhaling into the mask shouting, "GAS! GAS! GAS!" We were taught how to administer first aid to those affected by a chemical agent, by using the Combo pen that contained a shot of atropine.

Each day we had refresher training on various weapons and then had the pleasure of firing them. We practiced with the Carl Gustav 84mm anti-tank weapon and the 66 light anti tank weapon. I know I shouldn't say it but it was great fun, particularly the part when you've fired the weapon and then you watch the missile hit the target which was usually a scrap armoured vehicle positioned in the distance. The reality of all this training was that when necessary, firing one of these weapons at a target for real would cause death and devastation. At the time I was alright with that because they were the enemy. They were trying to kill us so there could only be one winner, and, with God's help, it would be us. When I say us, I mean the Coalition forces that were amassing against Iraq. There were now several armies that made up the allied effort, including Arab nations too.

As a Christian I had to think about whether I was comfortable with my job as a soldier, as I could be in a position where I had to take life. I'm not sure that I was willing to fight to prove our politicians right, it was more about playing my part as part of a team, supporting my mates and protecting each other. Bottom line was that we all wanted to return home, unscathed with lots of war stories to tell, and a medal, of course.

My feelings at the time were that murder was a sin as described in the bible within the ten commandments. Lawful killing was an occupational requirement when called to do so. There were rules of engagement, and we were bound by the Geneva Convention, that outlined how we were to treat the enemy. That said, there was still something carnal within me that wanted a fight, wanted an opportunity to be exposed to combat. But this wasn't so much about lawful killing and the Geneva Convention. For me, it was more about the condition of my heart and that internal struggle of loving everyone, even the Iraqis. These people had families and hopes and aspirations and wanted to live their best life, like me. I had to trust that God would guide me and I would do the right thing when the time came. I didn't particularly have a desire to take another life and ordinarily it would be the infantry that would be most likely to encounter the enemy. I just knew that whatever happened I wouldn't let those around me down, and I would play my part whatever that would mean, even taking the life of the enemy.

Whilst at Sennelager, I met Nick who was to be my crewman once we got to Saudi Arabia. The CET had a crew of two, an operator and a commander. Nick would be operating which essentially meant digging the main Challenger Battle Tanks in. This allowed the tanks to sit at ground level giving them better protection from air and ground attack. Nick was from the West Midlands too. He was a little younger than me and had very little experience operating the CET. He confessed that after completing his course he had spent little time on the CET. This didn't bode well for me as I was probably going to have to unnecessarily go over procedures, which wasn't ideal in a theatre of war. It was going to be challenging enough performing my own role as well as babysitting Nick. It wasn't his fault as his role prior to being deployed was as a combat engineer, (Oggy). He'd been assigned to a CET crew, as on paper he had passed the course.

I soon discovered that Nick was a crack shot, when practising firing the General Purpose Machine Gun, (GPMG) in an anti-aircraft role. The GPMG is an effective piece of kit and can fire 750 rounds a minute and was widely used by all three services, army, navy and air force. On this particular training session, we had practiced stripping and assembling the weapon. Now came the fun bit where we all had a crack at shooting down a fast-moving model airplane, that simulated enemy aircraft.

The GPMG was mounted on a larch pole, which allowed you to stand and fire the weapon that could swivel 360 degrees. Each of us had a belt of 200 rounds to use and our number two was a second person that would watch over the shoulder of the firer and tap his left or right shoulder to help guide his shooting. There was a tracer round one in every three. A tracer round lit up so effectively that you could see your rounds heading towards the target, or not!

I had my go and, although I'm not a bad shot, this was the first time for me aiming at a fast-moving target in the sky. There was no shame in not hitting it as only one out of about 30 of us hit the aircraft that day, and guess who it was? Yes, it was Nick. As he squeezed the trigger, I could see his tracer rounds obliterate the model aircraft. He'd only fired about two bursts and hit it on his second burst of fire. There was clapping and cheering as a red-faced model aircraft operator approached us holding bits of the shredded aircraft in his hands. Nick was still standing beside the GPMG and, I could see as the man approached, Nick smiled bashfully and said: 'Sorry mate' and mingled into the group. The model operator had taken it personally which we all found hilarious. Serves him right for smugly doing loop the loops prior to being shot down.

Whilst lying on my bunk after the day's training, I would think of Em but was reluctant to open that box of emotions as I knew I wouldn't be seeing her for some time. I didn't have the time to sit and reflect on how I was feeling as it would only lead to 'what ifs' and 'if only'. I concentrated on building relationships with the people I was with and preparing myself for what was to come. I was constantly checking my kit making sure everything was ordered and in the best possible condition.

Our time at Sennelager was drawing to a close and quite a few of the lads were keen to have a night on the town. I went with them for a beer, but gracefully declined their offer to join them at a peep show. For those of you who are unfamiliar with a peep show, it's a small room with a large glass window separating the customer from the lady undressing provocatively. It's your own private sitting. When back at camp there was the swapping of stories and graphic descriptions of what they saw and did. Each to their own I guess but this was squaddy behaviour and I probably would have joined them a few years ago before becoming a Christian.

I didn't judge them because I had the same carnal urges, especially as there would be no female contact for however long. The slightly disappointing thing was that some of the guys were married. As a man I struggled with those urges and despite believing that since giving my life to Christ, and being a new creation, I still felt that pull. Thankfully, I resisted, and a lot of the guys noticed that and later told me that they respected me for that.

I dreaded being a hypocrite so really did try and live the life, despite my thought-life sometimes telling another story. I felt responsible for being a witness to all of those that didn't have a relationship with Jesus. If I behaved in a way that didn't demonstrate faith in action, then what difference was there between me and a man that didn't believe in Jesus and behaved like I did. I had to walk the talk, as well as being the best soldier I could. Just because I was a Christian didn't mean that I couldn't be strong and good at my job. Being a Christian made me a better soldier and allowed me to tap into power that was supernatural, changing circumstances in the natural.

I constantly had a struggle in my mind that originated from my times watching porn before I was a Christian. The love of the female form and the distortion of how women should be viewed and treated wrestled with what the eye viewed as pleasurable. This was a private battle I fought and for a long time this enemy of my soul took up residency in a private room in my heart. I did believe at the time that God could take away this unhealthy desire, and I really wanted him to, but for some reason the habit didn't go. I felt very guilty as often it led to masturbation and that made me feel unfaithful to Em. It wasn't a good feeling as it was a contradiction in my life alongside, most of the time, me being a loving, caring man of integrity. Was the problem exaggerated because I was a full red-blooded man? Did all men struggle with this? Perhaps not all men, but as I journeyed in life, I came to realise that the vast majority of men struggle with sexual sin.

That said, men who don't have a relationship with God, feel they aren't accountable to anyone, so they develop their own truth and values, some secret and some not. Conversely, the Christian has a conscience that is accountable to God. We have commands and guidance on how to live through the teachings in the bible. I knew that Jesus said that we would be more than conquerors in him. I would have settled for just being a conqueror. I had the head knowledge but still wasn't getting the breakthrough that I expected. Perhaps I was simplifying the process, because it wasn't just about the temptation and the pleasure, but something far deeper that was going to need to be worked through. I just know that I wanted to please

God but my trust wavered at times because I couldn't see results as swiftly as I would have liked in my life.

Being away from my wife for so long was going to be a real struggle emotionally, physically and spiritually. Em was my best friend too and we used to get great comfort and encouragement from praying together. We were very playful too and I cherished our intimate times. There was a tangible chemistry between Em and I that excited me. I loved her femininity and her gentleness. She was real hoot too with a great sense of humour, often giggling together in the dark before going off to sleep.

Training at Sennelager completed we were on our way to Saudi Arabia with a stop off in Cyprus to refuel. I felt quite calm and pondered quietly during the flight with my Sony Walkman playing a Randy Crawford tape. There were a few lads larking about, joking and laughing, some were sleeping, and others seemed to be reflecting as I was. I started to think about how many of us would return. Would we defeat the Iraqis? How long would this whole thing take?

Wisdom/Reflection
- *Don't worry, things may not turn out as you fear*
- *Solid friendships are like gold during times of uncertainty*
- *Invest in your friendships, be generous, so that both parties can withdraw from the balance in times of adversity*
- *Distance can make the heart grow fonder, reuniting brings joy*
- *When anxiety and fear come knocking, let hope and faith answer the door*

9.
The Real Thing

On arrival in Al Jubail, I immediately sensed the temperature change as we exited the aircraft and were reunited with our kit. I glanced around, taking in my surroundings and noticed all the military hardware, that was familiar to me but now painted a sandy colour.

Once we had collected our kit, we were herded onto coaches to be taken to a transit camp nicknamed Black Adder. As we travelled to the camp, I looked out of the coach window and noticed how many mosques there were and how barren everything looked.

My initial feelings were that I didn't like Saudi Arabia. It felt artificially built up where we were. I'm sure there are some picturesque parts that are steeped in fascinating history and tradition. There didn't seem to be a welcoming vibe from the Arabs. Despite us being a liberating force that was also preventing Iraq invading their country, there didn't seem to be much of a welcome. Perhaps I'm being unfair, and it could just be down to cultural differences. I just felt an oppression in my spirit, almost like there was an invisible control over the population.

We were soon accommodated in a tent that housed around 12 of us. We were all Sappers so that was a good start and there was a natural sense of camaraderie, as we were all from the same Corps. It didn't really matter that we were all from different regiments, we were all Sappers, so our roles were familiar to one another. Doc and I were in the same tent and so was Dave Patrick who would become a very close friend of mine. The rest of the lads were a jolly lot and we had no difficult characters in our tent. A couple of them were quite young, Billy from the Wirral was just 17, not long out of training. The most senior rank in our tent was a Sergeant, who I hadn't come across before. He kept himself to himself and didn't really provide any leadership.

Routine was critical to keeping us focused so there was a lot of weapon cleaning and preparing of kit as we may have to be mobilised at a moment's notice.

As we became familiar with the camp, we realised there wasn't really a lot here. As the camp developed, they provided an open-air cinema, that was well received. It seemed strange watching movies under the stars on the edge of the desert. Hot showers were located at Camp 4. Certain units had the monopoly on the buses that shuttled to and from Showersville. We decided that we were well overdue a hot shower so me and one other blagged our way onto one of the buses, that was mainly occupied by Army Catering Corps personnel, known commonly as slop jockeys.

As we sat minding our own business, feeling blessed to be on our way to a hot shower, the sound of a weapon discharge rang out within the bus. This could either be that the bus was under fire or there had been a negligent discharge by someone on the bus. We had SMGs but the cooks had the newer SA80. Our first thought was that we were under fire as just that day we had been briefed to be vigilant as there were rogue Iraqi elements that were in Saudi Arabia to commit acts of sabotage.
The driver stopped the bus in the confusion. I crouched down low and scuttled quickly down the aisle of the bus and shouted to the driver to open the door. He looked at me with a stunned look but opened the doors fumbling as he did so. My mate followed me, and we stayed low making it into a ditch, taking up a fire position. My heart was racing and as we looked at each other we wondered what we should do next. All sorts of thoughts rushed into my mind like, what if the bus was hit by an RPG or small arms fire?

After a few minutes I sensed that the reason for the loud bang had been discovered. We cautiously returned to the bus and could see a group huddled around one of the seats near to the front. It transpired that one of the lads was playing with the safety catch on his weapon and clearly at some point must have pulled the trigger with the safety off. He was sitting on the outer seat and his mate was sitting closest to the window. The chap who had discharged his weapon was a deathly shade of grey. His weapon was taken from him and made safe.

There was a Corporal on board from his unit that took charge of the situation. As I took all the detail in, I could see that the lad sitting closest to the window was cradling his hand. As I glanced over to him, I could see that his hand was bleeding. The bullet had travelled straight through the fleshy part of his hand and out through the side of the bus. He was in shock and didn't say a lot. I looked at the outside of the bus and could see the exit hole where the bullet had tumbled causing two exit holes. There was no way this could be sorted unofficially. I later heard that the cook who discharged his weapon received a fine and an entry on his file. Suffice to say we didn't get our hot shower that day, thanks a lot, slop jockey!

Due to the anticipated chemical threat from Iraq, we were required to have various vaccinations that would protect us from some nasties that could be delivered via Scud missiles. One morning we queued up outside the medical tent and received jabs for anthrax, plague and a couple more that I can't remember. Dave Patrick was in front of me and opted to have all the jabs. His last jab was for plague and immediately after it had been administered, I saw his head go bright red and then he collapsed to the floor like a sack of spuds! I helped get him to his feet and he was given a seat to come round. I was next so I opted for all of the jabs apart from plague! We were also issued with NAPS tablets that were to be taken at regular intervals during the day. They were issued as a protection from the effects of nerve agent poisoning.

Every day we would practice getting into our NBC kit as quickly as we can which included fitting our respirator. Everyone took this training extremely seriously as no one wanted to die of nerve agent poisoning. It wasn't a nice way to go, it was slow and painful.

As we settled into our lavish accommodation it was still lacking some creature comforts. Thankfully, Doc was a very able carpenter and set to work to make me and him a set of bunk beds. Somehow, he acquired them and knocked them up in no time. We were the envy of our neighbourhood, but Doc wasn't taking anymore orders.

We discovered that there were some U.S troops nearby so one evening we ventured into their camp to make friends. It didn't take long before we were invited into a billet for a chat and a beverage. Wherever we went our weapons and respirators were always carried. I was issued with a Sterling Sub Machine Gun, which the Yanks loved the look of. The fact that a wet blanket would stop its bullets didn't matter to them. One guy offered me $500 and his M16 assault rifle in exchange. I was sorely tempted but graciously declined as I didn't fancy a court martial for giving away the Queen's property.

Iraqi Scud missile attacks were almost a daily occurrence now and I now know that our special forces were busy trying to locate and destroy the mobile Scuds, behind enemy lines. For us, it meant donning our NBC respirators and protective clothing, often leaving it on and sleeping in it. Thankfully, the Patriot missile intercept system took out almost all the Scuds before they hit their intended target.

We were sad to hear one day early on during the air campaign that a Scud had got through and hit a military installation in Al Jubail, killing several service personnel.

Camp Black Adder was quite wide open and had no perimeter protection. It was decided that we needed an earth bund constructing around the whole of the camp perimeter. That was a job for us, so we started to plan how to get started immediately. I visited the Yanks because I was aware that they had some plant equipment. They were keen to help and before I knew it I was driving a Caterpillar D6 Bulldozer out of their compound. There were several of us that were qualified to operate the Dozer, so I drew up a rota and we got started straight away. It felt good to have a purpose in doing something that was benefiting lots of people, potentially saving lives. We completed the bund in the early hours of the morning. When the camp arose in the morning there was a buzz of comments, and we were held in a good light for cracking on through the night to get it finished. We received a formal thank you too from the Camp Commander, that put a smile on our faces. The bund seemed to bring a reality to the threat as we were now in a defensive position.

Mail started to arrive including parcels from folk back in blighty that wanted to support the troops. The parcels were evenly distributed so everyone had something to open. They contained boxer shorts, sweets, magazines and other bits and pieces that were gratefully received. We were all given a supply of 'blueys', the blue folding letter that was a convenient item doubling up as writing paper and folded into itself as an envelope.

I had started to write to Emma and every time I did, I couldn't avoid opening that box of emotions that most of the time was kept tightly shut. Sometimes the mists in my mind would go to a dark place where I entertained thoughts of the future. Would I survive this? Did I really sense God calling me to the Police Force or was that my imagination or some random crazy thought? Would I be injured, and would Emma still want me if I was? I was too young to die and I hadn't loved Emma enough and I wanted the opportunity to love her more. I wanted to grow old with Emma and have grandchildren that we could walk to the park. I wanted the opportunity to be a father. I wanted to have children that I could adore, and watch grow into beautiful people. Now none of this was certain and although nothing in life is certain, being at war changed the odds.

My letters to Emma were small talk really and reassuring her that I was alright. I could sense from her letters that she was putting on a brave face, but I knew that she was anxious and that this whole situation would take its toll on her.
Most days leading up to deployment to the forward area were filled with haircuts, troop runs and weapon cleaning. NCOs (non-commissioned officers) were also required to prepare and deliver training sessions on different subjects to refresh and test knowledge.

I found that I needed regular time to be by myself. If I didn't find time to pray and read my bible I got agitated and my spiritual routine helped me stay positive and hopeful.

The tent always had a murmur of chatter and laughter so I would sit outside the tent which made it marginally better. It didn't take long for the lads to notice that I was spending time reading outside. They were respectful but curious and once they discovered that I was reading the Bible, they started to ask questions and were particularly interested in whether Iraq was mentioned. Once they knew that Babylon was ancient Iraq, a flood of questions followed wanting to know if the bible prophesied their fate. Although I wasn't interested in theological debates, we did have some interesting conversations about God. Most were fascinated at me appearing normal but being a Christian too. I told them that I was praying for all of them and they were genuinely appreciative, acknowledging that they needed god's peace for what was to come.

The Sergeant in our tent became more and more isolated and he was visibly anxious about the future. He didn't want to talk and verbalised that he just wanted to be back home with his wife. I was really surprised and disappointed that he, as a senior man both in rank and age, was openly fearful and unhelpful in helping others that were less experienced and needed his leadership. We all wanted to be at home with our wives but what we thought and what came out of our mouths were two very different things.

For the whole of my time at Black Adder before going forward, he remained invisible and disconnected from everyone else in the tent. I was later to discover on returning back to the UK that he was on the front cover of a broadsheet paper prodding the ground for an enemy land mine with a steely look on his face. I saw the picture and smiled. I'm not sure I could have pulled that off knowing that I displayed very little leadership and didn't actually go to the front. It takes all sorts I guess. I wonder what stories he told his grandchildren. Hopefully, truthful ones about how he struggled emotionally and how his mental health debilitated him. That would be a powerful story that was true. No shame in that.

The air campaign seemed to be going well, so the time was drawing nearer for us to collect our vehicles and move to the Forward Maintenance Area, (FMA). Supplies and equipment were being transported up the Main Supply Route (MSR), in a constant stream of traffic. Accidents were bound to happen and they did. News reached the camp of a serious accident involving a British Army vehicle. Unfortunately, a Lieutenant Colonel was killed, due to an Arab driver falling asleep at the wheel, travelling in the opposite direction. The Saudi police were involved and arrested the Arab driver. In Saudi they have the state police and the religious police. Our Military police were also involved in the investigation. I later learned from one of the MPs that the Arab driver had confessed to falling asleep at the wheel and that he was sentenced to death by beheading! The MP that relayed the story was present at the beheading as part of the procedure. He was ashen grey when he shared the story and was visibly shaken. I was amazed at how quickly justice was served. It could have only been a couple of weeks at the most. A big contrast to the UK or particularly the US where prisoners remain on death row for years.

Whilst at Black Adder Camp we received the devastating news that there had been a 'blue on blue' contact, also known as friendly fire. One of the U.S A10 Tank Buster airplanes had mistakenly targeted a British Warrior Armoured Personnel carriers. All the soldiers inside were killed. Understandably, we were very angry at the time and spat out insults about trigger happy Yanks. On reflection how was that pilot feeling, knowing he had killed a complete section of British Troops? Over 30 years later, I'm sure he relives that moment he pulled the trigger. Sometime later, on my return to the UK, I would get to see the Warrior vehicle that was destroyed in the friendly fire incident. I was shocked to see the damage that had been caused and reflected on the families that were now living with the catastrophic loss of their loved ones.

I had been given my notice to get ready to leave Black Adder Camp. I hadn't seen Nick Jacobs, my crewman since arriving at Black Adder, understandably so as he was tented with the guys from his regiment that he was familiar with. Essentially, Nick and I were strangers and really needed to build our relationship, as we would be living and operating sometimes under pressure in close proximity of each other. The CET crew compartment is quite compact, and it requires things to be organised and put in their rightful place.

Just before leaving Black Adder Camp we were paid a visit by General Sir Peter de la Billiere, Commander in Chief of British Forces in the Gulf. We were warned about his visit the day before so made sure we were presentable. We hadn't received our full sets of desert combat uniform yet, so most of us had to mix and match with our green, northwest Europe combat jackets with desert combat bottoms, or vice versa. We looked like a right rag tag lot. That said, we were clean and presentable and ready for our auspicious visit from the 'Top Brass'.

He arrived on time with his entourage and we were assembled in a horse shoe shape. There were quite a few of us formed up in three ranks. As he approached us, we were called to attention as the formal salutes went on and then we were stood at ease, ready to hear what the General had to say. The General had an air of authority about him but was friendly at the same time. He smiled as he approached a parked Land Rover and jumped up onto the bonnet so that he had a view of all present. His talk was inspirational as he shared his own experience the first time he was deployed as a young soldier. He was a good storyteller and was quite animated. He had the respect of the men listening due to his army service. He was a soldier that had been places and had served in the SAS. We listened. He explained that we would be deployed initially as BCRs (battle casualty replacements). He reflected on his role as a BCR many years ago and how frustrated he felt because he wanted to get in the thick of it. He told us that there would be a lot of waiting around but that we were to remain focused because we could be called upon at short notice. His talk lasted about 10 minutes and then he jumped down from the Land Rover, talked to some of the guys at the front and was then whisked away, presumably to another camp.

I was impressed with his speech and later we all agreed that we were glad that the General was leading us as he seemed like a common-sense type of bloke.

My previous regiment, 21 Engr Regt, had been in the Gulf since mid-1990. They had collected their vehicles and had been training in the desert for a few months. Support Troop 1st Fd Sqn, my previous troop, were settled in and, now that I was going forward, I longed to meet up with them. These were guys that I knew well, and if I was going to get into a spot of trouble, these were the guys I wanted to be with. No disrespect to Nick but I didn't know him and I knew that on his own admission he wasn't very competent on a CET.

I can remember hearing the anticipated casualty figures on our side and that made me more determined to get crewed with someone else so we could perform at our best. I felt quite bad for feeling this way, but I didn't want to get injured or die because I didn't want to offend Nick.

Em had been informed back in the UK with the other wives whose husbands that were deployed, that if we died as a result of nuclear biological or chemical effects, then our bodies would not be returned home. At the time there was a real sense that this was going to be a bloody war, so we weren't overreacting.

I was constantly reminding myself of Psalm 91 and The Lord's promise to me. I had to constantly refocus my thoughts that naturally drifted towards, 'what ifs' and 'if onlys'.

Dave Patrick had become a very close friend of mine and, as our time together drew to a close, as I was going forward, we started to think of ways that we could be deployed together.
Dave wasn't CET-trained but was a tough resourceful Yorkshireman. Dave was a little older than me and was a man that could get almost anything sorted. He was resourceful and a loyal friend. I know it sounds dramatic and over the top now, but my thinking was who would I prefer to get in a tough spot with, perhaps even spend my last moments with? Dave was also a rip-roaring laugh and optimistic in his outlook. How could I swing this swap though? I'm sure Nick wouldn't have minded but how would it work administratively. Dave was happy to go absent without leave (AWOL) effectively and take all the blame, leaving Nick at Black Adder Camp.

I so wanted this to happen, and I think we could have blagged it but there was something inside of me saying it wasn't right. It's what I wanted to happen but was it what the Holy Spirit wanted? I once read that the Holy Spirit won't work outside of the truth. Bottom line I needed to trust that, for whatever reason, Nick was the man I was to be crewed with.

I had made some deep friendships whilst at Black Adder Camp. I was sad to be leaving but didn't want to stay as that would mean that I miss out on any action. I looked around our tent wondering what would become of us all. I knew that if we survived, I would be in touch with some of these guys again. Some were friendships for this season, others could be for life. Black Adder Camp had become very cosy and convenient. I could see that some had become very attached to it, making it their home. The availability of a tuck shop, hot showers, open air cinema. I was ready for the desert and

the experience of being part of a Battle Group. This is what I had trained for whilst posted to 21 Engr Regt in Germany. I wanted to be issued with our CET and equipment so we could start getting familiar with it on the ground, and, more importantly, see how much Nick could remember about operating the CET.
The day came when Nick and I, along with others, left for the Forward Maintenance Area (FMA). We were transported by coach or rather an old type of bus that looked like it should have suitcases strapped to the top as it travelled along the dusty highway.

The Iraqis had been subjected to round the clock bombing from the coalition air forces. We were told it was going well and that we had control of the skies. As we neared the FMA I could see plane trails that I hadn't seen before. They were very high up and covered the sky. I would learn later that these belonged to the mighty B52 bombers that the Americans flew.

We soon arrived at the vehicle allocation area, and I was shown around the CET that had been freshly painted in desert colours. The Quartermaster had a clip board with an inventory that was checked off as we inspected the vehicle together.

Everything was there including buoyancy floats in case we had an amphibious task! I only knew of the Euphrates River, but I knew that some of the Wadi's could fill up around this time of year. I just couldn't see how some of this equipment was going to be of any use in a mainly arid desert. Hey, maybe we would get to Baghdad and have some need of the swimming equipment then, but I very much doubted it. I suspected that our main task would be excavating with the powerful front bucket. Moving earth to provide defences for our tanks and other armoured vehicles. We were also used to lay metal matting for vehicles to prevent them getting stuck in muddy conditions, particularly on the approach to bridges.

The trouble with the buoyancy aids were that they were big and bulky and were carried in the bucket. As I walked around the CET, I started to plan what kit I was going to ditch. This could be risky as if called upon to complete a task but not having the equipment could be embarrassing and potentially a disciplinary offence, not to mention putting other lives at risk for not being able to operate properly. I'm not usually a rule breaker but I am in favour of being pragmatic so that we could get the job done quickly and effectively.

I was a confident operator of the CET and had a lot of experience in getting the best out of the machine. They could be quite temperamental and were renowned for guzzling lots of oil and breaking down. As previously mentioned, I was a qualified instructor too so, hopefully, this would benefit Nick as I reacquainted him with the CET. I could see that we had been issued with an Auxiliary Lifting Attachment (ALA) too. This was mainly used as a mini crane but had a limited lifting capacity. I had used it for real but not very often. Once again it was cumbersome and awkwardly shaped. This usually ended up being dumped in the bucket too. The bucket that we needed to keep clear for the likelihood of being called at short notice to dig tanks and armoured vehicles in.

We were also issued our ammunition for our personal weapon. We were given 500 rounds of 9mm ammunition each, as well as six hand grenades, smoke grenades for the CET smoke dischargers and a '66' Light anti-tank weapon. Like us, many were collecting their vehicles, from Challenger Main Battle Tanks to Warrior armoured Fighting Vehicles. It looked like there were hundreds of vehicles spread out over quite a large area.

Nick and I climbed aboard our CET and started her up to make towards where we were to stay until we moved forward with the battle group. On starting the Rolls Royce engine, I was pleased to hear the deep grumble of the exhaust that blew out an initial plume of fumes. I checked all my instruments and, thankfully, there were no red lights illuminated. I could see that Nick was sitting awkwardly to begin with, probably daunted by the reality of sitting in the machine that would be providing us with protection and could be taking us into some hairy situations.

We parked our vehicle up and started to arrange our kit. There was our personal equipment then there were the tools and equipment to keep the CET functioning. I could see that there were other engineer vehicles nearby and I was looking forward to meeting the crews so we could start building relationships. This was critical to getting on and helping each other out. We loaded our magazines which each took 30 rounds, and we stored all our unused ammunition. We loaded the smoke grenades into the CET dischargers. These were used to provide cover from smoke if we needed it. If I had to discharge them the likelihood would be that we were in real trouble. Our bergens, that contained all our spare clothing, toiletries etc. were stowed on the top deck for easy access. We couldn't find a specific place for the anti-tank weapon, so Nick put it in between our bergens which seemed like a good idea at the time, we'd later have a narrow escape with that decision!

The weather wasn't what I expected for a desert environment. The sky was mainly overcast sometimes with a slight breeze. The temperature was around 5-6 degrees in the morning and rose to the early 20s as the day progressed. At this point I felt great. I had my vehicle, and I was in the desert with a battle group. We were closer to the enemy and were reminded of this several times a day as the bombers flew over our position. Not long after you could hear the rumble of explosions as the B52 bomb payload hit the Iraqi positions. As we had control of the skies there was a constant flow of bombers heading towards their positions.

The sight of the bombers soon went unnoticed as we began to prepare our machine and equipment. It wasn't long until I met the officer in charge of the Royal Engineer element. He was an ex Met police officer who applied for a commission to become an officer. I wasn't sure what to think of him to begin with. He appeared quite aloof and, as I observed him, I could see he was quite dismissive and wanted everyone to know that he was in charge. I was quite chilled and was mindful that my own leadership-style was to be visible but approachable, keeping things light. The last thing you needed in this environment was a stress head, that created a toxic atmosphere. We were all experienced soldiers that pretty much knew our role and that emanated a quiet confidence. Time would come when we would have to be more transactional and direct, but for now it was about settling in and preparing.

The other lads that were set up close by were a friendly bunch and quite humorous which I loved. Our troop Staff Sergeant (Staffy) was a nice guy too. He was an experienced guy but, like us all, had never operated in a combat zone. We all carried this as a sober reality so there were no egos here. We just all wanted to do our jobs well and get home. Very importantly Nick and I got our lean-to up, which in essence is a canvas type tent room that attaches to the side of the vehicle. We had been briefed about Camel Spiders, scorpions and snakes. I didn't particularly like any of them and stories had already begun to do the rounds, about how Camel Spiders bit you in your sleep in order to then eat your flesh that they anaesthetised!

I was a bit of a clean freak in terms of things being put in their place. Thankfully, Nick was pretty tidy too. It was so important to know that you could find things in their right place in the dark as well as in daylight.

We were pretty much left to our own devices in terms of routine. We had a briefing in the morning and in the evening that I, along with all other NCOs, had to attend. On the second day of being in the FMA I conducted a full inspection of the CET so that we could request missing parts or replacements as soon as possible as we could move out at any point.

Thankfully, there wasn't much to do on the vehicle as it appeared quite new. The tracks needed adjusting that included taking a link out which, thankfully, was uneventful. Nick was taking it all in and showed that he had some knowledge that was growing daily. We had the opportunity to take the CET out for a spin and I was pleased with Nick's confidence in handling the machine. I was still uncomfortable about having all this equipment that I didn't think we were going to need and could well hinder us. I'd made my decision; I was going to ditch it and if there were repercussions, I would take full responsibility. I asked Nick to drive a little further out to an area that was more isolated from other vehicles and people. He looked at me quizzically and I just nodded in the direction that I wanted him to go, with a look that said don't ask why. Once we'd got a suitable distance away, I told Nick that I wanted to give him some practice digging with the earth moving bucket. He was enthusiastic and jumped out of the crew compartment to empty the bucket from the buoyancy floats and ALA.

I briefed Nick about what I wanted him to excavate, and he got to work straight away. It was so good seeing our machine doing what it was designed to do. The ground was harder than I had envisaged. It certainly wasn't soft sand like in the Laurence of Arabia film. It took quite some time but Nick was getting the hang of it, which I'm sure boosted his confidence. Once he'd finished I shouted over the hum of the engine for him to come down and join me on the ground.

Once he was down with me, I explained my thoughts about dumping the buoyancy floats and the ALA lifting equipment. Nick just looked at me with a vacantly fearful look. I explained why and he trusted my judgment and he was reassured about me taking the flak if it came to light. We hurriedly dumped the kit into the hole that Nick had dug, and he jumped back in the CET and proceeded to fill the hole in. Job done! God help us if we have to cross a river!

I was content that our vehicle was prepped and ready to go forward. Nick and I went over the controls on a daily basis and were constantly reviewing where we had put stuff, to see if it was the best place.

I had developed a pain at the base of my spine, a bit like a painful spot. I went to see the medic and he told me that I had an ingrown hair. He tweezered something out of the boil and the pain reduced almost immediately. Apparently, he extracted quite a length of hair that had coiled and grown under my skin creating a lump that had reddened. Nick teased me, telling me that I had a condition called 'Baghdad Boil', Which was quite common in the desert, and involved sandflies biting you. Thankfully, this was not Baghdad Boil, but the diagnosis had stuck and Dr Nick named our CET Baghdad Boil and sketched a caricature of Saddam with a boil on his bum. Nice.

The evenings were very special in the desert, despite the fact we were there to destroy the fourth largest army in the world. I would sit alone on top of the CET before getting into the lean-to. The stars seemed close enough to touch. The sky was so black and I'd never seen so many stars. One night I remember looking up at the moon and thinking that this was the same moon that was shining over England. The same moon that Emma could be gazing up at, thinking the same as me. In one sense I felt connected to Em by the moon. As I stared at the moon, I got emotional and whispered: 'I love you Em'. I had an intense feeling of missing her and I would have done anything for a hug at that moment. It was an 'if only' and that was going to lead to a dead-end as Em couldn't be here with me.

The mornings were quite special too. Often quite nippy with a gentle breeze. One day I got up before the sun and quietly crept out of the lean-to and climbed up onto the CET to have a prayer time and read my bible. The sun was rising behind me and as I closed my eyes to be still and pray, I was aware that there was a bright light shining through my eyelids. Brighter than looking toward the sun with eyes shut. I sensed that I was not alone and felt very peaceful. I was scared to open my eyes in case I was confronted with something supernatural. It didn't matter to me whether I saw something or not as I could feel the presence of the Holy Spirit with my eyes closed. I felt very reassured that God knew about this war and its outcome. I felt privileged that His presence was there with me. I, his son and He, my Father.

Nick and I practiced some more with the CET, manoeuvring and digging. Whilst rattling past one armoured vehicle, I looked down to see what I think was an officer getting out of his lean-to brandishing his Browning 9mm pistol and pointing it towards us and shouting. He looked like a deranged man wearing no footwear and half dressed. I told Nick over the intercom to put his foot down and make for our position. Clearly this man had been awoken by our rumbling by and wasn't happy about it. His extreme behaviour may just have been an indicator to where he was in his mind. Sharing of feelings wasn't really the done thing and many of us had become prisoners to our own thoughts. It wasn't that others wouldn't listen if someone was having a hard time. It was more about not wanting to burden anyone else who may have had issues of their own. Secondly, you didn't want to worry others that you weren't up to doing your job.

I noticed that some were finding it tough, and their struggle usually manifested in either becoming noticeably withdrawn or easily irritated, resulting in outbursts.

Our Lieutenant, (Troopy) remained distant but when he did appear he irritated those around him. He had an air of superiority that wasn't appreciated. We were all relatively senior and weren't enamoured by his approach. On one occasion he gathered us all together and gave us a telling off about something trivial. It seemed like he wanted to use the occasion to stamp his authority. We had a mindset that we had nothing to prove and needed to remain relaxed but focused. Troopy was intense and made the men feel uneasy, so much so that one of the guys told him to calm down.

Troopy became more irate and this guy told him that if he didn't change his approach he may have an accident. This unnerved Troopy and there was an uncomfortable silence for a moment. Everyone knew what the guy meant, including Troopy. I felt uncomfortable but the guy who made the comment continued to stare at Troopy, who broke the stare and walked off. You could be thinking that this was a sort of mutiny or insubordination. It's a unique situation preparing for combat, and it takes a special leader that understands people and how to read the social setting. Troopy didn't and was relying on his rank rather than who he was as a leader. There was a saying in the army that you can respect the Queen's commission but that doesn't mean you had to respect the person carrying it. These were a good bunch of guys that followed the rules and there was no cause that I could see to berate them. Troopy had had a shot across his bow to think about his approach. I'm not sure it would change.

Nick had made friends with two guys that I didn't know. They were designated to our vehicle in terms of food and sleeping arrangements. Nick got on with them as they were smoking partners but they weren't my type of people. They whined a lot and had a negative view on most things. I noticed that they tutted and dragged their feet when asked to do tasks. I felt irritated in their presence as I realised, I liked time to think and plan. I just hoped that their negative attitude didn't rub off on Nick. As and when we moved forward, they would remain here, thankfully.

Wisdom/Reflection
- *Leadership at its best demonstrates putting your people first*
- *Being trustworthy will reassure your people and build relationships*
- *Take time to listen, because often it's what's not said that will speak the loudest*
- *Take time to be alone to think through how you're feeling and turn it*

into a prayer for thanksgiving, strength and peace
- *Sometimes despite our fears and insecurities if we're called to lead then lead we must*

A poloroid picture taken with a camera that had been donated and sent out to the troops

Me brandishing an iraqi assault rifle in Kuwait

A quick photo during the ceasfire period

Changing a hydraulic ram in the middle of the desert prior ro moving forward.

Me taking a moment having dug some of our tanks in

Tired and ready for a brew.

10.
My war diary entry extracts

February 22
We are at G-2 which meant, if all went to plan, we would be going in in two days' time. For the last few days our training had intensified and there was a feeling that things were about to shift.

I had a pleasant surprise visit from my old Staffy, Spence, along with Juels and Hev. My heart leapt when I saw them pull up in their CVRT armoured vehicle. We laughed and talked about old times. Being with people that really knew me was a tonic and I was sad that they would have to leave. I didn't even know how they found me but I was glad that they did.

If I was going to die then these were the guys that I would choose to die with. They left and I returned to my CET with a lump in my throat. That night as we formed up for our evening briefing at the back of Staffy's vehicle, our attention was drawn to loads of rocket flashes in the sky. Because it was pitch black it looked like they were heading for our position! I couldn't believe what I was seeing and I felt adrenalin surge through my body.

I instinctively ducked and sprinted back to my vehicle zig zagging as I went. I glanced back momentarily and everyone else seemed to be panicking too so I didn't feel that I was overreacting. I hid with my weapon and respirator to hand, behind the tracks of my CET.

As I watched the bright white lights that were rapidly making a trail in the sky, it dawned on me that they were travelling away from our position not towards it! I let out some laughter of relief and was joined by raucous laughter from many directions as others emerged from behind or under their vehicles. It turned out that it was an MLRS, (Multi Launcher Rocket System) not far from our position that had targeted some Iraqi positions. MLRS is a devastating piece of kit. Each rocket contains 644 bomblets that rain down on the enemy, penetrating armour as well as taking out personnel. It was surreal to think that after seeing the rockets fire, minutes later there would be death and devastation wherever they landed. Families would be unaware that their loved ones had died that night.

I later spoke to a Sergeant who had driven into the position that had been targeted by the MLRS and he said it was pure carnage. Body parts everywhere and many armoured vehicles destroyed as the bomblets pierced the armour and killed those inside. It was apparently a Brigade strength position that was totally annihilated.

February 23
In the morning briefing we were told to expect a lot more bangs tonight. I was paid another visit by Spence who told me to be ready as he needed another CET and had asked for mine and just me. I was so pleased that he had returned, and I was up for going with him. I just hoped the powers that be authorised the move before it all kicked off. I felt emotional that I could be going through this experience with all my pals from Support Troop. Spence told me to be ready to move and hopefully he'd see me soon. I waved him off and returned to my vehicle with a spring in my step. I decided not to share my news with Nick at this point as it may have demoralised him and, in any case, it wasn't a definite yet.

I was made aware that there was going to be a church service today. I was desperate for some Christian fellowship and someone to pray with. It was a lonely road and despite having quiet times with God it always helped to have human encouragement. It would be interesting to see how many would attend the service that was to be held in an open space where the padre had set up a makeshift altar.

As the time came for the church service to begin, I could see soldiers walking towards the altar from all directions. It was a moving and powerful sight to see. There was no machoism here, just men that seemed to want to connect with God whilst they could. All with respirator and weapon they found a place to sit and waited quietly. I could see the padre in his robes standing at the altar, waiting for everyone to settle. I was astounded at how many had attended. Each soldier appeared to be sat alone with space between us all. This was a time to be alone and this moment of privacy was where our hearts communed with God about the unknown and entrusting our future to him.

The padre followed the Church of England order of service. His talk wasn't really a sermon but more like a call for us to get right with God. It was literally calling as there was no amplification or mic so he was shouting out his message. I remember him saying that tomorrow some of us may not be alive and were we confident about where we were going to spend eternity. He encouraged us to make our peace with God and give our lives to him. As I sat there and reflected on his words I began to weep and, as my tears hit the gravelly sandy ground, I thought of how short my life was and of my dear wife who, at this moment, I missed intensely. My thoughts turned to the men who today put their trust in God and called out to him in their hearts. It always touched me when a person made the most important decision of their life and beyond. Nick didn't come to the service, and I can't recall us talking much about spiritual things. That said I'm sure Nick enjoyed having some time to himself whilst I was gone, as we did live in each other's company for a lot of the time.

At 20:00 hours Saudi time the deadline for Saddam to withdraw his troops had passed so it looked like we were going in.

February 24
It appears that one of our main boom hydraulic rams has broken. Not what you want to discover so close to going in. We had bodged it with a bolt for now, but this significantly affected the operation of the earth-moving bucket. I needed to get it fixed asap. Thankfully, we didn't have to wait long for a replacement. Troopy told us to start fitting the ram so we got to work. It was going to be a long night. All of the other vehicle crews were aboard their vehicles and ready to go. Line upon line of Challenger tanks and Warrior personnel carriers were ticking over and ready to go. I needed this ram to go on without any complications. I didn't want to be left behind as we were told that there were pockets of Iraqi Units that hadn't been swept up. I didn't fancy coming across them in such a vulnerable position.

I got Nick to sit in the crew compartment and operate the lever that lifted the ram up and down so I could line everything up on the ground. I was aware that Troopy and my Staff Sergeant were pensively watching us. I was under pressure and needed Nick to switch on. The ram was quite heavy for one person but doable. Nick needed to be precise with the controls to line everything up. The new ram was in position and now it was time for Nick to work his magic to help line up the holes that the pins would go through to secure the ram to the bucket.

I could hear tanks starting to rev their engines and shouts from commanders. I physically felt my blood rush as I thought I'm not being left behind! Up to this point I had been patient with Nick, but we had been trying to line things up for a few minutes now. I was aware that I was about to lose it as Nick didn't seem to be getting the urgency of the situation. I glanced back and saw Troopy look at his watch and beginning to walk towards his vehicle.

At this point I looked at Nick venomously and shouted: "If you don't sort your fuckin self out, I'm gonna come up there and rip your fuckin arms off!" I'm horrified as I write this because I know that this isn't an acceptable way to behave. I can only assume that the pressure of the situation brought out this guttural side out of me.

Interestingly, Nick hit the lever after my outburst and the pin lined up and the ram was fitted!
Staffy saw that we had got the ram fitted after my rant and he shouted over: 'Well done Corporal Borg'. I knew he was referring to my resorting to violent threats to get the job done. and I'm not saying that this is the best form of leadership but it focused Nick's mind for that moment and got the job done.

You'll be pleased to know that I apologised to Nick, I think he was surprised that a good Christian boy could show such aggression but understood the stress I was under. I hasten to add that I haven't had an outburst like that since, and don't intend to either.

February 25
We moved to the 'Buffer Zone' that was about 30km from the Iraqi border. Today the weather is heavy rain and thunder and lightning have

started. When it thundered, I could hear the static travel down the radio antennae and into my headset. We hadn't had mail for several days and understandably so. Usually, a Chinook helicopter would fly in with sacks of mail once a day. For now, I would have to make do with re-reading the letters Em had sent previously. I saw my first creepy crawly today as I walked back to my vehicle from an O Group briefing, I spotted a small Camel Spider. It's quite an ugly sand-coloured creature, funnily enough, that looks like a cross between an insect and a spider. No matter how small, I gave it a wide berth and nodded respectfully as I passed.

I hadn't heard the BBC World Service news bulletins for a few days as Troopy had asked to borrow my radio. Since moving off we had been battened down the whole time which means that our hatches were closed to give us the best protection.

It was quite cramped, and Nick and I were feeling it, sustaining the sitting position for such a long time. We were told that we would not be moving from our current position until 05:00 hours the next morning. It rained through the night and there seemed to be a lot of activity outside and in the skies as our aircraft continued to target the Iraqi positions.

February 26
I didn't sleep well and it's been raining all night. We're now moving towards the Iraqi border. The desert landscape seems to have changed and is far more undulating. We'd decided to get some fresh air so travelled with our cupolas up so we could get a view around us. This was acceptable at the time as we had been given permission.

I heard a whooshing sound to my right and, as I glanced around, I saw an American Apache helicopter gunship hovering adjacent to us. I could see the pilot clearly and he was looking at me and smiling. I gestured to him that I wanted to take a picture, which I did as I hurriedly located my Olympus Trip camera and snapped away. He nodded his head, gave a thumbs up and then accelerated away at an amazing speed. I was aware that we were part of a very big organisation that was multinational and very powerful. As we passed through the Iraqi Border, I saw a sign made from a lorry bonnet that had writing daubed on it saying: "Welcome to Iraq … The Big Red One". This must have been written by the U.S First Infantry Division who were known as The Big Red One where their nickname was created from their shoulder patch, (a large red number 1) in World War II.

The day we went through into Iraq, the weather was dull and rainy. I remember looking down at the wet ground that had turned into a quagmire from the large amount of traffic pouring through. Its not how I imagined the desert to be. I wondered if this was the usual weather for this time of the year. There were concerns that the dry warm weather would be detrimental to our vehicles, clogging up the air filters as well as drying out the parts that needed greasing regularly. But this weather was more like what we were used to in Europe.

We were now part of a large convoy moving through. We would have been sitting ducks if Iraq had been able to take to the skies. It was looking more like the M6 motorway in rush hour. Thankfully, it was flowing nicely so we kept moving. We passed quite a bit of Iraqi military hardware that had been blown to pieces, along with several Iraqi corpses.

I noticed an abandoned British lorry that I could see had blood spattered in the cab. I later learnt that a British soldier had left his cab to pick up a war souvenir that he had spotted. I gather it was ordnance that exploded in the cab. As we passed abandoned artillery pieces, I noticed that some of the guns had instructions in English on them. Probably guns that we had sold them when we were on speaking terms with Iraq.

As we continued on that day, I witnessed a small helicopter whizz past and head into the distance in front of us. The helicopter had a large dome attached to it and had no armaments that I could see. As we continued on, around 20 minutes' later, we saw the same helicopter flying back past us. What I saw next was awesome; around 10-20 Apache helicopter gunships making towards where the smaller helicopter had just come from. The smaller helicopter had marked up the enemy armour ready for the apaches to lock on to and destroy. I never saw the apaches again but I'm sure they caused devastation to the enemy positions.

We stopped at a temporary location in the Iraqi desert and were told that we were on 15 minutes' standby for Nick and I to move forward. Evidently, our CET was needed with us as its crew. It was dark by now. We were tired but knew we had to stay alert as we could get the call at any moment. We waited and waited but weren't called forward.

The Coalition forces were steaming ahead and were facing little opposition at this stage.

February 27
We continued to move forward from last night's position. There was a trail of destruction with Iraqi armour littering the landscape. There were scorch marks on the ground where they had exploded. Turrets were blown clean off the tank's chassis. It looked like the Iraqis had been taken by surprise. Some of their armour was facing in the opposite direction from where we came. This was due to the disinformation that was portrayed, making them believe that there was to be a large amphibious assault.

As we headed towards Kuwait, which was about 20km away, I noticed French Foreign Legion soldiers that had taken positions to protect one of our flanks. I nodded to one of the soldiers on the ground and he acknowledged me, nodding back.

As we trundled on, I noticed one of our infantry sections had adopted a goat that had been loitering nearby. I feared for the goat's future, as it served as a type of mascot for now but knowing the infantry, I could imagine that goat would be on the menu very soon.

We would periodically stop for half an hour or so. During that time some went off to explore some of the enemy trenches, looking for war souvenirs and memorabilia. I preferred to stay in my vehicle as there were reports of trenches being booby trapped by the fleeing Iraqis. One of the guys had found the paymaster's trench and came out with a brief case full of Iraqi Dina notes. The money was quickly distributed to all who wanted some. The whole brief case was probably worth about £50 in their currency.

We came across an enemy anti-aircraft gun that was loaded and ready to go. It was quite an archaic bit of kit, but we liked it so attached it to the front of our CET and towed it away! When we arrived at our next stop for the night, we set up the barrel of the anti-aircraft gun, so it was pointing to the sky and hung a bucket from it with holes in and used it as a shower, unloaded of course! I was surprised to see that the loot that the Iraqis had plundered from Kuwait was stored in their trenches. Video recorders, stereos and other electrical equipment that, clearly, they wouldn't be able to use in their trenches. There was the distinct smell of rotting flesh nearby too, which turned out to be goat's that had been butchered leaving the head and other bits strewn near to the trenches.

Despite the high threat level, to date we hadn't been subjected to a gas attack. A lot of the time we wore our respirators for the first 48 hours. Our CET had its own filtration system, but we weren't taking any chances, so even when we were battened down, we wore them. The NBC state had been lowered so we kept our respirators nearby but not worn. Nick has been snapping with his camera getting pics of destroyed vehicles and abandoned equipment.

Reports were coming in that our reconnaissance vehicles such as the Scimitar and the Scorpion were taking out the Iraqi main battle tanks! This was impressive as the role of the reconnaissance units was to press forward and report back the enemy strength. Their vehicles were small and fast so ideal for the job. It wasn't expected that their relatively light guns would be able to inflict such damage. Apparently, they were popping turrets off the Russian made T55 tanks, often with the commander of the tank heading skywards with the detached turret. Very soon our main battle tank crews became unhappy with the newly-found capabilities of the recce units as they weren't getting the opportunity to take out the enemy tanks which was their main role really. The plan was that the recce troops go forward, spot the enemy then allow the Challenger tanks to roll past and do their thing.

Our forces were moving incredibly fast and so the leapfrogging between the recce troops and main armour needed careful co-ordination. A serious consideration for the commanders was not letting the rate of pace become our enemy. Supply lines needed to be sustained and, thankfully, it wasn't yet a problem.

The 1st Division of the so-called elite Iraqi Republican guard had been destroyed and the rumour going around was that two more days at this intensity would finish the Iraqis off.

Thought about Em today and how beautiful she is.

February 28
I had a good sleep last night, probably due to the expectancy that this could all be over soon. It's interesting how I was so keen to get out here and be part of it, but now that I am here, I want to be back home. It's probably because I don't feel I've had the full experience as my expectations were very different. I'd read books by soldiers on the frontline and their experience of having to wait around a lot. This certainly was our experience. I at least wanted to fire my weapon or operate the CET underfire. I realise I've got to be careful what I wish for. These were my fleshy manly desires, but my spirit was saying bloodshed and war should be avoided wherever possible.

I had slept on the transmission decks on the top of the CET. Rain wasn't expected so I was willing to take the risk of sleeping under the open sky.

Nick and I were organised in the mornings; washed, shaved, fed and weapon cleaned. I attended an O Group briefing mid-morning and was told that a ceasefire had been agreed and was in place since 08:00 hours today. The second in command to Saddam had been to meet with President Bush to discuss terms I think. Despite the ceasefire I could still hear explosions. Perhaps it could have been us destroying Iraqi ordnance or fighting was continuing. It seems that this is going to be quite a swift war. I was encouraged to hear that President Bush had asked his nation to get on its knees and pray. I think this is tremendously powerful when the leader of a nation acknowledges the power of God to change world events.

Morale, at the moment, is high and since the ceasefire every vehicle is now flying a Union Jack from its radio antennae. As far as the eye can see, flags are flying. We've been warned that we may have to spend some time in Kuwait, how long we don't know yet.

We're on our way to Kuwait now, which is about a 100km journey. We've passed a number of makeshift prisoner of war (POW) camps. Iraqis can be seen lining up to get fed. They look a sorry lot, some without boots and proper clothing. Although a number of Iraqi soldiers were killed in action, the large majority surrendered. The relentless air bombing campaign and the lack of discipline must have affected morale. They were glad to see us as we were a guaranteed meal and care, more than they probably received from their own people.

The convoy is moving quite slowly, at the moment, mainly due to a minefield ahead. Time for a snooze.

March 1
Awoke at 06:00 hours to watch the sunrise. We've still got at least 42km to travel before we get to Kuwait. The convoy has been stationary for some time, but nobody knows why. As usual, it's a case of 'hurry up and wait'.

I've had a yearning today to have more of God in my life. I want to go to the next level with him. My thought-life has wandered during this time as I've been surrounded with death and destruction. I feel like I need a spiritual shower to wash off all this man-made worldliness. I long for a touch from The Father to bring me closer to Him. I'm very aware of my inadequacies and my need of his power to enable me to live a life that is enriched with his goodness, so I can pass this on to others. At times I haven't been the best witness to Nick but living in close proximity to someone 24/7 has its challenges.

We're now in Kuwait but you wouldn't know it as there was no indication of a border. The journey was quite sporadic and towards the end on Route Fox it got quite interesting. There had been quite a firefight here as tanks were still smouldering and others were still on fire with flames shooting out from the turret of some of the tanks. As the main threat of the enemy had diminished the temptation to jump down and explore for souvenirs, was great. Although a bit of a souvenir collector myself, the risk of injury was at the forefront of my mind. We'd made it this far unscathed so I was determined to stay in one piece.

I still hadn't received any mail and didn't expect to. Maybe when we got settled in Kuwait the mail might catch up with us. I was so fortunate to have three or four people that wrote to me regularly, including Em. Faithful friends from Histon Baptist Church encouraged me with verses of scripture and kept me up to date with local news at home. I marvel at the night sky every night and in the morning, I'm surprised at how much dew there is on the ground. The Kuwait desert landscape is more of what I expected, soft sand and dunes. Ceasefire is still on.

March 2
Last night a glow could be seen where the Iraqis had set light to the Kuwaiti oil refineries. There are Iraqi positions close to us that looked like they had been surprised and fled in a hurry. There was still food on some plates, something that looked like rock cakes, along with lots of tinned food, including sweet corn and what looked like tomato puree! There were also bags of flour everywhere.

One of our officers, along with some others, did some trench clearing nearby and came back with quite a booty, including posters of Saddam, RPGs (Rocket propelled grenades), AKM assault rifles, communications equipment, helmets as well as a recent music hits tape in Arabic! Happy with their haul they went on another sortie later and came back with an anti-aircraft gun and a few more assault rifles. No doubt a lot of this memorabilia would make its way back to the UK and would be proudly displayed in numerous NCO and Officers' Mess cabinets.

Stories of fatalities started to circulate along the line and I was saddened to hear that some of our guys had been killed during Iraqi contact and skirmishes. Because of the speed of the coalition assault, inevitably pockets of Iraqi units were left behind, this meant in effect that they were now behind or to the side of our positions. One such account involved a REME vehicle that was travelling along and encountered by an Iraqi tank. The REME (Royal Electrical Mechanical Engineers) are the guys that work the magic to get our vehicles fixed and back on the road. They are support troops so probably not the most adept as infantrymen.

Although they will have had their personal weapons they would have been lightly armed. I understand that they were alone and probably travelling back to their unit. This wasn't unusual because they were like the AA of the army, expected to assist broken down vehicles wherever they were. Unfortunately for them they were spotted by the Iraqi tank commander who engaged them with his mounted machine gun, fatally wounding one of the crew. News of the contact soon reached their unit and a hunt ensued for the rogue Iraqi tank. Various Units were on the lookout and soon the tank was located and taken out by one of the infantry anti-tank weapons, a Milan I believe.

There was another incident where a large number of Iraqi soldiers holding a white flag approached a British Warrior Armoured Fighting Vehicle. This had a section of British soldiers in the back. Two of them alighted the vehicle to conduct the prisoner taking drill whilst the gunner inside the vehicle covered the two soldiers on foot. As one of the soldiers approached the Iraqis the crowd of them parted and one fired an RPG directly at the Warrior. Unfortunately, the rocket cut straight through one of our soldiers and bounced off the Warrior. As the Warrior had been engaged it opened fire and, to my knowledge, there were no survivors. There were a few instances where Iraqi tanks flew white flags with their gun turret to the rear and when approached would traverse their gun and engage. This was a crafty tactic that often didn't go in their favour.

I felt quite irritated with Nick today. I think it's just because I'm very much an activator and like to get things done, and to be doing stuff productively, and when things need to be done, I like to snap to it and get it done. Nick was quite lethargic and not particularly using his initiative. Perhaps he's struggling in some way, but it was sometimes hard to tell because he didn't share that much about anything. These were extraordinary circumstances and a lot to process. Now that the end looked in sight it was almost as if our minds started to catch up and start to process everything that had happened and what we had seen.

I've found it challenging to merge both being a good soldier and maintaining my witness as a Christian. Under stress I sometimes forget the bigger picture of God having my back and wanting me to depend on him. I so prefer to be self-reliant, particularly when it's going well but happy to give God a shout when the wheels come off. I'm learning in this cramped environment how important it is to keep short accounts of wrongdoing and saying sorry when it's called for. There's no way you can live in such close proximity and hold grudges or be of a sulky disposition. In the circumstances, I think Nick and I have managed quite well. I've had to bite my lip on a number of occasions but I know that Nick would have had to do the same too.

Peace talks commence tomorrow, so hopefully we'll have more of an idea of which way this is going to play out. There's lots of talk about how we should push on to Baghdad and get this thing sorted in one swoop. If not, the feelings were that this whole situation would come back to bite us on the arse.

We were treated to some American MRE (meals ready to eat) ration packs for tea. They were of far superior quality than our compo rations. I had diced turkey with gravy and Nick had Chicken a la King.

March 3

Today started with a briefing where we were informed that we could all be home very soon, but I'm not banking on it. Because we are engineers there could be a lot of reconstruction of basic services, like water supply to be restored in Kuwait City. We've been used today to excavate an area to be used as a compound for all the captured Iraqi equipment. I was amazed at the range of equipment, some French, some British and a lot of Soviet and Chinese. All of it was made safe and then I had a bit of a mooch. I was astounded at the condition of their kit; it was of poor quality and, as I understand it, the better more modern equipment was mainly issued to the Republican Guard and other elite units. Their bedding consisted of a large rolled up mattress with heavy blankets tied to it. Not exactly compact and easy to carry. Most of the kit we commandeered was probably used by conscripts drafted at short notice, so in effect they weren't really professional soldiers. No wonder so many gave up as soon as they saw us.

My relationship with The Lord is quite good at the moment, although not easy, I feel like I'm being refined, and that's seldom easy. I'm quite self-critical and often feel like I could do better, but when I'm tired and/or stressed those thoughts turn toxic and are unproductive. I agree that we are constantly learning as people and don't mind the challenge of self-reflection and making changes for the better. It's also about managing my expectations of myself and of others. I'm sure we often create pressure on ourselves due to a distorted view of ourselves or a situation due to our state of mind at the time.

Despite what's going on around me at the moment I'm still reading my bible and a Christian devotional book. I don't feel too good about myself. I want to make the most of this experience but feel at times I'm unfaithful to God because of my dark thoughts. I'm really missing intimacy and my thoughts are constantly invaded by sexual thoughts that are unhelpful because they can't go anywhere. I know all the guys struggle with this and make themselves scarce when the urge becomes too intense. There's a stash of porn that's available if you know the right people to provide you with some graphic assistance. I know this may seem perverse and inappropriate to some, but it's the reality of being in an environment that is absent of normal sexual relationships. As a Christian man I believe what the bible teaches about where sex is appropriate, and that's within marriage. Clearly Em isn't here with me, so I'll just have to cross my legs for now! It's interesting though because when men are deprived from intimacy there is a mood change and, here in the desert, guys seem to get ratty and irritable and I'm sure that along with other things this doesn't help.
I wrestle with myself so much on this issue and those of you that are reading but don't share my beliefs will think I'm crazy. Masturbation, using porn is healthy and understandable in the circumstances I hear you say. Some of the teachings of Jesus seem beyond my capability. The bit when he says that if we think of a woman lustfully in our minds, we commit adultery. Well, there's no hope for me then! This is my struggle; I passionately believe in Jesus and am so grateful for dying for me and wiping my slate clean, in terms of everything I ever did wrong.

Now I can live with a clear conscience and rely on his forgiveness daily as I journey through this life. But, as a person, I like to see progress and if I keep falling at the same hurdle, it's either because I'm not approaching the challenge correctly or God's power isn't strong enough to conquer some of these issues that are sinful. I know God can do all things, after all, if I believe he created the world and is bigger than the universe, then my issues should be a walk in the park. If I constantly feel like I'm letting God down that affects my spiritual morale and I think that I'm taking advantage of my relationship with God, which I hate.

So, I have this battle going on inside me; my human nature that wants me to succumb to all my urges and desires. Conversely, my spiritual nature says that I can overcome sinful temptations through his power and not my willpower. There will be some Christians that are somewhat more liberal in their views and would say I'm being too hard on myself. I disagree, as in my spirit I feel convicted not condemned and know the Holy Spirit understands my behaviour and temptations but says that isn't his best for me.

Unlike some, I do take the bible literally; so I believe that God created the world in six days. Yes six, 24-hour days. I believe that Jonah was swallowed by a large sea creature. I believe that there were a first couple called Adam and Eve. I believe that Noah built an ark. I believe that God parted the Red Sea to allow the people of Israel to escape from Pharoah and his troops. I believe in the virgin birth and that Jesus is the Son of God as prophesied long ago. I believe that he died by being executed on a wooden cross by the Roman authorities. I believe that he died and on the third day he rose again. I believe that through his death he made a sacrifice, once and for all, for all people. I believe that as a result of what Jesus achieved everyone can be born again of His spirit and have a new life forgiven and set free in this life and then in the life to come, to spend eternity with Him.

So, there you have it. I've given you both barrels of what I call the gospel. This stuff is real. I believe that there is a spirit known as the devil, who deals in evil. His business is to steal, lie and destroy. He hates God's most precious creation ... YOU! But Jesus says that he has overcome the world and that when we have a relationship with him, we have all the resources to destroy the works of the devil. This is about love and loving all people because of what Jesus has done and the love he has shown and lavished upon us.

If we only take certain parts of the bible literally and believe that other parts are symbolic or actually meant something else then we are faced with the creeping doubt of rationalising this and that, thus removing the full power of God's word. Faith is a matter of the heart not of the head. I trust that

He knows best, and I take him at his word. In my eyes he can do anything and is the God of the impossible. Naïve, I hear you say. I don't think so. I have witnessed the power of God and, as a man, recognise that I'm not self-sufficient and have eternity in my heart. The difference between me and a man that doesn't believe is that I've come to a point of recognition of my need of God's forgiveness and the need of his love and guidance as I navigate through this complicated life. We all have a God receiver, you've just got to decide whether you're switching yours on to receive the signal.

March 4
The compound we had excavated was fast becoming full of captured equipment. a lot of T55 Russian built tanks and Chinese built T59 tanks. There were several Intelligence Corps' people milling around gathering information and I understand speaking to some of the POWs.

Where we were excavating was uncleared territory, so we had to be mindful of munitions and possibly mines. There were enemy trenches nearby that were constructed with breeze blocks and had colourfully tiled floors! We discovered whilst we were there that the Iraqi troops were being paid with counterfeit money, much to the disgust of the Iraqi soldiers who had been betrayed by their own government.

A smaller excavation that we were asked to do was a ladies' toilet, for the Intelligence Corps personnel. This was classed as an on-the-side job that cost the lucky ladies seven US ration packs (MRE), which were the favoured currency at the time. Unlike us, the Iraqi troops preferred fresh meat for their meals. Strewn around their position was rotting goat and sheep carcasses.

Wisdom/Reflection
- *Journalling in significant seasons of life is productive often after the event when looking back*
- *Your environment can bring out the worst in you. Revisit your values and align your behaviour accordingly*
- *The best decisions are made taking into consideration all the available information*
- *Choose one or two advisors that value the truth*

11.
Liberation

As we entered Kuwait onto the main Basra Road, the full horror of the air campaign could be seen as carnage littered the road as far as the eye could see. The smell of death and corpses was everywhere and many of the vehicles that were hit were still smouldering. I remember watching a drove of donkeys just standing by the road trying to make sense of it all. Groups of children lined the road cheering and asking for something in Arabic. We assumed they wanted chocolate and sweets so you could see soldiers chucking down goodies from their vehicles. One of the other crews reported seeing kids eating cigarettes as they were so hungry.

As most of the fighting was over there seemed to be a real appetite now for trophy collecting. I noticed that there was a bit of a frenzy as soldiers looked for something that they could claim as their own. Some had their own personal AK47 assault rifle, others like myself collected helmets and other equipment, as I couldn't imagine being allowed to take a weapon home. One of the officers spotted a Toyota Landcruiser that the Iraqis had commandeered and painted desert camouflage. It had been abandoned and was in good condition. He got in it and drove it away, just like that! I learned later that he drove it all the way to the port at Al Jubail and arranged for it to be loaded into a shipping container. Spoils of war that he continued to drive when back in the UK.

Although the cease fire was officially in force, there was still sporadic contact in Kuwait City where die-hard Iraqi units were holding out. I would later discover that Doc and Dave Patrick were deployed to Kuwait City and the surrounding area to work for the Army War Graves Service. A harrowing job of recovering the dead and burying them. Although we had seen corpses along the way, they had seen and recovered very large numbers of Iraqi dead.

As we made our way back to Saudi Arabia the journey was slow due to the volume of traffic. The main highway was lined with grateful Kuwaitis shouting and cheering. Some were in cars tooting their horns weaving in and out of our vehicles. Flags were hung from the overpass bridges and there was a real feeling of euphoria as it became known that Saddam had given up his invasion. 'Free Kuwait' banners could be seen everywhere along with people dancing and flag waving. I felt happy for the people of Kuwait and felt relieved that this mess seemed to be over. The tension seemed to lift off Nick and I as we gave each other a knowing look that said we were going to survive.

I started to unwind and thoughts of Emma became more frequent. I missed her so much and I couldn't wait to hold her and just do the normal things in life, like going for a pub lunch or for a walk near the river. I started to think about becoming a father and how if I had died over here then there would be nothing to carry on my DNA and who I was. I felt relieved to be alive because some hadn't made it, and some were maimed with life-changing injuries.

As we approached our compound where the vehicles were to be left, we were cheered by British troops that hadn't gone forward or were performing duties in the rear echelon. It felt great to arrive in a familiar area where our people were stationed. I couldn't wait to have a night's sleep on a camp bed, and even better a proper bed when I got home snuggling up to Em. The relief of just being out of danger changed our whole demeanour. We were relaxed and Nick and I were getting on so much better. I apologised to Nick for being a prat at times and he reciprocated. We acknowledged that we behaved differently under stress. I was glad that Nick had seen me at my worst and was probably confused due to me professing to being a Christian and at times behaving badly. Over the time that we were together Nick and I had some deep conversations about faith and I know he took in what I was saying. Thankfully, we always made up and I made sure that I apologised where it was called for. In the circumstances I think we carried ourselves well and finished our time together on good terms.
With the vehicles handed over we took our personal kit and headed for camp where we would be allocated to a tent.

The next morning I got to hear about an opportunity to get involved in a project helping wildlife that had been damaged due to the leaking of crude oil into the sea by Saddam's forces. It was classed at the time as an ecological disaster. I was keen to get involved and was the only Royal Engineer to do so. I think the others were happy to just chill and wile away the days until we got on that big bird back to blighty.

The next day I reported to a building that seemed to be part of a complex. I was joined by some other British Army volunteers along with some US personnel too. We were led into a room where I could see a number of people sitting at tables holding birds, cleaning them with a light detergent solution that didn't strip the oils from their feathers. I could see mainly cormorants which were quite big birds. Those that had been cleaned were put in cages ready to be released to a rehab pool. We were shown around the various treatment areas and the process of registering the birds, through to cleaning, rehab and then finally release. The rehab pool was basically a swimming pool that had been covered with a number of large camouflage nets to prevent the birds from escaping. They seemed to have a way of filling the pool with salt water and there were even live fish in it so the birds could dive for their lunch.

The Saudis had volunteers helping too and it soon became known that the survival rate of the birds treated by the Saudis was very low. We soon discovered the reason for this, as they were using kerosene to clean the birds. I watched one of the US volunteers become very animated with one of the Saudis as he took another dead bird to the bin. The American was very angry but trying to remain in control but clearly dumbfounded by the lack of knowledge of how to do things properly. In hindsight I wondered why the right approach wasn't agreed from the outset. Perhaps people working in silos and not communicating could have contributed to the issue.

Being involved in the wildlife project took my mind off the last few weeks where life had a very different focus. I felt like I was contributing to something that was helpful and wholesome. Each day I watched as more birds were saved and released to safe zones for them to continue their life in the wild.

The highlight of the project was the rescue of a Hawkbill Turtle. I'd never seen one before and couldn't believe how big it was. Weighing in at 72kg, it was impressive in size and stature. The turtle had been rescued on one of the beaches and it was almost totally black in colour from being covered in crude oil. Thankfully some TLC and a lot of cleaning brought it to a good place in terms of recovery. Today was the day that she was to be released, and I felt privileged to be one of the team taking her back out to her nesting island. There was another guy from the Lancers Regiment that was on the team too. We were both looking forward to the trip out in a chinook helicopter. We were to visit two locations, known as the Jana Islands I believe. The first stop would be to drop off the turtle and then we were tasked to pick up 40 US marines from the second location.

I helped to carry the turtle out to the waiting vehicle, along with three others. We had placed the turtle onto a sheet of timber and we each took a corner to spread the weight.

The National Wildlife Commission were leading on the operation and had come complete with camera crew as well as a handful of biologists. We were soon up in the air and life felt good. I loved adventures like this, particularly involving wildlife. It took me back to, as a young boy, searching for lizards and owl pooh. I would never have dreamed as a 12-year-old that I would be flying to a desert island to release a Hawkbill Turtle.

As we neared the nesting island, I could see the beautiful turquoise-coloured water and the near white-coloured sand. The weather was warm, and it was bright, so I wore desert combat trousers with a green vest and my desert hat. Just to think that a couple of weeks previously we were dressed in full combat kit and a lot of the time in NBC suits with respirators. I knew which I preferred.

We carried the turtle out to the lapping waves on the shore. It was so quiet and peaceful and there was a feeling of accomplishment as the team prepared the turtle for its release. I was very thankful to be alive and gave a glance upwards to the clear blue sky, thanking my Heavenly Father for bringing me this far. I often wonder if you don't have God to thank, then who do you thank when you are grateful, let's say for being delivered from danger or watching your child being born? Who do you thank for a beautiful day or a special experience that isn't due to any one person?

I used to get frustrated when I was quizzed about why such a loving God would allow such suffering in the world. Despite the gift of freewill and the freedom to make choices we still put the blame at his door. Sure, God could have made us as robot-like figures to just do as we were programmed, but that's no basis for a love relationship that is most important to him. Yet when things go well and we are elated, content, joyful and happy, those who blame God for the bad don't recognise him for the good. I don't get it, thankfully The Lord is patient and bears with us, always desiring to connect with us.

The camera crew were in the water, and we were just waiting to be given the signal to lower the turtle onto the beach. As we did the turtle paused then slowly made towards the water. The crew, in their wetsuits and waterproof-cased camera started to swim after the turtle, and within seconds it was gone. As we walked back along the beach, we started to collect driftwood and debris that had washed up from passing ships. I spotted a large Union Jack flag hardboard and a USS Missouri mug. I later learned that the Missouri was a famous US Navy battleship. We started fires and burned all the waste. As we walked back to the Chinook I noticed that the craters could still be seen from the last batch of turtles that had hatched.
What an experience! One to tell my grandchildren, but certainly not your gripping war story of blood, guts and acts of heroism. But nonetheless something that will remain with me as a cherished memory.

Next, we were off to the second island to pick up the US Marines. As we landed they were all kneeling in a huddle waiting for the back door to the Chinook to drop open. The air load master RAF sergeant made his way down to the door and as it opened the marines started to make towards us. As I watched, the RAF Sgt, who was quite a big guy stood at the entrance and bellowed: 'Unload your weapons first!'. Thankfully, he had noticed that their weapons were still loaded and that could have been a disaster once the helicopter was in the air.

After an eventful day, I returned to my tent to find that a lot of the guys had left and were on their way back home. I decided to move tent to join some of the lads that I knew, as space had become available in their tent. This was the tent that we first lived in when we arrived where Doc had made us bunk beds, but now there was fake grass carpet and lights. Clearly there had been some modifications made whilst I was gone. There was a sense of parting and the finality and probable ending of some of our relationships as we all returned to our different units. Although I would stay in touch with some, others were friends for a season and this is a lesson I learnt well, so that I could manage my expectations with friendships. There was some address swapping and plans for reunions, but, even with the best intentions, I realised I would never see some of these guys again.

Thankfully, I got to meet up with Doc and Dave before I flew home. We went swimming at the R&R centre and had quite a feast afterwards. We really were resting and recuperating. We all visited the US Seebee camp and watched a film called 'Memories of me'. We didn't think much of the film but were grateful for the entertainment, nonetheless. Doc and the others were at a Camp 4, so I went back with them to their accommodation where we swapped stories and a few souvenirs. I wouldn't have liked to have had their job as they seemed to be affected by what they had seen. Both sort of laughed nervously and I could sense they were masking how they really felt. Recovering headless bodies and body parts, day in day out, was bound to have an effect. Although I had seen many corpses along the way, I didn't have to get close enough to smell them or even look at their faces, or what was left of them. I understand that eventually people can become desensitised, but I believe eventually there will be a price to pay with a person's emotional health if it's not dealt with.

On March 17, I flew back to the UK. We were waiting on the tarmac with all our kit for a couple of hours prior to boarding the Kuwaiti Airlines Jumbo 747. I met up with some of the lads that I had originally been with during out training in Germany prior to being deployed. It was good to see them but there was a sombre atmosphere, and everyone seemed to be dealing with their own thoughts in their own world. Most of us were either reading or sleeping and I guess thinking about what was awaiting us when we got home. I was the only one from my regiment in Waterbeach so wondered whether they were expecting me and whether there would be transport arranged. I wondered whether there would be people at the airport to welcome us home. Would Emma be there? I imagined my mum and dad being there too. I was so keen to get home. I want to hold Emma and give her a big kiss. I wanted us to have a lovely meal together and to have a glass of full-bodied red wine. Although I wasn't much of a drinker, I did like the odd pint of ale or a glass or two of wine. What would we talk about, and would Em see a change in me?

We boarded the aircraft and I found a seat. I couldn't believe how big this plane was. All the seats were taken, and the Kuwaiti flight crew were very friendly and couldn't do enough for us. As we took off and left the ground there was a tremendous cheer from everyone on board as we're all glad to be out of that place. I'm sure Kuwait is a lovely country, but I would rather have visited in better circumstances.

I could see Geoff Sussex, an Army Padre sitting not far from me. I had spotted him before he had seen me so I approached him and smiled at him. He looked tense and tired. We gave each other a hug and I think he was pleased to be able to chat to a fellow Christian. I treated him to a Lion bar and we sat and chatted for some time. When he spoke about his experiences, I could feel the pain and anger emanating from him. He had a faraway look as he relived what he was recounting. He told me how he and others with him had come across Iraqi soldiers that were hanging from lamp posts. They rightly cut them down and buried them with dignity. One could only assume they were either deserters or had committed some misdemeanour. Geoff had a special place in my spiritual journey as he baptised me shortly after I had become a Christian.

The flight lasted for seven hours and it was dark when we landed at Brize Norton in the UK. I was excited but hesitant at the same time. I didn't know how I'd behave and whether I'd get emotional. This was unknown territory, and all I needed right now was to be held. I know this sounds wrong in a way, but I wanted my mum to comfort me. I wasn't really a mummy's boy but there's something about the love and embrace of a mother. She would tell me that everything was going to be alright. I know my mum had worried throughout me being away. We had a special bond and, as the youngest of six, I often got special treatment to the disgust of my siblings. That said, being the baby of the family, I did get looked after by them too.

We alighted the aircraft and collected our kit. I immediately felt the familiarity of home. I was so glad to see everything in a colder, duller climate, even the baggage attendants and the cleaners and ground crews were pleased to see us. As we walked to the main arrivals' area it became apparent that no one was here to meet us. Did Em even know I was coming home today? I was a little disappointed and realised that there wasn't going to be a joyful reunion. So back into task mode now to establish whether there was any transport laid on. I could see a line of white buses that seemed to be travelling to set locations. I could see a queue of lads from Scottish infantry regiments, who I remembered were stationed not too far from me. I asked the driver whether he would swing round and drop me off at Waterbeach. He agreed so I stored my bergen and webbing in the storage and took my weapon with me and found a seat.

I was the only Royal Engineer on the bus and, initially, I got some looks as if to say: 'Are you lost?'. I looked out of the window and before I knew it I was asleep only to be nudged what seemed minutes later to a gruff Scottish voice saying: "This is your stop pal'. I nodded appreciatively and exited the bus thanking the driver kindly. Slinging my bergen over my shoulder I walked through the camp gates, to the guard room. There I was met by a corporal sitting at a desk. I briefly explained my circumstances and gave him my details. He took possession of my sub machine gun and then asked me whether I had any map co-ordinates of where any dead were buried. I paused for a second as I had seen lots of dead but hadn't buried them, so the answer was no. He smiled at me, said: 'well done mate' and handed me a bottle of beer. So that was that then.

Our Army living quarters weren't far from camp, about a five-minute walk. The houses in Waterbeach were generous in size and well laid out. It was a great improvement on our first army accommodation in Anderhorst, Nienberg. As I walked home it felt very surreal as by now it was the early hours of the morning. The likelihood was that Em would be fast asleep. As I walked along Capper Road the tarmac felt good under my feet and although it was dark, I could see that the daffodils were out. I was overcome with emotion as I walked, and a tear rolled down my cheek. Things could have been very different, and I was grateful to be alive, and I was grateful to be in love with such a lovely woman I could call my wife. We had so much still to live for. We were so young, both of us just 23 years old, and had experienced very little of married life together.

As I approached our front door I paused and said a prayer asking that The Lord would give me the strength to be the best man I could and to be everything Emma needed from me. I prayed that from this day on our marriage would grow from strength to strength. I was hesitant to knock on the door as I felt bad disturbing Emma's sleep and I'd dreamt of this moment whilst in the desert but now here I was worrying about what I might find. Would Emma feel the same about me? Would I be able to adjust and live a normal life?

I knocked the door loud enough hopefully for Em to stir but not too loud to alarm her, or the neighbours.

I waited quietly and expectantly for that familiar sound of footsteps coming down the stairs. Here she came, I could see her silhouette with the backlight from the light upstairs. I heard Em's quiet voice say: 'Who is it?'. I replied in a similarly hushed voice: 'It's me'. I heard a fumbling with the lock on the other side of the door and then the door flung open and there she was.

As our eyes met Emma collapsed and fainted. I lurched forward and caught her in my arms. I held her so tightly and I never wanted to let go. I picked her up and laid her on the sofa in the front room. She came to crying and looked up at me saying: 'You're home!'. I held her again but for longer this time, feeling her soft skin against my face and the smell of her clean skin, slightly scented. Em's soft and shiny hair was longer than I had remembered. Her amber eyes looked warm and friendly even at this early hour. As we held each other, it was as if her love for me was soaking into me, and I just wanted to remain in this place. Everything was so different; from living in a cramped armoured vehicle, I was now in our home with furnishings and comfort. I felt as though I was contaminating this lovely environment with my well-worn desert combats and dirty boots. It seemed like an age before we let go of each other and started to talk. I was aware that as we started conversation my eyes were wandering around the room taking in my surroundings, the vases of flowers the tie-back curtains and the pictures on the walls. I hadn't thought much of our home when I was away but now the familiarity brought me comfort and safety.

Emma hadn't been notified that I was coming home but had been told by one of the other wives that her husband had seen me, so she knew that I was alive.

Em had lost a lot of weight and had lived off her nerves whilst I was away. I could visibly see that it was a big relief that I was home and able to take the reins on some of the responsibilities that married life brings. I held her hand and stroked it as I gazed at her wedding ring, reflecting on the fact that I was married and that this was my wife. Life in the Gulf was such a contrast focusing on everything army and male.

We talked for a while and it was mainly Emma updating me about family news, church and how she had coped. I didn't want to talk about my life away, so Em suggested that I have a bath and get some sleep. A bath sounded very luxurious and to sleep on a bed sounded heavenly.

Squeaky clean I climbed into bed and Em joined me. Feeling her close to me was a blessing and as my head sank into my pillow, I drifted off into a deep sleep that seemed to unwind my mind and was a medicine for my soul. I felt truly blessed that I was loved and, in a place, where I could build and develop this season of our life.

Wisdom/Reflection
- *Be aware that it may take time for your emotions to catch up with what you have just experienced*
- *Keep your emotions appropriately visible. Don't bury them but reflect on them as close to the event as possible. Emotional build up is corrosive*
- *Remember to include God in what and how you are feeling. He's interested and has the solution*
- *Have a confidante that you can vent on, expressing how you feel*
- *After a significant life event you are going to need time to heal and recover. Be intentional in making time for this*

12.
Transition

The following days were filled with talking time where Em and I engaged with our dreams once more. We planned to get away for a holiday abroad so in August 1991 we visited Malta and had a relaxing time connecting with my family over there and planning the next stage of our life. I was ready to start a family and Emma not so at the time. Em loved children but wanted more time for just the two of us.

I think my desire came from a place of relief that I was alive and wanting to have a legacy that was borne out of our love together. Three things that I really love are, babies, flowers and fragrance. I had imagined what our little girl or boy would be like. I wasn't sure whether Em was less keen for other reasons. Em sometimes felt nervy and low. By nature, she was cautious and more deliberative than me. Em needed more time to process and think through the options, whereas I was more intuitive and proactive. There are benefits for both approaches, and somewhere in the middle is probably about right.

Looking back, I think I was being quite selfish in just looking to my needs because of how I felt at that time. I had given less consideration to Emma's feelings, she would be carrying the baby and going through the transformation of becoming a mum. I know that not having her mum around affected Emma's outlook on her role as a mother. Although my mum was around it wouldn't be the same. There were issues that Emma held in her heart that I didn't fully understand or appreciate. I hadn't lost anyone close to me so didn't know the pain of loss.

The time for me to leave the Army was fast approaching. I had passed my final interview for West Midlands Police so Emma and I had to consider where we were going to live and what Emma would do for a job once we had left Waterbeach. The Army had cocooned me from real life. Most things were provided for us, and the administrative side of life was very simple in the Army. Life in civvy street seemed a little more complex and a bit more dog eat dog. I had been warned that the camaraderie wasn't there, and I'd have to watch my back.

My last few weeks in the Army were free and easy. I was able to keep fit, going out for runs and playing a fair bit of sport. Those of us that had served in the Gulf were well respected and left alone in terms of duties. We had a new Sergeant Major join our Squadron and he was making his mark. During an inspection of our kit he looked me up and down and then looked at my webbing that had dabs of desert cam paint on it. He looked at me and said: 'Did you go over there then?'. I said: 'Yes, Sir'. He said: 'Well, you're not there now, get it sorted'. I said: 'Yes, Sir'. That was translated into chill out sir, there are bigger things in life to worry about. The reality was that I was on wind down and didn't care much now for trivial barrack room crap. Part of it was me and others felt qualified to have personalised webbing because we had done what every soldier wants; to go to war. The Sergeant Major hadn't gone so I sensed a little bit of sour grapes. That said I did paint over my webbing as ordered.

To the very end, the Army tried to persuade me to stay on. Why I don't know, as I considered myself just about average. I received an 'O' grade confidential report, which was my annual appraisal. The 'O' stood for outstanding and was quite exceptional.

Wisdom/Reflection
- *Don't let your passion for something drown out the views or feelings of those closest to you*
- *Even when you have a good reputation, rules still have to be followed, you're not above them*
- *It is tempting to slacken off when you know you're moving to another job. Don't! End things well to the end*
- *A man wants to leave a legacy, an inheritance. The greatest being a daughter or son*

13.

War and Peace
RIP – Michael Derry

Just prior to leaving the army I received some devastating news that a good friend of mine called Des had been involved in a serious accident whilst riding a moped in Lanzarote. I first met Des when he joined Support Troop at 21 Engineer Regt. He was a Yorkshire man from Wakefield. He was a light-hearted and friendly guy, but a thinker too. He had the face of an angel and was handsome and fit. We had spent some time on the CET together on exercise and always had interesting conversations interspersed with times of laughter.

Des had committed his life to Jesus and became a Christian whilst we were together in Support Troop. Des had got to know a friend of mine called Michelle, who I'd known since my secondary school days. Michelle was a strong Christian and was instrumental in encouraging me in my faith. Des and Michelle had started to see each other. Their relationship seemed to progress quickly as they soon considered a future together. They visited Lanzarote for a summer holiday and whilst out there hired a moped to get around the island. A drunken tourist driving a car collided with their moped throwing Michelle and Des off with significant injuries.

Word soon got back to support Troop that Des had been involved in an accident. I had moved to the UK by then, serving with 39 Engineer Regt. I received a call from Troy, who had also become a Christian whilst I was with 21 Engineer Regt. Both he and Des used to attend a fellowship group Em and I used to lead at our flat. Troy had been allowed to travel to Lanzarote as a representative from the army. I took a week's annual leave and we booked flights and were on our way to Lanzarote a short time after receiving the news. Troy and I had been praying about what we were going to do whilst we were out there. Des was in a critical condition and the decision had been made, regretfully to turn off his life support machine.

Michelle at the time was in a coma with serious head injuries and a fractured spine. Troy and I were gutted with the intended outcome for Des and refused to believe that this was his time until we felt we had it confirmed from The Lord. Bottom line, we believed that God could do the impossible so were prepared for our aim to be to ask God to raise Des from the dead. This was heavy stuff and I know sounds crazy to those of you with no faith or even those of you that do believe! We loved Des so much and refused to believe that someone like him could be taken so soon, a young man in his early twenties. Michelle was alive but still seriously injured and we were also praying that we would see her healed too. I loved Michelle dearly and the whole situation saddened me.

Troy and I decided to fast until we got to Lanzarote, so no food just water for what turned out to be three days. We travelled light with just a small rucksack containing the essentials. During the flight a lovely air hostess asked us what we would like for our meal. We politely declined the meal and explained that we were fasting. She looked at us with a puzzled expression and then moved on to the next row of seats. Me and Troy looked at each other and laughed knowing that she probably thought what a couple of strange men we were.

Whilst praying about what we were to do when we got to Lanzarote, we sensed that we should find a church and seek the guidance of the Pastor. We felt that we would be shown the Lord's will through him. We walked for a few hours, following our nose. In hindsight we could have done some research and figured out exactly where the churches were located on the island. This whole trip was flying on the seat of our pants as we felt we were being led rather than going on a planned excursion.

Eventually we saw a large white wall with the word Evangelista written in large letters. We gathered that this must be a church so made our way towards it. We pushed the door, and it was open. We walked into an open area that was set out as a place of worship. We looked around and then were met by a man who said that he was the Pastor. He looked at us suspiciously to begin with but soon realised we were tourists that needed his help. He took us into a little office, and we explained why we were visiting.

He looked at us thoughtfully as I explained about the accident and Des and Michelle's injuries. By this time Des had passed as the decision to remove life support was made. Thankfully, the Pastor understood English and although was a bit surprised by our intentions to pray for Des to be resurrected, he was gracious and told us to come back tomorrow. In the meantime, he would seek The Lord for guidance. We were pleased with how our meeting with the Pastor had gone and felt reassured with his response. We felt that this was the man that The Holy Spirit had arranged for us to meet. We had a restless night that night because we had agreed that whatever the Pastor advised we were to take it as the Lord's guidance. That meant that we may not be here for Des and that he really will have died. But then if the Pastor agreed that we were to minister to Des then that would build our faith immensely, feeling that God was going to do it after all.

The next day we returned to the church where we met the pastor. He greeted us and took us into a side room where he gestured for us to sit down. I glanced over at Troy looking for some sort of non-verbal response of reassurance, but he smiled sympathetically and then lowered his eyes to the floor.

The pastor was straight talking and immediately informed us that we were not here for the healing of Des as this was a divine taking from The Lord. We were here for the healing of Michelle. Both Troy and I were in a daze knowing now that we would never see Des again. I burst into tears because of the reality of the situation. My good friend was no more, and we would be leaving Lanzarote without him. In a sense we were relieved too that we had been guided and although not the answer we were looking for, it seemed right. The pastor prayed for us and then we left and made our way to the hospital where Michelle was being treated.
Our faith was strong and endorsed by the instruction that we believed the pastor had given us, from The Lord.

This wasn't going to be an easy ride as Michelle had serious injuries, a fractured skull in several places, severe swelling to the brain and significant bleeds on the brain too. Her spine was broken at the T9 and she also had a fractured jaw in several places as well as extensive bruising all over her body. Would this really happen? Would Michelle recover from the potentially life-changing injuries she had sustained? The doctors had informed Michelle's mum that they didn't expect her to live, but if by some miracle she did she would never walk or talk again due to potential severe brain damage.

This was putting our faith on the line. Everything in the natural was questioning how was this going to happen? She had recently come out of a coma and a long road to recovery was expected.
Michelle's mum, dad and sister had flown over from the UK to be with her. They were at the hospital when Troy and I arrived. They were in the canteen having a coffee and were so pleased to see us and thanked us for coming. They didn't know the full story of why we were there, and we had no intention of telling them as they may have objected and prevented us from seeing Michelle. That would be totally understandable in the circumstances as they wanted their daughter to have the best chance of recovery.

Although they had an understanding of faith, I'm not sure it stretched to what Troy and I were about to do. What would the consequences be if we prayed, and nothing happened? What if we made things worse trying to get her to rise up and walk? These were high stakes in terms of how it would impact on our faith journey and how it would impact on Michelle, her family, and the hospital staff, as well as those that would hear about what happened throughout her life. I loved Michelle's parents and had fond memories of their hospitality when I used to go to Michelle's house after school, but I'm not sure how they would respond to mine and Troy's intentions to heal their precious daughter in Jesus' name.

We were shown to the ward and were ushered to a waiting area for visitors and told to wait there as there were doctors with Michelle. Troy and I looked at each other realising that this was it. We were putting our faith on the line. Humanly speaking we could get in trouble for what we were about to do. Doubts rushed into my mind about why we shouldn't do this. It is irresponsible, it is insensitive to other people's feelings, it is wrong, how do you know that what the pastor advised is right?

Pangs of fear started to stream through my mind and body as my heart raced. What if she wasn't healed and she couldn't get up and walk? As I was being attacked in my mind by doubts and fear we heard a curdling scream come from the direction of Michelle's room. We later discovered from her sister that when the nurses adjusted her bed or changed her sheet, the vibrations caused excruciating pain for Michelle. How on earth was she going to walk if her body was so sensitive to pain?! On hearing the scream, I had a bit of a moment where I stood up and walked away back down to the corridor to the way out.

Troy followed me and asked what the matter was. It felt to me that this was a sick joke that God was playing. First, he takes our friend and now he tortures us with hearing Michelle in pain despite telling us that we're here to heal her for him! Troy calmed me down and reminded me of why we were here, and all our doubts were pressing us to leave the hospital and then wonder our whole lives what could have been if we had persevered. We returned to our seats and waited some more.

I could see Troy's lips moving silently as he focused himself in prayer. I was really proud of Troy being such a young Christian on his journey of faith, but so bold and obedient. He was a special friend that would later have many trials of his own in life. Troy had a real interest and passion for the bible and was often seen with his head buried in it, gaining knowledge and wisdom that he would then share with others.

One of the nurses called over to us and motioned for us to go in to see Michelle. Troy and I moved towards the room knowing this was it. We had agreed that he would support me in prayer as I declared the healing over Michelle.

On entering the room, I could see Michelle and she was very still, lying on her back. The room had ambient soft natural light filtering through the windows. It was very quiet, and I sensed that we weren't alone and that there was probably an angelic presence in the room too. I was unusually calm. I felt like I was just about to start an important exam, with the confidence that I was well prepared and knew all the answers. Troy made his way to the right side of the bed and sat down on the chair that was positioned close to Michelle's head, I sat on the left side at the foot of the bed.

Michelle's eyes were closed but she was conscious. I observed her for a few moments and could see that she had substantial bruising around her head and neck, the rest of her body was covered by the bed clothes. Troy had started praying with his hands clasped and his head down. I could hear him praying in tongues, so I started praying too. I wasn't sure whether Michelle knew we were in the room, so I said hello to her in a hushed tone. She opened one eye and said: 'Is that you Kev?'. I stood up so she could see me easier, and I smiled telling her how glad we were to see her. A period of silence followed as I looked at her intently and my body was filled with a supernatural faith as I said, 'Jesus is going to heal you today Michelle'. She paused and then replied in a croaky quiet voice, 'I know'. I felt no fear or doubt, and that was because The Holy Spirit in me had taken over. This was His dance.

'Michelle rise up and walk in the name of Jesus!', Troy continued to look down, but his prayers seemed to intensify in speed and tone of his voice. Michelle stared at me, and the upper half of her body sat up almost as if it was pushed into that position. I moved forward to pull her bedsheets back to allow her legs to swing over the side of the bed, at the same time I took hold of her hands to help support her. I could see that she had a colostomy bag as well as several drips attached to her. I was in unchartered territory but still riding on the adrenalin of faith I continued to help Michelle to her feet. Troy was now looking up with his mouth agape, welling up with emotion at what he was witnessing.

Michelle glanced towards the WC in her room and said, 'I want a wee'. Troy and I laughed which broke the intensity of the situation. Michelle was now standing up and the toilet was about five paces from where she stood so I led her to the loo. She sat down and took a sigh of relief. Not quite sure how it worked with her having a colostomy bag, but she was grateful to be sitting on the loo.

I walked her back to her bed, and as I positioned her to get back into bed, I heard the room door open. It was Michelle's sister, Julie. She looked at Michelle and then at me holding her hands, wide-mouthed she gasped and hurriedly closed the door, running back to the canteen to report what she had witnessed to her mum and dad.

Once in bed Michelle lay down and drifted off to sleep. She must have been exhausted. Troy and I looked at each other in amazement. What had just happened?! We were indeed here for Michelle's healing; the pastor was right. Everything had connected and come to pass. We were elated and our faith levels had just rocketed. We left Michelle asleep and returned to our hotel room. I understand that the hospital staff were astounded that Michelle had got out of bed and walked. We were quite cautious of bringing it to their attention as, if I'm honest, I was concerned that we would get into trouble. I think Julie must have shared what had happened.

Troy and I felt high on the goodness of God for what we had witnessed, but at the same time we felt emotionally drained. Our room was pretty basic with just enough room for the two single beds. I wanted to get my head down and felt unusually tired. I sensed that in the spiritual realm something was brewing, what that was I didn't know, but it felt spiritually tense, not in a good way. I'd felt this unsettled feeling before, not knowing where to put myself and not being able to put my finger on why I felt that way.

I hit the sack whilst Troy stayed awake. He needed time to unravel the day's events and read the bible. I lay on my back on the well-worn mattress and drifted off to sleep. Almost immediately I felt myself transported into a murky inky dark place that had an evil presence about it. I couldn't see anyone, but I sensed a presence that I didn't like, in fact, I hated it because the tangible entity was anti God.

A noise started to generate in the space that was the sound of opposition. There was anger, fury and blasphemy present and in response I started to say the name of Jesus, hoping it would protect me and take me out of this gloomy place of wickedness. Although I could see no one or nothing I could feel myself being dragged down and, with a shout, I pleaded the name of Jesus, at the same time waking up akin to breaking the surface of the sea coming up from a deep dive.

Breathless and agitated I looked over to Troy's bed and he was praying whilst staring at me wide-eyed. I shared with him about the place I had just been in my dream and the fact that something was trying to drag me down. Troy looked scared as he had also witnessed something whilst I was asleep. Whilst reading his bible he could hear me murmuring and my body twitching. As he continued to observe me he could see that I was slowly slipping down the bed as if someone was pulling me by my feet. This freaked him out, so he fervently started to pray. We both sensed that the forces of darkness were not happy with what had occurred with Michelle getting healed by Jesus. We were doing warfare in the spiritual realm and our only protection was The Lord of Heaven's Armies. The Bible talks about dark princes over different geographical areas that oppose the purposes of God in the heavenly places. In the book of Daniel, it was the Prince of Persia that resisted Daniel's prayers. It seemed like the Prince of Lanzarote was having his say.

Despite sensing the spiritual climate being oppressive, I was exhausted and lay back down to sleep once more. Unusually, I was asleep almost instantly and was back in the place of darkness and evil. For the second time, I experienced again what had occurred the first time, including being dragged down. This time though Troy was watching me slide down the bed in real time and shouted my name to wake me up. I told him that it had happened again and he looked shaken and said that I had started to move down the bed again. We both agreed to pray and use the weapons the bible talks about that demolishes the enemy's strongholds.

We prayed on the armour of God that is written about in Ephesians 6 and aggressively against the powers of darkness. After all we were both soldiers and up for a fight, but this wasn't a fight of flesh and blood, this was against principalities and powers and wicked powers in the heavenly realm. As we prayed, we could hear something outside our room door; a demonic sounding voice shouting in a tongue I have never heard before. It wasn't human that was for sure and both Troy and I heard it.

Our room had a window that looked out onto the corridor that had a view all the way down to the other rooms. As our prayer intensified, we could hear the voice protest and then as if the evil spirit was walking away down the corridor, the voice continued to shout but moving further away until we could hear it no more. Troy and I looked at each other in amazement as we couldn't believe that it had gone in response to our telling it to go in Jesus' name. We both felt a massive sense of relief and the spiritual atmosphere had changed. We both felt peaceful and lay quietly on our beds reflecting on what had just happened. I fell back into a deep sleep without the spiritual oppression. The rest of the night passed without any further interference. I would like to think that God deployed an angel or two to watch over us.

In the morning, I awoke and recalled a dream I had to Troy. It was brief but hugely significant as to what had taken place whilst we were in Lanzarote. I could see a road starting on the ground but leading all the way into the sky and beyond. Then I saw me and Troy making our way down the road from the sky to earth. It was so steep we were walking down as you would coming down a very steep hill or mountain. We were met at the bottom by Emma and some other friends. They asked us where we had been and we looked up and pointing said: 'Up there!'.

Michelle would go on to make a full recovery and later train as a teacher attaining a first-class honours degree. She later went on to train as a minister within the Church of England. She's now married with four grown up children and is grateful for her life.

Wisdom/Reflection
- *There is an unseen battle waging between good and evil, whether you believe it or not, matters not. It's happening regardless*
- *Jesus Christ is above all and holds all power and dominion. The power to heal, protect and save*
- *Where there is trust, obedience and faith in Christ, extraordinary things happen*
- *Don't let what your eyes see limit your faith. God keeps His word*

Michael Derry. Gone but not forgotten

14.
From green to blue

House packed and ready for inspection, we waited as the housing quarters' representative went into great detail checking, with clipboard in hand, the condition of all appliances, carpets, walls and anything else that was visible and not visible, like the inner regions of the oven. Moving out inspections were legendary in terms of level and detail of the inspection. Emma and I had stripped the oven down to its bare carcass and then meticulously cleaned every part. Thankfully, we passed and on our way to Walmley in the West Midlands where we had bought a small two-bedroom townhouse.

I had left the Army in October 1991 and was due to join the Police in December that year so I had some time to spare. Thankfully, I passed the police home visit where Em and I were visited by a police sergeant who came to our home and asked both of us some questions about our lifestyle and how we thought we would adapt to life in the police. He was a pleasant guy and we appreciated the visit. I also had to pass a fitness test and a final interview before a panel of three people, one was a senior police officer, the other was a woman from HR I think and another man who represented some type of committee related to the police.

I was asked several scenario-based questions that were designed to test my moral courage and people skills. They seemed to like my answers and commented on how I saw things in black and white. I think that may have been because I was quite decisive in my responses, particularly around what I believe was right and wrong. They were probably chuckling to themselves inside thinking, naïve boy, wait until he's faced with some of the challenges the public and colleagues will throw at him. Nonetheless, they must have liked my responses as I passed my final interview.

I flew through the fitness test and was only beaten by another applicant that was previously a Royal Marine. Compared to the military the fitness assessment was a walk in the park. Back then it was two laps around Tally Ho police training centre, running as fast as you can, along with some upper body tests in the gym.

Around the same time whilst having a quiet time, reading my bible, I sensed the Holy Spirit illuminate the following scripture; Proverbs 24 verses 23-26, which says:

These are the sayings of the wise:

To show partiality in judging is not good. Whoever says to the guilty, "you are innocent". Peoples will curse him and nations denounce him. But it will go well with those who convict the guilty, and rich blessing will come upon them. An honest answer is like a kiss on the lips.

I decided to do some volunteering at the local leisure centre so called them and they asked me to drop a CV off at the centre and they would let me know. The next day I dressed for the occasion in a plain blue navy suit and regimental tie, shoes highly polished. I was met at the enquiry desk by one of the managers who asked me who I was here to see. I explained the fact that I was dropping off my CV as I wanted to volunteer if they could use me to help with physical activities.

I explained that I had just left the Army and was in between jobs, joining the police in December. He looked at the CV that I was holding out for him to receive, and he smirked and said: 'No thanks' and walked off. I stood there for a moment not quite able to compute what had just occurred. Why had I evoked such a response? Did my breath smell? Did I look dodgy? Was my approach wrong? I looked around and realised I was on my own in the reception area. If I hadn't been taken by surprise by his response, I would have savoured exploring with him what his problem was. I couldn't get too physical as I was about to join the police. My human desire was to grip him and get him to modify his attitude. This clearly wasn't appropriate and remember, at this stage of my life, I was still a bit rough around the edges in terms of pent-up aggression and a good Christian response to this particular challenge.

Emma and I received the wonderful news that she was pregnant, and we were delighted that, firstly, Emma was able to get pregnant, and, secondly, that we had a home of our own that we could bring baby back to. Emma and I had shared a lot with each other prior to trying for a baby and she was in a place of wanting to be a mum and the preceding months had been a time of preparation for us as we sought advice as a couple from older wiser friends that we considered as mentors. I was so grateful for Em's graciousness and humility as she carried our baby.

In December 1991, I joined West Midlands Police. Having waded through some administrative paperwork we were taken to stores to collect our uniform and equipment. We were quite a large intake and, from my initial assessment, from a diverse range of backgrounds. There weren't many ex-forces' recruits and, for the first time ever, I was working with women too. Everyone seemed friendly and excited to be in the police. It was viewed as a good job that had good prospects and the pay wasn't bad either. That said, initially I took a pay drop as I was well paid in the army due to my rank and other qualifications.

I was very comfortable in the company of the people on my intake. It wasn't as thuggish or as hard-hitting as the army. I was really interested in other people's stories of how they came to this place in their life. All were local to the West Midlands area, and some had families, others were single but most of us were in our 20s or 30s. I was very conscious not to give away too much of myself too soon. There were others though that were quite extroverted and wanted a lot of the airspace. I was happy for that as I was taking it all in, building a profile in my head of every individual, and I'm sure some were probably doing the same with me.

Having received all our kit, we were required to wear it every day we attended Tally Ho police training centre. We had all sorts of induction training before being sent off to Police college at Ryton-On-Dunsmore.

Em and I had moved into our small two-bedroom townhouse on Walmley Road, the previous owner incidentally was a policewoman. All our furniture fitted nicely into our home, and Em and I set out to make it our home by getting some friends to help us decorate.

Before long I was at Ryton for the week returning home at the weekends. We were members of St John's Church and, thankfully, Emma had friends from church as well as family close by. I was immersed in learning my new job and wanting to excel in classes that we attended.

On arrival at Ryton, we met our instructors who were all sergeants, one of whom would become a dear friend of mine. We were introduced to each other in class for the first time. Some I had met at Tally Ho prior to Ryton. We had to do the usual of saying a little bit about ourselves by way of an introduction as well as sharing needs, fears and expectations. Some fully embraced this and shared their hearts on the first day. I cringed inside thinking that this was too much too soon. I couldn't believe how emotional some of them were and I wanted to burst out laughing but thought better of it.

The police was quite mushy and cuddly compared to the army, where you were discouraged from sitting in a circle and sharing your feelings. I was used to just being told to crack on, so this was all very amusing. I didn't want to appear that I wasn't engaging in the exercise, so I gave just enough and nodded considerately whenever someone shared something special to them. Don't get me wrong, if someone shared how say a bereavement or traumatic situation had affected them, I would respect that, but there was some stuff that was shared that was quite wet and in my view wasn't for group consumption.

I liked having classes with both genders. I got on well with the girls and got used to them bringing something different to the table, in terms of perspective. I would learn how important that different perspective was as I journeyed through my police career.

Whilst in class we were encouraged to volunteer for certain roles that meant some responsibility. For example, a volunteer to march the class around the site. All students were required to march around camp, either as a squad or as an individual. I was quite comfortable organising a team of people and marching them around the camp, but, at this early stage, I kept my counsel and allowed a guy called Tom to volunteer. He was quite a loud character and had shared with the class that he had military experience from his time in the Territorial Army. There was another ex-army guy in our class called Jason, we glanced at each other and smirked looking down. The Territorial Army volunteers were known as STABs when I was a regular soldier. STAB stood for Stupid TA bastards. They were the weekend warriors that trained as soldiers on the weekends and during holiday periods. To be fair, they should be commended for the giving of their time and, ultimately if called upon, to serve their country in a time of war.

So Tom got the job and once class had concluded for the morning, had the onerous task of marching us to the dinner hall. We formed up, eventually, as the majority of our class had never marched before. The term form up in three ranks was alien to most so I didn't envy Tom and I was curious to see how this was going to pan out. It's really embarrassing if people are out of step or talking whilst they are marching. Just the basics of stepping off on your left foot and swinging your arms shoulder high. We would be getting drill instruction formally so, for now, I guess anything would do.

We formed up and Tom, shouted: 'By the left quick march ... Left, left, leffety left and left!'. What followed was like an act from Fred Carno's circus. There were some hopping and some skipping. I tried to keep the step regardless but knew it was going to the rats. We halted bumbling into each other, and some started to blame Tom who tried to respond but the consensus was that we should have a new drill leader and I was elected on the spot and graciously accepted, as I didn't want to be subject to an embarrassing episode like that again.

After providing a few basic pointers we arrived safely at the dinner hall with some of our pride in tact. I sensed at the time that there was some resentment from Tom that he had been ousted and it had gone so well for me. I understood how he could have been feeling and would gladly relinquish the role back to him, if he could indeed perform the task. I knew very little about him so gave him space and avoided any conversation to do with drill. When I was in the army it was a necessary evil, it allowed a body of men to act as one with one person giving the words of command. If I could have got away with not having to march around, I would have. Some loved drill and usually went on to do their drill course at the Guards Depot in Pirbright.

This wasn't the first time I would have direct or indirect conflict with Tom. One evening we had all sat down for tea after a day full of lessons on criminal law and police procedures. The long tables were arranged in rows, with the sergeants and other senior ranks sitting at the top of the dinner hall slightly separated from the rank and file.

I was sat at a table with a number of our class that had formed as quite a close group. One of the girls called Emma was having a hard time absorbing all of the information and doubted her ability. She was a lovely person and came from quite a humble background so was very proud to have got into the police. We were speaking words of encouragement and empathising with her. As we sat eating and listening to Emma, I noticed that someone off one of the other nearby tables was flicking peas over to our table.

This happened several times and despite us trying to ignore the infantile behaviour, the peas kept coming. I looked over at the table and gestured them to stop as I couldn't identify who the culprit was. I also indicated that Emma was upset so needed the pea throwing to stop. It didn't. A second volley came over and I could see that it was Tom that was vaulting the peas over to our table. This caused a major irritation to those on my table and I decided this was the time to act. I was angry inside and wasn't in the mood for childish behaviour. I walked up to the offending table and took hold of the vinegar bottle, looking at Tom I said: 'I asked you to stop'. I put my one hand round the back of his head to hold it steady whilst I shook the vinegar bottle aiming it at his eyes. After several shakes I released his head and left the scene to the sound of Tom letting out a bit of a whimper.

As I write this, I am embarrassed and shudder to think did I really do that? Regrettably, I must confess that I did. Looking back, I hadn't long left the army and had to think carefully about my conduct otherwise I was going to get myself into trouble as technically this was assault. Thankfully, I wasn't ostracised by the class, in fact some felt Tom had it coming to him. For the rest of my time at Ryton I kept my distance from Tom and he from me. It was hard to believe that our paths wouldn't cross again in our careers but, thankfully, they would and on better terms.

I still had a lot to learn in terms of managing my emotions and wanted so much to be a gentleman without losing my manliness. I was physically courageous and didn't mind getting into a scrape if it was for a noble cause. How was I going to cope with violent situations on the street, when confronted by those that have done wrong either by hurting others or themselves?

On reflection my behaviour was wrong and in hindsight I could have deescalated the situation verbally. This I would soon learn as I was exposed to many challenging scenarios where skilful communication would become critical.

I had a competitive edge that could go either way. I would learn that it wasn't always about me and that sometimes a more altruistic approach was preferrable. As I watched and observed the other students, I realised that I was quite hard and ruthless in my approach. I liked to get things done but at what expense? I would learn that the army was very driven and focused, in contrast to civilian life. Most of my friends and colleagues were far more laid back, a little vaguer in their approach. In fairness, that wasn't all of them, as some were just as and some more focused than me. Perhaps that was due to upbringing that helped form their values.

I had a good bunch of friends on my intake and most evenings we laughed until we cried. Most evenings were occupied by going for a run or going to the gym and then studying before going to bed. One of my good friends was Roger who was an ex Royal Marine. We used to go running together and push each other by increasing the pace now and again to see if the other would crack.

Unfortunately, Roger would have a nasty accident once posted to his unit. He was on Public Order training and performing a drill over uneven ground. He severely broke his leg and several operations later; he had his leg amputated. I remember him calling me and relaying the story and then, just matter of factly, said: 'I'm going to have it off'. He was talking about his leg. I paused and then we both roared with laughter over the phone. Thankfully, he started the round of laughter and I joined him. I think it was just surreal and shocking and that's how we got past it. Roger would have had a promising career in the police, but it wasn't to be.

We were trained in unarmed defence, a martial art whose name escapes me. I didn't really rate martial arts but valued some tips on how to restrain and defend myself, within the confines of the law. Some called it applying

Home Office approved pain. We had to practice the techniques on each other, and I always made an agreement with my pain partner not to go too hard as I wasn't very flexible. No point in injuring yourself on the practice run. Once the technique was having effect, you had to tap the mat to let your partner know that they needed to release. On one session we had an exercise where we had to pair up with someone and then try to wrestle each other to the ground and hold them there for a number of seconds until the instructor blew their whistle. I had been put with Jock who was 6'2" and about 16 stones (I may be being kind with the weight estimation). Jock was a big unit and certainly one that I would want on my side, he was a lovely guy too.

As we approached the mat I whispered to Jock: 'I'm going to kill you on this. He laughed because he got my sense of humour and quietly responded: 'We'll see'. We had to kneel opposite each other and then grapple for supremacy. The whistle was blown and we made towards each other hands outstretched and knees pressing hard into the mat. I advanced towards him keeping my centre of gravity low, which was easy for a small guy like me. As I made contact with Jock, I bear hugged him under his armpits and leaned my weight forward.

I can remember looking at his face as I made my move and seeing a vulnerability in his eyes immediately before he toppled backwards. This gave me great confidence so, as soon as he was on his back, I shuffled to his chest area and lay across him hanging on praying for that whistle to sound. The screech of the whistle confirmed my win. We both stood up and patted each other on the shoulder. As we walked off the mat Jock smiled at me and whispered: 'You little shit'. We both burst out laughing and returned to the bench. There is no doubt in my mind that in a head-to-head standing or needing to put weight behind a task, Jock would be my weapon of choice. He would remain a good friend throughout my career as we occasionally crossed paths.

Jock and I often car shared when going home for the weekend, along with a couple of others. We were proud to be police officers and couldn't wait to finish training so we could do it all for real. Carrying a warrant card reminded us of the power and responsibility we had and would look for opportunities where we could use our power legitimately, which meant whilst off duty for us. Any wise and well-seasoned cop knows that you don't go looking for incidents. Life was complicated enough when dealing with stuff in duty time. That said, if something cracked off that put a person in danger, then most people including off-duty cops would get involved.

On our way home for the weekend, we saw a car that overtook us at what was clearly over the 40-mph speed limit. The car was packed with young lads and music was blaring out of an open window. We caught up with the car at a red traffic light. As we approached the car, we debated whether we should show our warrant card and give some advice about the manner of driving and excessive speed. Yes, let's do it.

We drew up alongside the car in the other lane and gestured to the driver who made eye contact. Jock showed his warrant card and told the driver to drive within the speed limit. The driver looked at us and apologised. The passengers sheepishly glanced over at us and then looked down into the footwells. Job done. As the car pulled away, we watched it drive at a more sensible speed and then we all burst into laughter. It worked! When we returned to lessons on the Monday we shared our experience with the others, who looked for opportunities to try out their newly-endowed powers.

Weeks of training and lectures as well as square bashing (drill practice on the parade square) was developing us with a new skillset that provided us with academic and practical skills that would soon be put to good use for real as we were posted to our units across England.

One of our sessions that proved to be amusing involved drinking alcohol and attempting to drive. The scenario was created to test our knowledge and skills of the breathalyser procedure and the powers relating to stopping a vehicle. Those of us that were stooging, (acting as the offender) had to drink enough sherry to turn the breathalyser machine indicator light to red. This intimated that there was enough intoxicating liquor from our breath sample to surmise reasonable suspicion and arrest the driver in order to conduct a more accurate test back at the station. The Lion Intoximeter provided samples that scientifically are more accurate and provide the grounds to charge a driver for drink driving.

A few of us stooges guzzled the sherry and then tested ourselves to make sure we were suitably intoxicated before we went into the role play. I was surprised at how much it took before the light turned red. Others had a lower tolerance, and it didn't take many swigs from the bottle for their light to illuminate red. Please note, I am not advocating risking driving whilst being intoxicated. There are so many variables that many of us got different results every time we took part. Tiredness, an empty stomach and other factors affected the results. Nonetheless, a helpful exercise both in terms of learning the correct procedure and an understanding of how intoxicating liquor affected us all differently.

Soon the Passing Out Parade was upon us as all our training was complete and we were now ready to move onto our next phase of training that was completed on our respective divisional areas.

The day of our parade was a gloriously sunny day and the culmination of friendships forged and the closing of a memorable season in our lives. Emma attended with my mum and dad. Em was heavily pregnant and pretty early on had to find a seat as her ankles were swollen. During the parade awards were given out for various strands of work achieved. Our intake won the best at drill award, and I was awarded with a presentation truncheon with the training college crest on it, on behalf of the class.

There was a brief ceremony indoors where the then Chief Constable of Northamptonshire Police gave the address, that was a realistic and inspiring message, including wisdom acquired during his long and successful career. He also presented me with my Gulf War medal which had only arrived a week before the parade.

I started my two-year probation at Erdington Police Station. I was posted to a shift that covered Erdington, Kingstanding and Sutton Coldfield. I wasn't the only probationer on my unit so the tea-making duties were shared. Members of my unit were very welcoming and were a light-hearted lot and all had several years under their belt. There was a mixture of men and women, but the majority were men. I was soon to find out that Glynnis ran the station. She was the front office enquiry officer. She was a police staff member, not a warranted officer and was the mummy of the station. She was a great laugh and very compassionate, always offering a listening ear where required. She also knew all the gossip and wasn't to be crossed, as just a look could kill from Glynnis.

There were some real characters on our unit too. One of the guys known as Rick O was a throw back to the 70s. His hair was too long for my liking, way below the collar. He often wore slip-on shoes with his uniform and carried his Motorola radio in his hand as if it was a peacemaker revolver. He was tall and thin with angled features. His eyes were always narrowed and he had a moustache that needed to go. He would have easily got a part in a Clint Eastwood western if he'd auditioned.

Wisdom/Reflection
- *When starting a new job listen more than you talk*
- *Be curious about people that you find difficult rather than judgemental*
- *Look to someone who is well respected at work and approach them as a mentor. A teachable attitude is commendable*
- *When becoming a parent for the first time ensure that you pay attention to your partner being extra loving and thoughtful. (It's tough when you're tired!)*
- *Pray for your unborn child and have that together time of spiritual intimacy as a family*
- *A family that prays together usually stays together*
- *Anger is a legitimate emotion but keep it on a leash, lest it calls its friends aggression and violence to the party*

Me as a probationary constable having just joined West Midlands Police

15.
My first shift and beyond

My very first shift I was assigned to a prisoner watch. The detained woman had caused some damage to a church and seemed to be vulnerable. I made myself known to the custody sergeant and he pointed to a cell with a chair outside it. I walked over to the cell door and peered through the hatch to take a look at this woman that had been arrested.

As I looked through the hatch I was faced with this lady's naked boobs. I was shocked and knew that I needed to get my face out of the hatch pretty quick. She looked demented and I'm sure she had foam coming from her mouth. I then heard her shriek: 'Jesus didn't die for my sins!'.

I stepped back and informed the custody sergeant that she was half naked. I started to pray under my breath as I sensed this was quite a spiritual situation. I prayed for the woman and her current state of mind. Those that are spiritually aware would have said that this woman was possessed by a demon. It was like some of the people Jesus delivered from spirits in the Bible. This was full-on as she continued to howl and scream. I decided that I needed to pray that the spirit would be silenced. I could have easily rationalised that she had mental health issues and not bothered to pray but I just got a sense that there was something else at play here. Besides, Jesus did die for her sins and the spiritual influence was insulting my Lord and Saviour.

This may sound crazy to those of you reading that don't believe in spiritual warfare, but, as a Christian, the day you believe you are in a battle. I had read and been involved previously in occurrences like this. As soon as you believe that it's spiritual and you deal with the situation as such, you have a whole load of resources available for you to deal with it. For one, everything needs to be done in the name of Jesus. In my own strength and authority I am nothing and will have little or no effect on the situation. What Jesus accomplished on the cross by dying for our sins and saving us from an eternity without him.

The fact that he was raised from the dead signalled mission accomplished, allowing his followers to do the same things as he did. In Jesus' own words: 'even greater things than this you will do in my name'. Anyway, if I got the woman to be quiet I'm sure the custody sergeant would be grateful. This wasn't exactly in the police policy and procedure manual but I was going to give it a go.

I couldn't exactly stand up with my hand in a Jesus pose to rebuke the spirit, so I had to make do with whispering the prayer in the direction of the cell. I wasn't going to risk looking through the hatch again so I stood up from where I was sitting and whispered with a bit of a hiss to emphasise my words. Thankfully, there was a lot going on in the custody block so no one was really paying attention to me. The woman continued to shout and scream but when I commanded the spirit to be quiet in Jesus' name, something unusual happened.

The woman became strangely quiet – I was reluctant to look into her cell, but the sergeant realised she was quiet too and asked me to check on her. When I looked in she was sat on the floor with her top back on just staring at the floor. It actually worked! Not that I should be surprised but I was. Sometimes, even if you don't feel that you've got the authority, you actually have. Sometimes, it's not about how inadequate you feel or whether you feel you have the faith. It's believing that Jesus said we would do these things and it's more about trust and obedience. Thankfully, the woman remained quiet for the rest of the shift. Day one over.

My tutor Mick was a really nice guy and very knowledgeable as well as pragmatic. I would have to demonstrate that I was competent to patrol independently, but before that I would attend incidents with Mick who would allow me to deal with all aspects of the job. This would be followed by a debrief. My PDP (personal development portfolio) detailed all the competencies I had to accomplish. Mick would volunteer for jobs that came over the radio to enable me to get the experience needed to achieve the competencies.

A suspected sudden death call came over the radio reported by a concerned neighbour. Mick gestured to me to respond to the controller, volunteering to attend. As we were driving to the address, Mick was questioning me on what the correct procedure will be and asked if I had any concerns about seeing a dead body. I was ok with seeing death as I had seen many corpses during my time in The Gulf War.

The occupant in the address was an elderly lady living on her own. We knocked on the front door and shouted her name through the letter box. As I looked up, I could see that the curtains were still drawn. I looked at Mick and suggested that I put the door in. He agreed, so I stepped back and kicked the door forcing it to open. She had only put the Yale lock on so it didn't take a lot, but if the mortice lock had been on too it would have taken more than my right boot.

As we made our way up the stairs my senses were heightened, particularly, my sense of smell. I'd smelt death before so was expecting there to be an odour. We called the lady's name and identified ourselves as the police but got no response. I feared the worst. The living room door was ajar, and the lights were on. As I peered into the room I could see that the television was on and caught between channels, displaying the fuzzy static picture.

I saw immediately that the elderly lady had fallen and died where she lay. As I looked at her something didn't look right, and I soon realised that I couldn't see her head. As she had fallen her head had struck a wastepaper bin and was actually in the bin. Ordinarily, this would have been unfortunate but unremarkable. My mind couldn't make sense of what I was seeing. The bin was a Dusty Bin character from the 3-2-1 show hosted by Ted Rogers. So, all I could initially see was an elderly lady's body with a Dusty Bin smiling face.

Thankfully, the relatives hadn't arrived yet so we had the opportunity to perform the usual checks of the body. We did remove the Dusty Bin from her head but I must confess I did have a little chuckle to myself. I guess some would call this black humour and some may scorn and say that my chuckle was inappropriate.

Death is not nice and I was saddened every time I attended a death, because it impacts on so many and brings so much pain and often loneliness. I always prayed for the families and saw it as a privileged position to be there to offer that initial comfort and reassurance. Police officers deal with so many incidents in one tour of duty and processing the trauma in what we attend often had to wait.

The conversation in the car with your partner was what helped make sense of what we saw. Death never really bothered me and I learned that biologically we are just skin and bone. When the soul is gone, life is gone. It's a fine line between life and death.

As a Christian my thought processes went beyond death and to the afterlife. How different the prospect for the person that had a relationship with God and trusted and followed Jesus. They had the hope of the promises that Jesus declared and are recorded in the bible. For those that had no faith on their own admission believed there was nothing else apart from decomposition. Who knows for sure, but one day we will see. There are lots of testimonies of people that had died and come back to life and reported a spiritual experience where they saw Jesus. In fact, I learned recently that it's become a science, because of the numbers of people reporting the same or similar experiences. It seems mad that we meticulously plan and make provision for our lives but neglect to plan and invest in what comes after life. I have noticed that people tend to shelve death and the thought of it until life-threatening circumstances come upon them. Eternity is a long time and warrants serious consideration.

Back in the day, probationers were required to demonstrate their street craft skills on foot patrol. I was posted to Erdington High Street. I was told by one of my sergeants that once you put your big hat on (helmet) and leave the station the public won't know that you're new and will expect you to know directions to everywhere and be able to deal with every situation. Thanks for that sarge.

I left the police station and made my way towards the High Street. I transmitted on my radio to report that I was out on foot patrol, then raised my head, straightened my back and walked with a confident swagger. I nodded to people as I walked past and greeted them verbally if they looked friendly. An elderly lady looked at me with smiling eyes and said: 'Hello officer, are the officers getting younger or am I getting older?'. 'Both,' I said smiling and I walked on. As I walked, I felt my truncheon down the side of my right leg and hoped I wouldn't have to use it on my first foot patrol.

As I entered the High Street, I was aware of people looking at me and others were oblivious of my presence. I stopped on the corner and stood and watched, observing people. I saw a young man acting furtively. As I approached him, he turned in the opposite direction and quickened his pace. I broke into a jog to catch him up and then said in a commanding voice: 'You! Stop!'. To my surprise the youth stopped. As he turned around to face me, I noticed him try to secrete something down his trouser waistband. I told him to put his hands out in front of him. At this point I sensed that he was contemplating making off on foot so I grabbed his wrist and assertively took him to the side where I could maintain control of the situation. My heart was beating ten to the dozen and my mind was racing thinking about what my grounds for detaining him were and would I remember the words of the caution that I would have to recite if I arrested him.

The youth had started to perspire, and I could see beads of sweat on his forehead. By now members of the public were curious about what was going on. I needed to get him checked on the police national computer (PNC) and let the controller know that I had someone detained. This would provide me with some additional back-up if he decided to play up. The thought had crossed my mind as to whether he was alone. Would others come to his aid and harm me in the process?

He gave me his details and, instinctively, I didn't believe him. I decided that I had the grounds to search him, which he was unhappy about and started to move around. I told him we could do the search here or at the station and he reluctantly agreed. I searched his trouser waistband first and found a sharpened screwdriver. He looked at me directly and started to pull away from me, I yanked him back and said: 'You're going nowhere matey'. I arrested him for having the sharpened screwdriver and continued to search him. I found a credit card and some cannabis resin in his pockets. I clumsily put all the seized items in my pocket and proceeded to handcuff him.

By now, I had got an audience. Some were just curious, and others were clearly not fans of the police. There were no cars available to transport my prisoner to the station, so I had to walk him back. I felt extremely vulnerable and wanted to get to the nick as quickly as possible. I'd got this far and made my first self-initiated arrest, my prisoner escaping was unthinkable.

I arrived safely to the custody block and once the prisoner was booked in it transpired that the credit card was stolen and he hadn't given his correct details. He was charged and appeared at court where he received a community order. The screwdriver could have been used as a weapon or as an implement to break into cars. He denied having it as a weapon.

Wisdom/Reflection
- *Remember to wear your spiritual armour every day as you can never tell what the enemy is going to throw at you*
- *Preach the gospel and if necessary use words (St Francis of Assisi). Live out your faith in the workplace*
- *As iron sharpens iron so one person sharpens another. Make sure you're the one doing the sharpening, influencing the culture around you*
- *Debrief your day and speak out your emotions. Pray through those instances that challenged you and seek the Holy Spirit's counsel on the issues*
- *Take time each day to be silent and discipline your mind to enter a state of thankfulness*

Police driving course in the 90's. The legendary peugeot 405 Mi16

16.
Isn't she lovely?

Walking the beat was where I cut my policing teeth, because there was nowhere to hide. I learnt how to quickly assess and solve problems. As a cop you need a certain amount of empathy as we often turned up at the worst time in people's life. Discretion was also a gift that I had the power to use wisely.

One such occasion was when I was on foot patrol in Erdington. Not much was happening and it was getting dark – I saw an oncoming car with the driver not wearing his seat belt. I decided to stop him so I stepped into the middle of the road and raised my hand in a commanding manner, hoping inside that the car would stop! The car did stop, and the driver looked stressed.

He was an older man that was respectful and was probably thinking how young the police were these days. He pulled his car over and I asked him to alight his vehicle which he did. So far, he had passed the attitude test by his non-verbal communication. There was no tutting or rolling of the eyes and his stance was non-confrontational. I asked him what he wasn't wearing his seat belt and he looked down and just muttered: 'I'm sorry officer it's been a bad day'. I could have patronised him by telling him the hazards of not wearing a seat belt, but I'm sure he knew that. The focusing of the mind would come when he was informed that there was a financial penalty in the form of a fine for the offence.

I notified him that it was an offence that would mean a fixed penalty notice could be issued. He looked up and apologised again, almost resigned to the fact that this fine would add to his already challenging day. I told him that, on this occasion, I would be giving him advice but if I saw him not wearing his belt again then I would not be so benevolent. He sighed and sincerely thanked me. As I wished him well and continued patrolling he called after me and invited me to call in to his fish and chip shop any time, with his compliments. I took this to mean free fish and chips for life. Despite his kind offer I never did take him up on his offer. Being beholden to another as a police officer often compromised many a good officer, with allegations of corruption.

July 4 1992, a very special day as our daughter, Hannah Frances, was born. Emma was in labour for over 24 hours and on her own admission part of that was probably inexperience and Hannah not wanting to leave the cosiness of Em's tummy! Our midwife was a small Welsh lady called Miss Jones. She was old school and quite stern. She hadn't had children herself but was quite adept at helping mothers get theirs out safely and healthily.

I can still remember the moment that Hannah popped out. There was a scream of relief from Emma and I could see immediately that the baby was a girl. I was overcome with emotion and was all fingers and thumbs when the midwife invited me to cut the umbilical cord, which I willingly did. We were now parents and we had our own little baby girl that came into this world as a result of our love for each other. We agreed that this beautiful little girl would be named Hannah and her middle name would be Frances in memory of Emma's mum whose middle name was also Frances. I took my responsibility of being a father seriously and saw it as a massive privilege to raise children. The bible had a lot to say about how we should raise our children and I was passionate about our kids having a vibrant faith of their own. We continued to pray for our little Han now she was in the world and gave thanks to The Lord for his blessing.

Emma's pregnancy was relatively trouble-free and she was a joyful expectant mum-to-be. During pregnancy Em had a job that she could do from home. A friend of ours mentioned the job to her as she was finishing with the company and a vacancy would be available. This was ideal as Em could do as much or as little as she liked, and her income depended on how many units she made. The job was making colostomy bag covers, that made the colostomy bags look less clinical and unsightly. Rolls of material were delivered to our home and then Em would cut them around a pattern template and then sew them together on a sewing machine. She particularly liked making the ones for the children that had Disney character material, that, hopefully, cheered up the children. Em would pray over each cover she made, asking God to bring comfort and healing to the person receiving the cover.

As I adjusted to being in the police, the shift work and processing of incidents that I had attended; I realised that with the changes of new home, new job, becoming a parent came challenges that I hadn't considered.

Emma, despite being a superb young mum, started to struggle with her mental health. She increasingly felt flat with a low mood. We though to begin with that it may just be the baby blues as her body adjusted to being post-natal. Em felt guilty about the way she felt and I tried to reassure her as much as I could. Em had bonded with Hannah and we loved bathtime and holding her, feeding her a bottle of milk. The mornings were the most difficult for Em, and, when I was on an early shift, I used to worry about leaving her with Han, because I knew she struggled.

I had to have my head in the game for what the day would bring at work. The thing about being a police officer was that you never knew what you were going to face from day to day. It could be that you had to deliver a message to relatives that their loved one had died or attend a serious road traffic collision, or a suicide. It was a challenging time of life and although the joy of being parents was always in our hearts, life often presented circumstances that we had to manage. Emma was a night owl so I would normally do the bath routine with Han and Em would sit at the table making colostomy bag covers. She would aim to make 200 a week and would often be sewing into the early hours of the morning. I loved this woman so much. She was a grafter and a wife that still managed to give me the care I needed and invest in our little Hannah. Em was a natural with little ones and I think she got this talent from her mum who was a nursery teacher.

It was evident early on that Hannah was going to be a world changer. She couldn't wait to talk and used to speak with her eyes when she couldn't form words. Hannah wasn't going to wait around and was a determined little girl. She was walking at just over 10 months and wasn't going to wait for anybody. We could see at an early age that she was very perceptive. She wouldn't be pushed around by other children at toddlers but was intensely kind when she saw a need.
As a shift would come to an end, my thoughts would turn to thinking about

Han and looking forward to spending some time with her when I got home. I used to maul her and then get told off by Em for leaving red marks on her face from my stubble.

Despite being financially challenged and tired we were very happy as a family, and it was a good feeling when we were in for the night together with our little one. God was leading us and caring for us and we were confident that all would be well and this was just part of being young parents.

Emma's low moods in the morning seemed to get worse and after visits by health visitors and appointments with the GP the consensus was that Em would benefit from some medication to help with her mental health. Em started taking anti-depressant medication, but, at that stage, post-natal depression wasn't mentioned. Emma's dad had been on anti-depressant medication all his adult life so we did wonder whether Em's illness could be hereditary.

I didn't really know how to cope with how Em was feeling and felt more at ease being a provider than a carer. If I'm honest, I could care for Em to a point but once I'd done all the things to try and make her feel better, and she was still low and feeling hopeless, I went deeper into providing and that often meant doing more of the routine with Hannah so Em could rest.

Depression did bring a sadness to our home and I can remember thinking that it shouldn't be like this. We should be enjoying being a young family, watching Hannah grow. There were flashes when Emma felt that she could function and that was usually later in the day. But while we were waiting for the medication to kick in things got darker and I found it increasingly hard to hold everything together.

Lack of sleep, worrying about Em who seemed lifeless, looking after little Han and learning how to be a cop, started to take its toll. I visited my GP as I thought I was going to pop under the competing demands. The doctor listened to me then took his pen out and gave me a sick note signing me off work for two weeks. I felt a failure and hated the fact that I was being signed off because I couldn't cope.

I went to see my boss at Erdington Police Station and told him about my situation. He was old school and I feared that he wouldn't be sympathetic. He stood there sternly looking at me as I explained how things were at home and my visit to the GP. He motioned for me to give him the sick note. He glanced over it and then ripped it up. He told me to take two weeks off but submitting this sick note wouldn't be good for my career or any prospects of promotion. I was grateful at the time for him squaring away giving me two weeks off and bowed to his career advice.

On reflection I'm not sure his advice was wise. It was well meaning but unwise. Being able to recognise that you're not coping and reaching out for help is a great strength. Perhaps supporting me by signposting me to other interventions and helping me to manage a structured return to work would have been more helpful. Thankfully, I can say years later, this is the sensitive approach of the modern police service. Later in my service as an Inspector I would have the opportunity to exercise compassion and support for those that were in a similar position to me.

Emma was a great homemaker and, despite her poor mental health, she made our home a lovely place to come back to. She loved dried flower displays and there were always fresh flowers in the house too. Em could cook several dishes very well and one of those was lasagne.

At that time we did most of our shopping at KwikSave. The quality of food was shocking but we were on a budget so we made the best of what we could afford. Emma always made me feel loved and despite being a mum and having challenges with her health, she always made time to hold me and hug me. I needed that so much and I'm not sure why, but I needed to be held. I had so many insecurities and felt that it was for me to sort myself out.

I knew that the Holy Spirit was in the business of transforming lives and setting people free from life patterns that are negative, in terms of attitudes and behaviours. I just felt that it was my issue and that I needed to sort it with the help of God. Later I would learn that it wasn't about my effort and good works. I was loved unconditionally and nothing I did could make God love me any more or any less.

My Catholic roots seemed to be influencing me to focus on good works rather than the miracle of grace, undeserved love. But I didn't want to take advantage of God's good nature and felt guilt when I sinned the same time over and over again. I felt that I didn't deserve the Father's forgiveness because of the way I constantly let him down. I would learn that as I repented and talked things through with God, our relationship would deepen, and the power of Jesus' sacrifice would reap its full power as it covered my mess. I found it hard to get my head round how God could love a man like me. This would take time to sink in as I continued to journey with Him.

As Hannah continued to grow we could see early on that she was going to be a passionate communicator. At ten and a half months she began to walk and was on a mission from an early age. Hannah always knew what she wanted. She brought such joy to our lives and a memorable time was when we went on our first holiday as a family to Rhossili in Wales. Our friend allowed us to use their static caravan for a week, so we had quality time with our little girl. One evening we wondered what we would have for tea as we hadn't shopped that day. As we walked along the beach with Hannah in the back carrier, we passed a fisherman. We stopped and watched him briefly and I asked him whether he had caught anything. He told me that he had caught one Sea Bass. He reached into his bag and took the fish out and said we could have it for our tea! So God was good by providing us fresh fish for tea ... no loaves though! Just kidding God.

Shift work was becoming the norm and Em and I started to form a routine that seemed to work. I was fortunate that when on nights I could spend most of the day with Hannah and do the bedtime routine too. This allowed Em to have a snooze and recover from the day's activities that usually included taking Hannah to the Wacky Warehouse ball pool or a local toddler group.

I was enjoying my probation period and, because I was working in a busy area, soon had all of my competencies covered, demonstrating the required skills to be a competent police officer. I was soon to be authorised for independent patrol and would soon be able to go on mobile patrol as well as foot patrol. I learnt so much whilst on foot and really honed my communication skills. There was no escape and I often had to deal with people who were very upset or angry, who usually wanted to vent on somebody. The police often get the brunt of the emotion in an incident. When in a patrol car you can choose what to stop for but when on foot there's no escape!

Wisdom/Reflection
- *Don't try and fix something that you are not qualified to fix or requested to fix. You'll get frustrated and disappointed. Be supportive and be guided by the person in need*
- *Ask questions rather than making statements, and then listen and hear what is said*
- *Sometimes your loving presence is enough*
- *Christian fathers we have a responsibility to create a harmonious atmosphere in our homes, despite what kind of a day we've had. (It's tough I know)*
- *Prayer and medical care complement each other, don't neglect one or the other*
- *Be mindful of your behaviour as even a baby will sense stress and disunity*

Hannah Frances is born

17.
On the Beat

Being a probationer, I often got the job of watching witnesses or prisoners in hospital. On one occasion I had to guard a man who had been stabbed through the neck with a kitchen knife by his girlfriend, who had discovered that he was having an affair. He was conscious but not saying much. I was there just in case someone else attended the hospital intent on hurting him. The hospital ward was quite quiet until I heard a bubbling and gurgling sound. I glanced over to the patient and watched as he projectile vomited a green substance that went everywhere, though thankfully not in my direction. I thought about this man some months later and was told he made a full recovery.

As I journeyed through my career, I often thought about the people that I had dealings with, wondering what had become of them and whether they were in a better place.

I was always curious about why people behaved the way they did. Often people would resort to violence because they didn't have the emotional agility to navigate through how they were feeling and why they were feeling that way. It wasn't always just about violence though as some people internalised how they felt about themselves and others without throwing a punch.

I remember attending the hospital with my patrol partner and being asked by a nurse to help her with a patient. I was intrigued at why she had asked us to help her. She led us to a cubicle that had its curtain drawn and then nodded towards the entrance indicating that she needed help in there. We paused for a moment and waited for an explanation from the nurse. She told us that there was an extremely heavy patient in the cubicle that she needed to lift and put into a chair.

I asked the nurse why he couldn't get in the chair himself as it was only a short distance from the bed to the chair. She smirked at me and told me that I would understand once I'd seen the patient. I pulled the curtain aside and I was aware that my mouth was open and that my jaw had dropped. My partner had a couple more seconds reaction time, so his mouth was closed by the time he entered the cubicle.

Before I knew it, I was speaking: 'Jeeps mate how did you get that big!' – I can't believe I had just said that but I did. Insensitive I was but I was surprised by his response. He told me that he used to be an ice cream salesman and that over time he began to consume a lot of his stock. At his worst he was eating four, four-litre tubs a day. He was eventually sacked due to the missing stock that he had eaten. He weighed in at 36 stones and was suffering in his health due to his weight. He had sores all over his legs and his buttocks literally touched the floor. He seemed to be a nice guy but very sad about his demise. We talked for a little while before lifting him. He explained that going to the toilet was difficult and sometimes messy. He hadn't seen his private parts for a long time. I had never seen such a large human before and I pitied him because his quality of life was poor. He had underlying issues that manifested in him taking comfort in food, or, in his case, ice cream. We managed to lift him into the chair to the relief of the nurse. We wished him well and went on to our next job.
When returning home from a tour of duty my head was often still buzzing from what I had witnessed. I may have attended up to 10 or more incidents all with their own level of trauma. Sometimes, it would involve me having to get physical and restrain someone or sit with someone having delivered a death message to them, notifying them of a loved one's death.

Walking through the front door to a two-year-old who is running towards you shouting 'Daddy! Daddy!' and a wife that just wants you to take over, was nice but tough. Processing a challenging day often had to wait until Hannah was in bed and the routine chores had been finished. I didn't really burden Emma with what had gone on during my day because it was often dark stuff that didn't really have the best outcome. Jesus was my confidant and I often stayed up by myself to pray through what my eyes had seen. I called it a spiritual shower. Every situation has a spiritual environment that will be influencing the situation. I would often return home feeling quite oppressed being in the presence of evil and chaos. I very rarely shared what I had seen at work with Em, unless it was something that had a happy ending.

I started to become cynical due to having to listen to people lie so often. I would weigh people up even when I was off duty and would be building a profile in my head of what sort of a person I figured they were. This subtle form of conditioning can be priceless on the streets but potentially damaging for social relationships, including family. Judging people's agendas can be costly as intuition isn't always right. But having this attitude paid off for me on the streets as I became adept at arresting offenders.

One evening we were spending some time with our Vicar, Barry Harper. He leaned over to me and said to me to be careful that cynicism doesn't erode my faith. That was timely advice and advice that I have carried with me since.

There were lighter moments too that created laughter for colleagues and the public alike. One such time was when a call came in that a cow had escaped from Sutton Park and was on the main Lichfield Road, that was busy with traffic and a residential area. I was the closest resource, so I attended the call. I could see members of the public gathering so I headed towards them to see a large brown cow on the driveway of quite an impressive house. I've never had much to do with cows, but I did know that they were curious animals and very powerful, especially when they were charging towards you.

I tried to look authoritative and walked purposefully towards the cow. As I did this the onlookers withdrew, expecting the worst. What noise do you make when trying to herd a cow? I was acutely aware that any street cred I had left could disappear with how I dealt with this cow. I didn't want to run after the animal because that would look like something out of Keystone Cops. I began to think that whatever action I took I was doomed.

There was an entrance and exit to this driveway and I would only be able to cover one. As I outstretched my arms to create a barrier the cow backed away to the exit. I had no choice but to sprint to the exit. Thankfully, having completed about three shuttle sprints a call came over the radio to say that the farmer was enroute with a cow box to transport the animal back to the park. As the radio transmission ended, the farmer pulled up with a big grin on his face. I looked at him with a disapproving frown that seemed to evaporate his grin. As soon as he alighted his vehicle, he started to speak cow language and before I knew it the cow was safely herded into the box. The onlookers returned and I received a round of applause.

Wisdom/Reflection
- *Don't let cynicism kill your faith. Bad things happen, but so do good things*
- *Exercise when at all possible, particularly if your job is stressful*
- *Take 10 minutes before entering your home environment to centre yourself by giving all of the day's occurrences to God*
- *Be intentional about smiling and look for opportunities to boast about other people*
- *Laughter is a medicine. Take it daily*

18.
Onwards and Upwards

Early on in my service I decided that I wanted to lead within the police by becoming a sergeant. The police style of leadership was very different from the army and the leaders in the police didn't seem as dynamic as I had expected. Because we are a disciplined service, I expected to be led by people I would follow anywhere. This wasn't always the case – in fact, I would say it was the exception rather than the norm. That said the police was a very different environment compared to the army. There was far more of a get-it-done attitude in the army whereas in the police there may be some dissent and chatter about a given task, rather than getting on with it. I would later learn that the get-on-with-it style of leadership didn't really fit for the majority of police scenarios.

I felt there was a deeper bond between soldiers than between police officers. In the army we were a close-knit community, both in and out of work. We spent a lot more time together sometimes for months on exercise. There wasn't the need for such close relationships in the police, I suppose, and there was the issue of the army being an all-male environment. The police seemed more civilised and your life wasn't your work culture. It was sometimes hard to get away from the army.

Once my two-year probation period was complete, I put in to take my sergeant's exam. This was a written exam that covered criminal law and police procedures. The pass mark was 75% and it wasn't something you could just do on a wing and a prayer. In the evenings I would revise, determined to pass first time, which thankfully I did. Early on in my police career I showed a leaning towards wanting to develop others too and, once out of my probation period, I was asked to become a tutor which I did enthusiastically.

My first probationer was a bright young lady called Sam. She was polite, efficient and well turned out. She had a great attitude and was willing to learn. We were on mobile patrol on the Wyrley Birch Estate when I saw a taxi turn onto the estate with one person in the rear. On seeing us, he slumped down out of view. I looked at Sam and said: 'What do you think?'. She hadn't seen what I had seen but was keen to investigate. I pulled behind the taxi and began to follow it. I sensed that the passenger in the taxi was going to get out and run.

I prepared Sam for the possibility, and I could see that her adrenalin was starting to flow. I released my seat belt ready to get out and give chase. Although the passenger usually alights the vehicle first, I didn't want to put Sam in that position just yet. I illuminated my vehicle's blue light, and I could see the taxi driver looking into his rear view mirror. He pulled over and I stopped our vehicle and sprinted to the rear passenger door. As I got to the door the passenger jumped out and lunged at me with a stabbing motion with his right hand. I was later to discover that this man had a sharpened chisel in his hand which would have caused me a significant injury.

At that time, the police were not issued with CS spray, stab vests or proper batons, so our protective equipment was fairly limited. Thankfully my reaction was quick enough to avoid any contact with him. He started to make good his escape, so I ran after him keeping a safe distance as he was extremely unpredictable.

Often offenders that are addicted to mainly Class A drugs, like heroin or crack, will demonstrate high levels of aggression and their thinking is irrational. I shouted to Sam to remain with the taxi driver as I continued to keep the offender in view. He eventually went to ground in some undergrowth. I had been giving a running commentary whilst chasing this chap, so reinforcements were on their way. My priority now was to ensure that the area was contained so that the likelihood of him slipping away was minimal.

Before I knew it, we had a police dog tracking from the taxi and the AO1 helicopter, was above doing a sweep of the area. By now there were enough officers to contain the area, so I returned to the taxi where Sam had detained the driver. I asked the taxi driver who his passenger was and where he had picked him up from. The driver became quite evasive, and his memory of the detail was vague. I asked him to open his boot and looking inside I could see black bin liners full of items that I believed to be stolen. I looked at the taxi driver and paused to provoke him to give an explanation. He shrugged his shoulders and said that he wasn't aware of what was in the bags. There's no doubt that he knew what the passenger's business was but he would always have a get out claiming he had no knowledge.

I could hear over my radio that the dog had located the offender, who was now in custody. It turned out that his pockets were filled with various pieces of jewellery and, while being arrested, he put up a fight so got bitten by the police dog for his troubles. It later transpired that the offender was very well-known to us and had recently preyed on the elderly community on the Wyrley Birch Estate, committing burglaries during the night whilst the occupants were sleeping. Years later I remembered the offender, Neil, and wondered what had happened to him. I was told by a colleague that he was still addicted to heroin and had been in prison several times since.

Wisdom/Reflection
- *Make a plan and stick to it. Build in realistic rest periods and timescales*
- *Intuition is a mix of experience and knowledge. Trust it*
- *Recognise the talent in others and where it depends on you help them to succeed*
- *Leadership is a privilege. Followers deserve good leaders*

Me as a sgt posted to Sparkhill, Birmingham talking to a distraught resident

19.
Number Two

Em and I were enjoying being parents and having a close circle of friends who were raising a family too. We kept in touch with Peter and Sue from Cambridge as they had a little girl the same age as Hannah, called Sarah. Both girls got on well, but Hannah was definitely the bossier one, but Sarah seemed to know how to deal with that and they would remain friends into adulthood, when they would become parents themselves.

We had never put a number on how many children we wanted but we knew we wanted more than one. When Hannah was around two and a half we were blessed with another baby girl, who we called Lydia. Lydia looked like a native Indian when she came out, red with lots of black spiky hair. I can remember getting odd looks from the midwife when she was born as I cut the cord, and then held her up like out of a scene from the Lion King, thanking God for her life.

Hannah was excited to have a baby sister, and it wasn't long before Lydia was Hannah's baby as she attempted to feed her a bottle of milk and read her books.

Emma started to dip a little with her mental health as her body began to balance after having Lydia. We had to go to the GP to review her medication as she could feel herself spiralling. Her medication had changed a number of times in order to get the one that suited her best. It was always a worrying time for me because I didn't like to see Em ill and because I was concerned about how I would cope with two little ones. Because we only lived in a two-bedroomed house, initially Lydia slept with us in our bedroom. The Moses basket was at my side of the bed so I had easy access so Em could sleep. Whilst she was waiting for her new medication to take effect, Em's mood was up and down and sometimes debilitating, where she couldn't get out of bed.

I was still on shifts but must have built up my resilience as I managed to keep going. Sleep deprivation is an awful thing though, as Lydia had colic for the first two years of her life and that meant a screaming baby. Despite doing all the right things she would still wake in the night and it started to wear us down.

Emma's medication had a mild sedative in it so she often was the last to be aware of Lydia's crying. After a prolonged period of crying in the night I snapped and in the early hours I can remember picking Lydia up with one hand and through gritted teeth telling her to be quiet. It was like I was in a trance just wanting the noise to stop. I dropped her back into her Moses basket. Thankfully, Emma called to me and came to my side, took Lydia and comforted her. I realised that night that I was not in the best place and felt horrified about the place I had got to, and I could have hurt little Lydia.

How single parents cope I do not know but I knew that I needed help. As Lydia was waking every night with terrible colic pain, we decided to put her to sleep in the bathroom. For our own sanity we needed some sleep even if it was the smallest amount. We were becoming hyper vigilant with every little movement or noise coming from the Moses basket.
Lydia, now a lovely young lady, accuses us jokingly of scarring her mentally, by putting her in the bath to sleep. I must clarify that the bath was empty and it was only for a short period of time to give us some respite. Providing for Hannah's needs, emotionally and developmentally, as well as having Lydia, was a challenge at times and we would both take turns when I wasn't at work to get some kip when we could. I know that when I was at work it was very hard for Emma who was always well turned out and wearing a smile.

Emma naturally had a kind and sociable disposition, so it was really noticeable when that beautiful shine became dim. She would often grapple with feelings of guilt because she wanted to be more for the girls. I was in awe of how she managed the girls and the home, as well as loving and supporting me. Emma would later coin a phrase with our girls that sometimes seven out of ten was enough. She learnt this through her own experience of sometimes trying to be everything to everyone.

It was so important for us to have a network of good friends around us to provide mutual support when needed. Our friends from St John's Church were a Godsend, particularly when Emma was struggling with depression. Meals would arrive on the doorstep and the girls would be taken out in order to give Emma time to rest. We knew that being parents was a privilege and that our girls were a blessing, but the role was relentless and because we were so committed to investing in the girls it took time and energy, which we knew would pay off as the girls grew up.

Despite being worn out we took great strength with meeting with close friends to pray. They say that a problem shared is a problem halved and that certainly was the case for us. We knew that raising a family would be pleasantly challenging but we still came before The Lord for strength and wisdom to do the right thing. Journeying with prayerful friends was a big part of our strategy for getting through this season. We were reminded that the joy of the Lord is our strength and that God would not put us through anything we couldn't cope with. We knew that just because we were Christians didn't mean life was going to be a breeze. The bible says that a righteous person will have many troubles, but The Lord will deliver them from them all. Our relationship with God was based on trust and obedience. Trusting that he would see us through with everything we needed and being obedient to his ways that we learned through the scriptures in the bible.

As I was the main earner in the family, money was always tight. We were constantly budgeting and sinking into our overdraft. I felt responsible for this and a certain amount of failure. I was raised with a provider ethos and felt that I wasn't providing enough. We were extremely frugal and our holidays were always based in the UK camping. We loved our camping trips and have many special memories of Dartmouth and other parts of Devon.

Wisdom/Reflection
- *Call for help when things get too much, and you feel out of control. Showing vulnerability is a strength*
- *Don't get into a familiar routine rut that obscures your view of how your partner is feeling. Don't ignore signs of poor wellbeing because they will only get worse*
- *Factor in couple time and individual time. Agree it and then make it happen*

- *Don't get isolated, stay connected to friends and church*
- *Take time to look into your children's eyes and speak words of blessing over them daily*

Lydia Carey joins our family

20.
Promotion

My natural leaning in the police was towards crime investigation. Usually, officers favour either traffic policing or crime. As I started to build my career towards getting promoted, part of my development was an attachment to the CID (criminal investigation department). These attachments were like rocking horse droppings. They didn't become available very often. You had to be recommended by your inspector and you had to have demonstrated your leaning towards that area of work. This was usually evidenced by the arrests you had made. I was fortunate in that I regularly consulted detectives for advice around some of my cases so my face was known. In fact, one detective nominated me for a Chief Superintendent's Commendation, which I received for outstanding investigative skills for bringing an offender to justice, for committing grievous bodily harm.

Whilst on my attachment I was seconded to a murder incident room. Tragically, a Kingstanding woman was murdered on her own doorstep by being stabbed repeatedly. I soon became absorbed in the case and regularly worked 14-hour days. In the initial stages of the investigation there is a lot going on so it's all hands to the pump to secure and preserve as much evidence as possible. The overtime was a welcome boost to my pay packet but being away from home was taking its toll. One evening having returned home, once the girls were in bed, Emma gently said that the girls hadn't mentioned daddy in the last couple of weeks. This revelation hit me like a sledgehammer and, even worse, was the fact that I hadn't noticed. That was a turning point in my career and my commitment to my family as I didn't want to be an absent father that the girls had little recollection of when they were young.

Em and I communicated well together and we always had a debrief at the end of a day, to either vent or laugh about some of the things life threw at us. It was a good way for us to take stock of how each other was feeling and to actually look at each other and remember that we were in this together.

I was soon to be promoted to sergeant and posted to Acocks Green. I wasn't familiar with this area and didn't know anyone. As a newly-promoted sergeant with only five years' service I knew that there were going to be challenging times ahead. Joining a shift with several constables that had three or four times my amount of service meant they would probably want to test my leadership, in particular, my decision-making skills. I felt quite alone and vulnerable, in an unfamiliar environment. It was always better when you knew people where you were going because they would vouch for you and spread the word that you were ok.

The other sergeant on the shift was an old sweat with over 20 years' service and I wasn't sure that he was going to be an ally either. It was often the case that when promoted with little service people wanted to see you fall because thoughts were back then that you had been promoted too early. This was unusual for me because I was used to making friends and then working well together, building relationship and trust. I was aware that I was behaving normally because I felt that the shift weren't sure of me. I guess that's normal and it would take time to build my credibility and get to know them individually.

Now that there were two sergeants on the shift I was posted to Edward Road Police station which was in Balsall Heath. I wasn't looking forward to moving there as it was quite an oppressive place as a community and had high crime rates, particularly around violence and prostitution.
The nick, (police station) wasn't a nice place to work from either. I was inheriting a team that was cobbled together from several teams so it wasn't that cohesive. I had heard that the last Inspector was bullied and a mutiny developed as a result of low morale. I'm sure there were two sides to the story but I would never hear the Inspector's side as he retired, on ill health I think.

In a recent reorganisation the sector sergeant position became a lonely one. You were it. You occasionally saw your inspector and only really had meaningful contact with another sergeant when you were handing over at the end of your shift.

My team that I had inherited were a mixed bunch. One openly admitted that he was only motivated by overtime and had a reputation of earning a lot of money as a result. Others were there to do the bare minimum. Others just kept their heads down because of some of the other strong characters on the shift. I had my work cut out and knew that they weren't going to go out of their way to support me in leading them. It's fair to say that I was taken advantage of due to me wanting to be supportive of them.

One constable who had just arrived on the shift and had quite a bit of service, asked to have nights off as his wife was suffering from depression. I allowed this but before long others then started to make requests that would impact on the resilience of the team. At times I wasn't balancing the needs of the organisation and the individual. It was a steep learning curve for me and I knew at times I was being played. The army-style of leadership wouldn't work here as some of these guys were more like mercenaries.

I'm saddened to say that I didn't like a number of the officers on the shift and I certainly didn't trust them. I would go home most days miserable due to having to be extra vigilant with what I said and having to check up on jobs where ordinarily I could empower staff to make decisions and get on with the job. It was the worst period of my career and I was despondent that they hadn't seen the real me. I don't think I had developed the emotional agility at that time and knew I was withdrawing from them which didn't help. I so much wanted to help them and have fun doing it as we policed a tough and needy part of Birmingham.

New Hope Mentoring Programme

Whilst serving at Edward Road there was a shaft of light by way of an opportunity presented to me by the then Chief Superintendent. He knew I was a Christian and sent me a newspaper article titled the Boston Miracle. Churches in Boston took more ownership for their neighbourhoods and mentored offenders returning to the community from prison. Homicides were spiralling out of control in the neighbourhoods and even in schools!

He gave me his blessing to explore the concept working in Balsall Heath. I managed to get some church leaders together and a guy called Richard who belonged to a local church but wanted to volunteer his time to make this concept a reality. Richard had just completed his degree in immunology and had a heart for transforming communities. We set up some key meetings with city leaders and other activists and started to gain momentum. This gave me a focus apart from trying to run a team that was challenging. It felt purposeful but was looked on cynically by other cops who didn't regard it as police work.

This was visionary police work that would enhance both crime prevention and reduction strategies. It was futuristic but I was aware that it wasn't hard police work where we were kicking down doors. I became more convinced that this was just putting a plaster over things. We needed hearts and minds to change and essentially the acts of kindness and commitment provided by mentors was more cost effective and more importantly life changing.

Richard started to apply for funding through several sources and we both attended meetings to give presentations about how this type of mentoring could work. Before long we had secured some funding and started to recruit mentors. Within a year we had made significant inroads to the prisons and with churches supplying volunteer mentors. We had developed a training programme and attracted the attention of the then Lord Mayor of Birmingham.

Our work had also been noticed by Faithworks, a national Christian organisation that co-ordinated community action across the country. They also held an awards ceremony to celebrate new and promising projects. We were awarded first place for our project that was called New Hope Mentoring Programme (NHMP). Having received this award, the Lord Mayor funded a trip for Richard and I to visit the project in Boston, where the concept originated. We returned from Boston inspired and motivated to do more to create significant impact in our communities.

As we began to grow, we were able to fund Richard's post as well as a Mentor Co-ordinator. Richard, on his own admission, was polishing up on his people skills, so I offered to help with recruitment and selection of the Mentor Co-ordinator. We had a number of applicants, but one drew my attention and stood out. Amanda had applied for the job despite a colourful criminal record that spoke of a life of hardship and vulnerability.

She was a scouser who said it as it was but had a warmth about her. She made it through the paper sift despite her past which I actually saw as a strength. There were still risks that we needed to be conscious of but I convinced Richard that we should get her in for an interview. Amanda was more surprised than us to have been given the opportunity. She was dressed smartly and was up for this. The interview went well and she was totally transparent about her past. Her story was a powerful and moving one. Here's Amanda's perspective of that part of her journey in her own words.

I had stopped any criminality after I became a Christian and had Misha in 1998. By the time she was almost three I knew I had to do something careerwise but didn't know where to start as I had left school with no qualifications and had 30 convictions! No easy feat. I initially signed up with St Paul's development trust in Balsall Heath to do an ILM scheme which was basically a YTS for older people. I started working in their nursery and was working in the kitchen and cleaning but it was exhausting and my brain was dormant, so I asked them if they had anything else. They transferred me to the Balsall Heath Forum to do an admin placement and I was told that I would be able to do an NVQ in admin which never materialised due to funding issues. I was there for about 18 months. There I met Richard, he was the faith co-ordinator and worked upstairs from me so never really had much interaction with him. Funding for my role ran out and I was therefore about to become unemployed once again, I was devastated.

The only thing I could think of to do was pray as I still had no qualifications and only 18 months' admin experience. I asked God for a job and pleaded with him saying if I haven't got a job I'm scared that I will go back to what I know.

I was looking for jobs all over and it was then I saw the role advertised for part-time admin assistant with the New Hope Mentoring Programme. I thought this looks good, working with offenders I reckon I could do that no problem so I called the number and enquired about the role. Richard answered and the first thing he said to me is that you Amanda, I said yes and he replied: 'I can't give you any special privileges because I know you'.

I replied: 'I don't want any, I only want an application form'. I was actually really surprised when I was contacted and shortlisted for an interview.

My interview was scheduled for quite late in the afternoon and I was really nervous most of the morning until I got a phone call from NHMP inviting me to come in earlier than scheduled. I headed straight there! Upon entering the interview room I saw Richard and a police officer in uniform, Kevin Borg. The first thing I thought was: 'oh no I'm definitely not getting this job'. I basically sat there and disclosed my whole criminal history and explained why I thought I would be ideal for the job. Once the interview was over Kevin stood up and gave me a hug which was the most surreal thing ever. Number one you don't get hugs in interviews and number two you don't get them from policemen either! I still had no clue if I would get the job or not but went home relieved that I had attended and been honest and upfront about my past. Not long after, I received a phone call telling me I had got the job. Shocked was an understatement but I was over the moon.

I ended up working for New Hope in several different roles and was there for nine years in total. I started part-time admin then was promoted to female mentor co-ordinator then when Richard left to go and live in Russia I was lead mentor co-ordinator. In that time, and with the help of NHMP, I passed my driving test, gained an NVQ 3 in adminisitration alongside an NVQ in team-leading and also completed my PTTLS (preparing to teach in the life-long learning qualification). I helped to train over 500 mentors and, most importantly, helped a multitude of offenders sort various aspects of their chaotic lives out.

My past became an asset and I was living proof that people can and do change. In 2009, we were invited by Sarah Brown to 10 Downing Street for a celebration of mentoring and they had asked for the member of staff, mentor and mentee that had most benefitted from our project. We were shortlisted from 500 national projects down to 30. I was chosen and visited 10 Downing Street and ate canapes with the prime minister's wife; another surreal moment!
Unfortunately, in 2011, we had a shortfall of funding and sadly had to close the project which was heartbreaking. Shortly before we closed Rachel Simpson the programme manager and I flew to Northern Ireland to train

a bunch of mentors who would be working within Magaberry prison, mentoring between Catholics and Protestants which was another valuable piece of work we did.

Before we had even closed, I was headhunted by both Anawim Women's Development Project and Sova who I ended up working for over the next three or four years on a research project around attitudes towards mentoring funded by the Ministry of Justice and culminating in a national hub for mentoring projects called 'Just Mentoring' which was launched at Westminister which I had the opportunity of attending.

All I can say is prayer works and thanks to God he turned my life around!

Amanda's story was truly remarkable and an example of how God moves when we pray and trust him. Richard and I had been praying for the right candidate and to be obedient to where he was leading us. Great things sometimes happen in unexpected circumstances. Amanda was one of those happenings.

Apart from setting up NHMP I felt that my posting to Balsall Heath was a challenging one. I faced several difficult situations where I stood by my integrity and this put me in a bad light, due to others' lack of standards. Others may have turned the other way, but I had the courage of my convictions and feared God more than man. This is where it mattered in terms of being open and honest. Some police officers thought they were cleverer than they were, and often became unstuck. I believed that once integrity was breached it was a bit of a slippery slope. I couldn't wait to leave the E3 area so started to look for a different job within the police.

Wisdom/Reflection
- *Your job is your job not your life*
- *Sometimes you need to go against the accepted norm and take a prayerful risk*
- *Growth occurs when you leave your comfort zone*
- *Go with the vision you've received even when you're not sure of all the detail*

21.
Number 3

In 2002 our gift, Constance Melita was born. We now had three girls and what a busy home ours had become! Hormones bouncing off the walls and dramatic tantrums were now the norm. Little Connie just looked on as her big sisters tried to make sense of life. They made a fuss of Connie as it was like they had their own real-life dolly. Heavens knows how she survived all the man-handling and dressing up!

At this stage of our lives, Emma had found a job as an administrator with a local charity. Her income was welcomed as it meant that our finances weren't as tight as they were previously. It was a helpful focus for Emma too, as she was interacting with people and had a job that had purpose in helping children and families with special needs. Emma had a real knack of connecting with people and making them feel valued and listened to. She had such a kind smile and a cheeky laugh too. Emma wasn't just about the softer skills though; she was a doer and liked to get things done. In our relationship, I usually initiated things, but Emma followed in closely to make sure they happened well. Anything that involved any form of confrontation, Emma left to me. That said, I'd witnessed her on a couple of occasions straighten her back and stand firm in her view, in awkward circumstances. It took a lot to get her to that place, thankfully.

We'd moved house by now into a larger house anticipating Connie's arrival. The move-in date was very exciting and, for us, the new home was a substantial step up. The house had previously been owned by a friend of mine, but I made an anonymous offer to not put him in a difficult position if he refused it. Thankfully, he accepted so I revealed my identity, and he was thrilled that we would be only the third family to live in the house. He did say that he would have raised the price if he had known it was me.

We celebrated our move-in with fish and chips and ate them on the living room floor amongst the packing boxes.

The hours leading to Connie's birth were calm and peaceful. After all, we had been here before and were quietly confident about the process. As Emma started to experience twinges, we looked at each other and, as planned, got the bath ready just to help Emma relax and maybe the warm water would help to ease the discomfort. We talked and prayed for a bit then Emma said that she thought we should get the bag and make for the hospital.

We arrived at the hospital and made for the maternity ward. We were shown to a lovely clean room and all the staff had smiley faces, so all was good with the world. At this stage Emma was in control despite the contractions having intensified. The midwives in the room were carefully monitoring the proceedings and were calm and professional. Then it was as if a switch had been flicked as the midwife without warning pressed a button and within seconds a crash team had entered the room, led by an Egyptian doctor, who I remember being very tall as he burst into the room. I looked up to see him jump onto the bottom of the bed and place both hands on Emma's pelvis pushing down quite forcibly. Nurses either side of him were fiddling with drips and things whilst watching the various monitors too.

I think I must have been gaping at them with an open mouth trying to take in what had just happened, and before I could close my mouth a baby had arrived. Apparently, Connie's shoulders couldn't get past Emma's pelvis so the doctor had to open her pelvis to give Connie enough clearance to get out.

In a second, I refocused and let out some words of reassurance to Emma, but it wasn't a moment of relief as there was still a sense of urgency in the room as something still wasn't right. A nurse was holding Connie, but I could see she wasn't the right colour. She was a bluey black colour and her limbs and head were lifeless. Emma was in good hands; my priority now was my precious little daughter. For a second, a thought flashed across my mind that she might not live.

My thought was broken by Emma gasping to go to be with Connie. I left the delivery room and followed the nurse who was holding Connie. Two or three minutes had gone by, and the nurse stood in the corridor looking left and right as if she didn't know where she was going. I watched impatiently for her to make a decision. She seemed to be asking where a certain piece of equipment was but with very little sense of urgency. I could feel myself boiling up and the words: 'Sort it out now!' came howling out of my mouth. The nurse physically jumped in shock and hurried down the corridor, the right way, thankfully.

I followed her with an intentional brisk walk almost breaking into a run. Connie still wasn't breathing and as the nurse carried her, I could see her head lifelessly bobbing about. I could see a doctor walking along the long corridor towards us. I immediately recognised him as my friend Chippa, who was a paediatrician, originally from Tanzania.

I met Chippa at St John's Church, where he and his family worshipped having moved into the area recently and we had befriended them. We would go for walks together with our children and visited each other's homes for meals. Chippa was still a distance away when I shouted: 'Chippa help!'. He must have recognised me by now, as we met in the middle of the corridor and he said with a friendly, wide smile: 'Give her to me nurse, it's going to be ok'. The nurse hurriedly passed Connie to Chippa who took hold of both of her feet and hung her upside down. I didn't want to question his actions but did wonder why we weren't heading for the equipment we were originally heading for. I trusted Chippa, who was passionate about his job and commanded a sense of great competence. Chippa slapped Connie firmly on her back and instantly she turned pink and let out a cry. I cried with relief on the spot.

Due to Connie's shoulders getting stuck in Emma's pelvis, she had to be x-rayed so she was placed in a very grand Silver Cross pram and I was directed to the x-ray department. All was well so I hurriedly made my way back to Emma who was recovering with a cup of tea and slice of toast. She was sat up in bed, beaming as I passed Connie to her. She was flushed in the face and a bit sweaty, but she looked beautiful to me. The next day, Emma and Connie were discharged. Hannah and Lydia were with Nan and Pops but knew that they now had a baby sister.

In the weeks to follow Connie would get used to being handled like a doll by her older sisters.

Connie was my gift form Emma. That doesn't mean that Hannah and Lydia were any lesser of a gift, but the timing of Connie was significant. Emma was reluctant to have a third child and, although I did want a third, Emma's wishes were more important as she would be carrying the child, as well as probably being the prime carer, as with our other two girls. Emma shared with me after Connie had been born that her reluctance wasn't around the logistics.

There were far deeper reasons. Emma had lost her mum to breast cancer when she was 17 and Gill, her mum, was in her late 40s. Emma didn't want to give me a child that would most likely lose her mother as she did. At the time I was touched by Emma's rationale and saddened that she felt she was under this self-fulfilling prophecy of dying young with cancer like her mother. In light of Emma's reasoning, I realised even more so what a sacrifice Emma had made. Despite her losing her mum I didn't want to accept the same fate for Emma and prayed many prayers renouncing that path for our future as we entrusted our lives to The Lord who was in control of everything.

Our lives moved on as we raised our three girls and only occasionally did I glance back in my mind to our conversation about Emma's health.

Thankfully, I was successful in getting a job at Police Headquarters. I was now the Force Youth crime co-ordinator. I was responsible for Youth Crime Officers across the force area as well as the Safer Schools Officers, who were based in the higher crime neighbourhood schools. It was a great job that I thoroughly enjoyed because of the minimal supervision and the freedom to manage my own workload and time. Working at Lloyd House opened my eyes to the working of the police within the higher echelons. It was certainly a lot cushier than working the streets.

That said there were different pressures, like researching and writing policy. Attending meetings and giving presentations. A whole different skill set was required, and it was a steep learning curve for me. For some of my work, I reported to an Assistant Chief Constable. This rank sits very close to the top of the tree and has a portfolio of many responsibilities that span nationally. He saw the work I was doing with the schools' officers and arranged for me to see how the police engaged with schools in the US. He'd arranged for me to be shown around by a police chief. I didn't realise I was going to be his personal guest staying with him in his home! He picked me up in a police pick-up type vehicle and was keen to know all about me as we travelled to his family home. We arrived in quite a rural location where his wife gave me a warm welcome as well as his son who was also a police officer.

We ate and talked around the table drinking beer out of jam jars. There was quite a lot of banter going on and I thought that they had poured the beer into a jar to see if I would drink from it. They finally convinced me that it wasn't a blag as they poured and drank their beer from jars too. Strange custom, but they were great hosts, and I learnt a lot visiting their schools, seeing how the police played a pivotal role in schools and were regarded as part of the team. I returned to the UK enthused and started to see how some of the practices in the US could work in our culture.

The girls were growing up fast and had busy lives full of playing with friends, ballet, Brownies amongst other things. I was so proud to be a father of three girls but I did struggle to understand how best to play a gentle and compassionate father. I realised that I was quite hard in my approach, not because I didn't care, quite the opposite. If I could see them doing something and I knew full well what the likely negative outcome would be, I would advise them of another way to go about it or just give a direct instruction not to do it.

I didn't like answering back and saw it as being disrespectful. This would often escalate, particularly with Hannah and I would shut her down with my authority as her dad. Not because I thrived on being the parent, it was more the stubbornness and refusal to take advice. As a child, if my dad said to do something, I wouldn't even question it, there was a presumption that he knew best and I trusted what he said was best for me. Even as an adult now, if dad has a view, even if I don't necessarily agree, I won't challenge him, unless it was something that I would die in the ditch for and threatened to compromise my values.

And then there's the example of my Heavenly Father and how he behaves. I felt such a responsibility of being a good dad, that my girls would adore and respect. I didn't have the emotional agility to deal with the stresses of life, tiredness and the demands of the girls. They were good girls, but I know that at times I frightened them when I lost my patience due to them being disobedient or wanting to be heard.

It sounds horrendous now, but as young parents Emma and I believed in physical chastisement. It was the last resort and often used when we were at the end of our tether. With a better understanding of how to navigate around child behaviour we may not have resorted to smacking as often as we did. Don't get me wrong smacking wasn't a regular thing, but some would argue that once is one time too many.

I can remember being smacked as a child and knowing that I had pushed mum or dad too far. Most parents don't wake up thinking that they are going to smack their child that day. As Christian parents we were keen to follow the Bible's teaching on raising a family. Spare the rod and spoil the child. What did that mean? Was there a place for smacking a naughty child that didn't heed previous warnings? Teach a child the way and when they are older, they won't depart from it.

Then there's the scripture that says, Fathers do not provoke your children to anger by the way you treat them. I so wanted to be that father that could nurture them, being kind and patient and a great example of a male role model. I know that I didn't measure up and felt that my own upbringing influenced and, in some ways, had shaped my response, despite me knowing what the right response should be. I seemed to be fighting against my past, to raise three well-balanced girls. Emma was so much a girly mother that it helped compensate for my manly slant on parenting. She naturally did the things that the girls loved and was far gentler and patient than I was.

I was just so intent on getting it right that I overcooked it at times and probably disheartened the girls with my sometimes-uncompromising standards. From an early age we taught our girls to use their manners and to be tidy where possible. If they were rude, they would be sent to their room, but conversely good behaviour would be rewarded. Emma and

I praised our children often, but I think I sometimes ruined the moment by then pushing them to improve on the good they had done. There was lots of cuddling time, and, being quite tactile, they had their fair share of daddy mauling them with a large helping of tickles too. The girls were very sociable and loved it when we had friends around. I was always so proud of the way they could hold conversations and read the room at the same time. Emma and I used to go to bed feeling very blessed to have such lovely girls. From the point of conception, we prayed for our children and saw the importance of covering them in prayer. We even prayed for their husbands before they were born. During pregnancy Em and I would lay hands on her tummy and pray that God would bless and guide the little life inside her.

Prayer was the spiritual life blood in our family. We would have regular family prayer time and Hannah and Lydia would roll their eyes when I got the bible out to read some scripture. I used to look at them sternly and tell them that God's word would save their life. I then used to get them to imagine a scenario where they were in a prison cell without having access to a bible. What verses would they remember to give them hope and comfort. A bit extreme I know but both Emma and I saw the importance of knowing God's word so that in times of trouble and joy we could remember His promises and in faith call the power of them into our circumstances.

I think the girls gave me some airtime because they knew I was streetwise as a cop and my occupation was cool. Bedtime was often a time when the girls wanted to hear a story of people I had arrested or something gory that I had seen. They were fascinated by badness but also by human behaviour. I would always try to end a story on a positive and before turning the lights out there were always cries for one more story dad!

Tiredness was one of my greatest enemies and often made me grumpy. Working shifts didn't suit me biologically and once I had a non-shift post my mood improved remarkably. Working office hours meant that I didn't have the opportunity to see the girls to school or pick them up. I usually arrived home in time for us to sit at the table and have tea together. I was learning new skills, so I was still tired but not so stressed because I wasn't dealing with traumatic incidents anymore.

Wisdom/Reflection
- *Don't take for granted the things that are precious and fragile*
- *Hold lightly to the things that are temporary, they're not important*
- *Recognise and identify your warning signs of burnout and how you can overcome them*
- *Take time to plan and manage your finances with your partner. Create a budget and monitor it together*
- *When starting a new position at work focus on building relationships*
- *Don't treat all of your children the same. They all have differing needs*

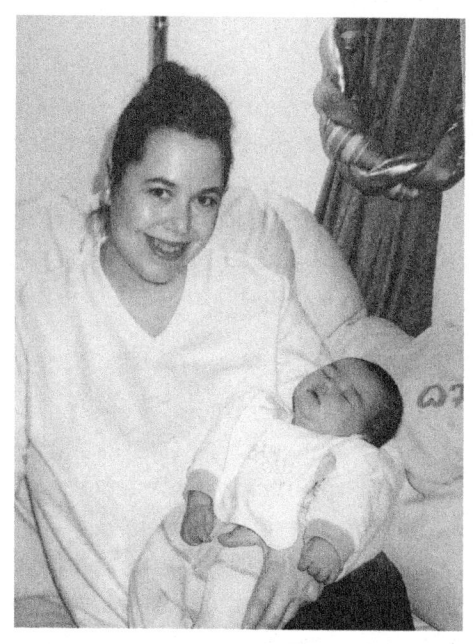

Welcome! Connie Melita

22.
Acacia
– The Vision is Born

Emma was awoken at 04.20 on October 16 2003, feeling that the Lord had spoken to her about starting a movement that helped young mums and their families suffering with pre and post-natal depression. As Emma had suffered with our girls it seemed that God was using our suffering to help others. This is often the case and some of the most effective charities were born out of adversity.

Emma shared her vision with me, and my view was that we should pray about it some more and, in the meantime, push the door to see if it was indeed from God. Often, we can have great ideas and they are valid and praiseworthy, but it's another matter whether they are called into being from God. Time is so precious and often in short supply when raising a family, so we really wanted to make sure that this was a God idea rather than a good idea.

It was evident early on that this was a God idea. It started very organically with Emma meeting mums in St John's Church, just chatting over a hot drink. Emma was a great communicator with a warm and welcoming smile, so it wasn't long before the befriending part of the service was up and running. Emma was a great networker too and before long she was meeting with health professionals to see if the service was something that they would value. Eventually GPs, health visitors and midwives would become referrers to what would be known as Acacia Family Support.

The Acacia tree was very symbolic for what the service stood for, and the symbol of an Acacia tree was confirmed by at least two other friends who felt that The Lord has shown them the Acacia tree either as a picture or vision whilst they were praying. I remember Emma telling me that the Acacia tree can survive in dry and arid land and provides shelter and food for many different animals.

For the next four years Emma would build and develop Acacia with a good friend called Rachel and many others, that walked with Emma as the vision was realised. As the service grew, organisations invested in Acacia and office premises were found and funding was awarded to deliver the exceptional service. Isaiah 41 v 17-19 was a key scripture Emma was given to support the vision.

Acacia was making a tangible impact with young families, saving mainstream services significant costs by getting upstream in a friendly and personal way. Who would think that later in the life of Acacia the Queen's Award would be given in recognition of the sterling work done by the team, that are mainly volunteers.

Whilst Emma was busy with Acacia, I was leading a charmed life in my posting at Headquarters. I had already travelled to New York and Boston to research how US law enforcement deal with school-based violence.

As Emma and I immersed ourselves in our careers, enjoying the challenge, I felt that our relationship was subtly coming under attack. I was spending time away at conferences and in the evenings, Emma was either taking calls or working on her laptop. With ferrying the girls around to their clubs and activities in between, there was very little time to invest in us.

Invariably when it came to bedtime, we were both whacked and offered each other a goodnight kiss then to sleep. This was a dark time in our marriage when many things converged. Church life was dull, and it suited us to become anonymous not really engaging but saying and doing the right things. Spiritually we were vulnerable and that naturally spilled over into our marriage. I knew Emma loved me and she cared for me, but a distance had emerged and rather than dealing with it, I put it in a box and detached myself.

I still engaged with the girls and enjoyed being a father, but, as a husband at this point, I was behaving out of duty, rather than love. I was sad inside because Emma was my best friend and I was so proud of what she was doing with Acacia, so I almost didn't want to interrupt or get her to stop, because it was such an honourable thing she was doing. It wasn't Emma's fault that I withdrew. It was mine. I realised that my heart was hardening, and this was a dangerous place to be.

Thankfully, I had two good friends who acted as accountability partners. I shared my struggles with them, but I was very good at minimising things and wearing a mask which defeated the object in some respects of having that accountability. I subscribed to the teaching, in terms of relationships as God first, then partner, then children. Some might view this as a bit legalistic, but the theory is that as you focus your time in getting closer to God then He will enable you to love others better, enriching all of your relationships.

There's a verse in the bible that says to love the Lord your God with all your heart, soul and mind. That made it quite clear that I'm to put the Lord first in everything. Easier said than done at times. The hardening of the heart is one of the most deadly diseases that occurs emotionally, spiritually and plays out into physical and mental health too.

I believe that there is an evil entity known as the devil. He goes by many names, from his name in heaven as Lucifer, to Satan, the deceiver, the father of lies, to name but a few. I know Christians that blame the devil for everything bad that happens to them, and I'm sure the devil is happy to take the credit. The reality in my experience lines up with what the bible teaches. There are three snares that entrap us in life, the world, the flesh and the devil.

In my situation, the world was applauding me, I was successful in my career and had a bright future ahead of me in the police. I had a lovely family with three precious girls and a wife that adored me as I did her. I did believe in our situation that the devil was playing his hand and was blowing his breath on my hardening heart.

There's another verse in the bible that says to be at home with the world is to be away from The Lord and to be at home with the Lord is to be away from the world. The latter is preferable as it was God that gave me favour with both him and people. The bible also says that promotion comes from the Lord too. I could psycho analyse my situation and come up with excuses from my childhood or some other trauma that helped shape my character. I do subscribe to a lot of that research, but I also believe in

personal responsibility to change negative behaviour.
I remember reading that a lot of what happened in childhood that shaped behaviour, isn't the fault of the child, but it is our responsibility to change unhelpful behaviours. I was quite needy and loved Emma cuddling me and physical touch is important to me. During this season this happened less and less. Emma appreciated words of affirmation and I know that the amount of time I listened to her and indulged in meaningful conversations reduced. Because we were known as a good family that had a good reputation, both in and out of the church, we were trapped by our own success. I didn't want others to know my business, as I was quite a private person in that way.

I was still calling out to God as my heart started to freeze over and my prayers at that time were very short and usually consisted of the word, help!

One evening it came to a head, when the girls were in bed. Both of us broke down in tears and shared about how we felt and reflected on how we had let it go this far before communicating how we felt. Thoughts and feelings aren't facts and often I was feeling things about Emma that were totally unfounded, and vice versa. It felt like I had been in a distant land, pretending to be at home. We both cried a lot that evening and said sorry to God for not honouring him in our relationship.

Some of you may be thinking that Emma didn't do anything wrong and what she was doing building an organisation was a commendable thing to do. If I may say that to not recognise the different needs between husband and wife during different seasons, is short sighted and more complicated than what's on the surface. I feel that men and women still have a long way to go to understand and celebrate the differences in gender.

Emma and I put some checks and balances in place as an early warning system to guard our relationship. We were more proactive too, in creating space for just the two of us. This is so important but many couples neglect this and focus all their attention on their children. It is possible to worship family more than God. This ultimately will unbalance the family dynamic and make a way for error and bad judgement to creep in.

Wisdom/Reflection

- When God plants a vision in your heart, He usually confirms it with His word and other godly people
- As a Christian couple you will witness the same things in your spirit. Use this to empower and unify
- Pray for your partner's purpose and be receptive to how you might play a part in God's plan
- Don't let what God has given you become a distraction
- Watch carefully and guard your marriage even in the good times

A family camping holiday in Devon

A family photo after church

23.
Serious and Organised Crime

My last year or so as a sergeant was spent running some innovative teams pioneering some new tactics to reduce gang violence. Due to our relatively poor detection rate for gang violence, we explored new ways to disrupt them. Housing legislation was used by our newly-formed unit to gain intelligence with a view to applying for injunctions in the civil court.

Here the burden of proof was to a lower standard, the balance of probabilities. This was easier to prove offences than beyond all reasonable doubt in the criminal court. We had some impressive results that put a senior gang member in prison, albeit it only for two weeks. This was the first time he had been convicted in 10 years. Previously significant police resources had been committed to trying to put this particularly nasty individual in prison.

During the trial of this notorious gang member, who wore a colostomy bag due to previous gunshot injuries, it was very challenging trying to find a witness that would give evidence. In any gang-related crime, the biggest challenge is getting people to come forward as witnesses, mainly because of the danger they then put themselves in.

The suspect had been arrested for breaching his exclusion zone that banned him from entering Birmingham City Centre. Prior to his arrest we had to collate the evidence that proved it was him at the scene of a particularly ruthless assault. With some clever technology that identified him by the metrics of his ear canal we were able to positively identify him as the main offender. As the offence took place in a busy wine bar, there were lots of people that witnessed the offence.

Thankfully, one witness was willing to attend court and give evidence. In the meantime, we had heard that other members of the gang were trying to find out who the witness was, in order to stop them giving evidence by any means. It was rollercoaster ride trying to keep the witness reassured that she would be safe. We had arranged for special measures to be put in place in the court. They have to be applied for in the court and authorised by the Judge. It's very rare to have all measures granted but on this occasion we were successful.

The witness would be giving evidence behind a screen with voice distortion technology in place too. The witness was collected in a plain police car with blacked out windows and delivered the witness to court via a private entrance. Once in the court, my witness was taken to a private room that was secure. At this time there were several known gang members congregating in the court and were clearly on the lookout for any potential witnesses. Tension was high and my primary concern was the witness.

The suspect was now in the courtroom having been transported from prison. I was speaking to some of my team about post-hearing arrangements when I was horrified to see the head usher escorting my witness through a public area of the court to the private entry into the court room! I couldn't believe my eyes! I looked in disbelief at a couple of the lads who were with me, and they told me that the usher barged in and said the Judge needed the witness now. Despite being told that special measures were in place, he arrogantly insisted on taking the witness. As we walked towards the court room the usher walked towards me and I asked him what he was doing with my witness. He responded by saying that he wasn't answerable to me and pointed his finger at my chest. I was livid but was holding it together until he pointed his finger at my chest. I instinctively grabbed his finger and pulled him down to the ground by it. He squealed like a pig, and I enjoyed the moment. He had no idea of the anguish and risk the witness had gone through. The preparation and plans that we had to make to ensure this was safe and smooth. This wasn't my finest hour, and my team were shocked at what had just happened.

They helped the usher up from the floor and he scuttled away saying" 'I'm going to report you to the judge!'. I still had this streak of aggression in me despite trying over the years to become calmer. As a Christian I know this wasn't the way that Jesus would have liked me to behave. I really struggled with this and although 90% of the time I was balanced, it just took certain triggers to set me off. It was normally around invading my personal space

or pushing/grabbing me.
I could usually resolve issues verbally by empathising and communicating in a way that de-escalated issues. I think what didn't help was that this was a high-risk situation. The case was adjourned after all that and the next day my boss, Dave Murcott, spoke to me saying that the judge had heard about the incident and wanted the name of the officer that was responsible for assaulting one of his court staff. Oh well, there goes my career I thought. I was happy to put my hands up because I wasn't going to try and get out of it. I was always taught by my dad to own up to the things that you have done. I asked Dave whether he wanted me to report to the court and he said no. Until the judge officially summoned me, we'd wait.

That night I prayed and told God that I would accept whatever came my way as it was me and although I felt justified, I knew it wasn't right. I knew that God saw why I did it. I'm not a bully and have protected victims all my career. I was asking for His forgiveness and mercy, but I knew I deserved to be punished. The summons from the judge never came. I later found out my Head of Department, who was a senior police officer had spoken with the judge and the full circumstances were conveyed to him. I was thankful for the backing from the top. On leaving the unit I was presented with a certificate that had a word art image of a pointing finger with a Latin sentence under that translated: 'don't point the finger'. I was privileged to work with a wonderful bunch of people that were committed to tackling gang members despite the risks.

Following my posting to the Multi Agency Gang Enforcement team, I was posted to the Serious and Organised Crime Unit, Team 3. This team was created during a time when gang-related violence was at unprecedented levels, particularly the criminal use of firearms. It was a newly-formed team that, looking back, was probably politically motivated, demonstrating that the police were tackling gangs. We had a close working relationship with our Firearms and Surveillance departments. We targeted known and suspected gang members daily. On forming the team I organised a bit of a team-building exercise that would also provide some fun and knowledge around firearms. The very helpful Firearms' department agreed to put on a range day for us so we could familiarise ourselves with the various firearms that were circulating on the street. It would also give us a bit of credibility when we came across firearms and had to speak to suspects about them. This was the first time for some of the team holding a firearm and firing one. We were treated to the Mach 10 machine pistol as well as a variety of other weapons. A good day was had by all.

My time on Team 3 was relatively short as I was successful in the promotion process to the rank of inspector and was summonsed by an Assistant Chief Constable (ACC) who congratulated me and told me that I would be getting my pips (inspector rank insignia) next week and I would be seconded to the Safer Birmingham Partnership, which was a multi-agency team that jointly worked to reduce and prevent crime in the city. Team 3 was high octane action and whilst I was with the team we recovered six handguns and arrested numerous offenders. The team continued to have some impressive results under the leadership of Dave Murcott.

Wisdom/Reflection
- *Great leaders ask more, than tell*
- *Sometimes you've got to go with what you don't know*
- *Some situations turn out well, but they don't always start that way*
- *Always try to do something that costs you without necessarily getting a return*
- *To stand by what you believe may cost you, but your integrity will remain in tact*

Team 3 SOCU group photo

24.
Working for the Top Floor — Strategic!

It was a poison chalice. Having just left Serious Organised Crime, dealing with serious offenders, I went to a job that was mostly meetings with non-police people that didn't really know a fat lot about crime. I was in charge of a small police unit within the partnership and was the main liaison point for our partners. This was a very political posting, where everyone was protecting their budgets and resources. I had to feed back to the top floor higher echelons at Lloyd House, (police HQ) and support the leaders of the partnership who weren't police too. Sometimes it was hard to please anyone, and I soon discovered that being away from the main police environment created a distance with colleagues and felt out of the loop. Some colleagues joked about my posting, but I knew that there was some truth in their jesting. I wasn't at the sharp end anymore now that I was working for the council they said, followed by a request for me to get them some bin bags. This posting was strategic and high level and, if done well, would be a definite springboard for the next rank to Chief Inspector for me. ACC Hyde promised I'd be there no longer than two years. I was counting the days.

I worked long hours on Team 3, but was now working 9-5, Monday to Friday, weekends off. This job was tiring in a different way. I had to read lots of documents to then brief senior officers and prepare and deliver presentations. This was a steep learning curve for me and there was little forgiveness for mistakes.

One day, I was on the top floor of Lloyd House where the great and the good live. The highest-ranking officers, including the Chief Constable. I was walking past one of the ACC's office when I heard him shout: 'Get in here!'. There was no one else in the corridor so I figured he must mean me, but I was puzzled because I didn't work for him. I turned around and stood in the doorway of his office waiting to be invited in. I could sense he was really angry and when he turned round to face me, I could see by his face that he was about to explode.

He was holding some papers in his right hand and started waving them about. He walked up to me and said: 'What the fuck is this?' and waved the papers in front of my face. I knew the blood was draining from my face and I could feel my heart pounding. I had to hold it together and establish what he was on about before I responded.

He held the papers in front of me and I quickly scanned them and could see that the report had nothing to do with me. He had collared the wrong person. I calmly explained that the papers didn't relate to me to which he sneered: 'Then fuck off and get me the person that they do relate to!'. At this stage I thought I don't deserve this treatment. I could feel my fist clench and my mind started to race with thoughts of whether I would get away with it if I punched him in the face. I so wanted to do it. I know, it's so wrong but you had to be there. He's a snivelling little man and was behaving that way just because of his rank. I felt on high alert inside my body just like I was about to have a violent confrontation. I had felt like this many times with incidents on the street, so I was very familiar with my body's precursors; dry mouth, shaking inside.
I paused and looked at him trying to telepathically convey that I could squash him like a fly but valued my freedom more than hurting him. I left his office and walked down the corridor feeling humiliated and was met by a friend of mine who was a Chief Superintendent. He could tell that something was up and, after explaining what had happened, he told me to keep my powder dry as I wasn't the first that he had vented on.

Later that day Jim called me to say that I would be receiving a call from the ACC to arrange a coffee. Sure enough the next day the ACC called me to say that he wanted a chat. We met in a coffee shop in Birmingham. He apologised for his behaviour and then smiled wryly saying he couldn't promise that it wouldn't happen again. So that was the measure of the man who couldn't commit for not having another tantrum. I understand that he was spoken to and advised about the way he treated people. Thankfully, I didn't have much to do with the man after that.

By now you must be puzzled by my ability to have raging violent thoughts and impulses and be this loving Christian man, that professes to follow Jesus. I guess the important point in this instance is that I didn't act on my impulses. Being human is tricky and the bible teaches that the human nature is constantly at war with the spirit nature. It's encouraging to know that the apostle Paul struggled saying why he did the things that he shouldn't do and the things he should do, he didn't.

As a Christian man I've found that I need strengthening daily and doing the right thing is a constant battle. I would learn to reflect and prayerfully ask the Holy Spirit to change me from the inside. I so wanted to be a man that could respond in a godly way even in challenging circumstances. If I listened to the accusations from the enemy, I would have given up a long time ago. Silencing the destructive thoughts is critical to moving forward and focusing on things that are noble and pure. Understanding that we are in a spiritual battle helps to make sense of why sometimes we are tested and feel the way we do.

I did think that becoming a Christian and becoming a new creation as the Bible put it, would mean a quicker transformation than I was experiencing. As I journeyed with Christ, I would learn that enthusiastic obedience brought on transformation quicker. Being obedient meant that I needed to know what to be obedient for. That meant reading and digesting his word and more importantly letting the Holy Spirit illuminate His word so that the full power and effect could be manifest in my life. It's very easy to become legalistic with what you read in the Bible and that's why I find it critical to have the Spirit and word.

He puts it in perspective and shows you how and when to apply His truth. The closer you get to The Lord the more subtle the whispers of the enemy become, even quoting the bible! My experience is that the devil deals in half truths and counterfeits, so it will do you well to know the word and receive good solid teaching to help bolster and reinforce what you have read.

My time at the Safer Birmingham Partnership was coming to an end. I had learnt how to think strategically, how to be more diplomatic and how to absorb a lot of information quickly, with the requirement to then brief senior officers on the content. I was relieved to be returning to a policing environment where culturally I felt safer, in terms of banter and letting off steam.

Thankfully, I was posted to Sutton Coldfield so super convenient for commuting and a familiar stomping ground from earlier days in my career. The way this posting came about was fortuitous and a blessing from the Lord. I love the way when you commit your way to The Lord, He directs your path. It is about trusting him no matter what and not trying to take over the helm. Now I don't want this process to sound too simplistic as my methodology is quite basic. I do commit my way to The Lord and then proceed to try all the metaphorical door handles to see which one turns and opens.

I'm sure that some of you that are far more patient and in tune would go to the right door after careful contemplation and prayer. I do commit my way to The Lord but then crack on to activate the plan. I am impatient but, in my defence, I do sense as I'm praying what way I should go. I guess it's different for all of us because of the way we process things and also our levels of faith. I usually get an uneasy feeling when I'm doing something in my own strength. I often journey with one or two advisors around significant decisions to confirm my direction or caution me on my intentions.

Whilst taking Connie to dance class one Saturday morning I bumped into a good friend of mine who at that time was the Commander of Birmingham North police area, which included Sutton Coldfield. I asked him whether I could spend some time shadowing one of his inspectors to ease myself back into operational policing. He went one better than my request and offered me an inspector's post as a permanent position. I enthusiastically accepted and started on the Operational Command Unit (OCU)the next week! Little did I know how much of a blessing being so close to home would be for the seasons of our life as a family ahead.

Wisdom/Reflection
- *Be silent rather than speak and regret your words later*
- *Take time to learn the priorities of your partners at work. Spend some time learning their business*
- *Do the right thing even when it goes against your agency's agenda*
- *People are more important than processes*
- *Others may be senior to you but never superior*
- *Even in the face of adversity and unfairness, be professional and exercise courtesy*

A visit to 10 Downing Street when Gordon Brown was Prime Minister, for a community initiative that went rather well

Carefree days before Emma's illness

25.
Back to my Roots

It was so good to be at Sutton nick as there were people there that I had served with earlier on in my career and the whole layout of the place was familiar and held fond memories for me. I didn't have to work hard at building relationships as there was a level of trust and friendship already in existence.

Being an inspector on a Response team was a good way to get myself back into mainstream policing. As the Duty Inspector, all the resources for the area are at your disposal. You are it in terms of managing threat and risk of anything that happens during your tour of duty. I loved it though because it weas leadership at its best. Empowering your teams and making decisions when it counts, often in dynamic, dangerous situations. I still had aspirations for promotion and had planned to invest 18 months as an inspector at Sutton, hopefully being successful in the Chief Inspector promotion process.

As a family I think we were in a good place. Emma was now being paid for the work she was leading in Acacia and we had worked through each other's needs. I was very content having a wife that I loved and children that brought us a lot of joy and laughter. All three girls were opinionated and had the Mediterranean fire in their bellies. They all had a great sense of humour and could be heard somewhere around the house role playing, dancing or singing.

Lydia had an exceptional singing voice and Em and I thought that one day she would sing before kings and queens. Her voice was of a very high standard for classical singing, but Lyd had a passion for musical theatre and would later be successful in gaining a place at the prestigious Arts Ed, the Andrew Lloyd Webber school.

Connie was entrepreneurial and we got a sense that money would follow her.

Hannah had the heart of a lion and became fierce when seeing the injustice in the world.

I had met my match with all three and they often held me to account which, looking back, was a good thing but not perhaps when I'd just got home having experienced a particularly challenging shift. I didn't share with them what I had had to deal with so I didn't really have a release valve. When it came to bedtime though they would demand that I tell them a 'real' story. I would select the lighter moments like the very fat man that had put on his weight by eating all his wares as an ice-cream salesman, (true story).

As the girls grew up, I was determined to ensure that our Christian ways weren't diluted by the world out there that they were being exposed to. We continued to say grace before meals, and we would battle trying to get them together to listen to a bible reading. They were all involved in church youth groups and would have their own quiet times where they could work things out with God themselves. We didn't want to live our faith out through our girls and wanted them to have their own personal walk with Jesus. After all, one day they would leave home and make their own life, so it was about them building their own house on the rock rather than the sand.

I was confident that the girls were more streetwise than most. I would share life lessons with them and warn them of some of the things out there that could cause them trouble. We used to have time discussing difficult friendships and what they should say to get out of trouble. I found that there was a lot of listening with our girls. They really valued just being heard, and Emma was better at this than me. I would listen to what the issue was and then come up with a number of options open to them, (usually three). For me it would be about choosing an option and then dealing with it. This wasn't always the case, and they would end up getting upset and I would become intolerant and tell them to get a grip.

Not the right response I know, but I lost patience when I thought that their response was emotional and irrational. I understand it's more of a man response than a woman one. Emma often had to be my follow up like the fragrance in the breeze, putting back in place what I had knocked over in my china shop! What irritated me most though was when they didn't listen or honour what I'd asked them to do. I wouldn't class myself as being overly tidy, but I did like some order, and this was often a struggle for the girls as they were untidy. I would be patient to begin with and ask for things to be put away and would ask again a little later, giving them time to respond. If the chore still wasn't completed, I would get frustrated and raise my voice, seeing this as an act of disrespect.

Then my little voice in my head, would tell me that they were ungrateful and didn't value what I said. They would then answer back despite my efforts to get them to put their clothes away. That would be the red light to me and often I would shout and revert back to how it was when I was growing up. I would always regret my behaviour and then justify it by thinking that if they had done what they were told this wouldn't have escalated. It's pretty much what used to happen on the streets too. Somebody would be behaving badly so they would be approached by an officer who would communicate with them calmly to begin with to establish what the issue was.

If their behaviour improved, they would probably receive some advice and that would be that. If they continued behaving badly and offences were committed, then the officer would escalate their communications in an attempt to resolve the conflict before dealing with the offences. If this didn't work there would be a final appeal by saying: 'Is there anything I can do to help you and stop you behaving like this?'.

Often that appeal would be met with a lot of abuse so now there was only one option, arrest and that usually meant some sort of physical confrontation. Once they had been detained and the handcuffs were off at the police station, often the prisoner would be apologetic and extend their hand to shake yours! I guess I carried some of that methodology into the home and it wasn't always appropriate. On reflection I was so intent on them getting the initial building blocks of their life right that I concentrated too much on the process rather than them. Most of mine and Em's thinking was around the girls and their development. We always tried to do the right thing, and I was unapologetic about sticking to following the principles of the bible.

We can beat ourselves up as parents looking back, wanting to do things differently but at the time there were many variables that influenced how we behaved and responded. As long as you can reflect and honestly say that you did the best you could in the circumstances and that you have learnt from your experience then it's time to move on and make today count.

I so wanted to be a man of God that lived by faith, but I didn't want to lose my masculinity. When the bible talked about being gentle and meek, I struggled. Of course, I wanted to be kind and, in the right circumstances, gentle too, but I didn't want to be a doormat. I am a straight talker, but also diplomatic. Discerning a situation would influence my approach. As a cop you become emotionally intelligent, knowing when it's going to kick off with violence or when compassion and empathetic gestures are called for.

I became adept at spotting bluffers; those who were lying or pretending to be something that they weren't, even in the church. I wore a mask and nodded at the right times but inside I knew they were fraudulent, and this affected how I viewed people. I would always be scanning for an agenda, looking for body language that would confirm my suspicions. I passed all this learning onto my girls and I'm not sure it was the right thing to do as in the process I encouraged them to become judgemental.

Hannah was my best student, and I could see her emulate me. I wanted her to be sharp, not to be anyone's fool. I can remember when she was having trouble at primary school with another girl who was bullying her. My advice was to follow her into the toilet and push her up the wall and sneer at her saying: "leave me alone or you'll regret it!'. I know you're horrified and disappointed with me for giving my ten-year-old daughter that advice. I understand the more noble route is to try and communicate sensibly asking for the bully to reflect on how they're treating others and to stop. I've not personally seen this be effective with youths. Adults maybe. I've heard far more of youths resorting to self-harm and suicide because of cruel relentless bullying.

I guess quite primitively I believe people respond to pain and often avoid it if they can. I know there will be lots of research saying that my advice was damaging and ill thought out. Perhaps that's true and I would add that

I can count on one hand the number of times I have had to resort to that approach and each time it was successful. I don't advocate or celebrate violence or the threat of it but on very rare occasions it can be the solution.

I would rather talk things through and am a great believer in restorative justice. I hasten to add that before resorting to the toilet encounter with the bully, the advice was to look for a solution through trying to understand the problem with resolution in mind. Better to take a city by peace than by force the book of proverbs says. I wholeheartedly agree, but also to choose wise advisors before going to war! So, there's my problem. I will still consider masculine solutions before perhaps praying about the situation. My initial instinct is revenge and if there is a physical threat towards me or my loved ones then my first thought is how to neutralise the threat or take it down.

I sometimes wish I hadn't joined the army or the police as both professions played to my dark side. I would have made a far better wildlife photographer or gamekeeper. I believe we are all built for a purpose with our unique character traits that when combined with others can be a powerful force for good, but, as with all things, can become toxic if corrupted.

My saving grace has been my walk with Jesus. He sees me and knows me. He makes me feel uncomfortable and unsettled about things and is the inspiration for transformation of behaviours and character. The amazing thing is that He gives the power and authority to take hold of parts of your life and turn them around, from physical healing to the healing of emotions and the past. This may sound crazy I know, but I've known Him for over 30 years now and I have a history with Jesus that shows his hand and power in my life. If you don't know Him, this will make no sense to you, and you may admire me for my faith, but you won't feel compelled to join me on this journey as you surrender to Jesus. This is a matter of the heart not the head. It's about humbling yourself and trusting Him with your life. There will be change involved but there is joy in the journey and just knowing that the greatness of the One that created all things, cares enough to be interested in me, and get this, He actually loves me!

Wisdom/Reflection
- *Where it depends on you aim for good endings as you don't know when you may return to the same environment*
- *Don't burn your bridges as you may need to use them again*
- *Time spent well creates growth and experience*
- *As a leader you often set the tone for the working day, make sure it's a bright one*
- *Set a learning culture not a blame culture*
- *Trust your people and they will trust you*
- *Use your sense of humour and have those micro conversations with your staff*
- *Make the tea every now and again for your department*

26.
2011
– And So It Begins

The year 2011 would prove to be an eventful one for what looked like all the wrong reasons, on the surface.

Mum was feeling unwell in November 2010, and I accompanied her to the hospital for tests. I had a sense that this wasn't going to end well. Mum had a routine operation to remove some polyps from her stomach and whilst removing them there was some suspicion about whether they could be cancerous or not. The radiologist informed mum that she would have to wait for the consultant's report. I took the radiologist to one side and pushed her for further information. Her eyes filled up and she said that there were some worrying images but that the consultant would have all the detail. She then hurried away.

It would transpire that mum had stomach cancer that would later spread to her liver. Mum's illness was relatively short but aggressive. During that time, we had many deep conversations about Jesus. I recalled with mum the evening she came with me and Emma to church. Mum was moved by the pastor's words and made her way to the front for prayer to respond to the call to accept Jesus. Em and I watched with tears in our eyes as mum gave her life to Jesus.

Now at the end of her life she pondered often and on one occasion she sat in the wheelchair in the hospice, looking into space. I asked her what she was thinking of and she said: 'Jesus'. Mum died in the April and as a family we had the privilege of being by her bedside at home as we watched her breathe her last. The priest and all my brothers and sisters were present. Dad looked over to me and asked me to pray so I prayed for mum just before she died. I entrusted her into the loving arms of Jesus, and we all said amen.

Mum was the epitome of selfless love and such good fun. Sensitive in listening and always wanting to help solve problems. She was a great cook and had lots of love to give but ,woe betide you, if you crossed her. She hated unfairness and usually fought for the underdog. I was so sad to see her go but my grieving process was cut short because whilst watching mum suffer with cancer, we received the devastating news that Emma had some abnormalities in one of her breasts, that turned out to be cancerous. Emma didn't attend mum's funeral because she was undergoing a pre op for a mastectomy (amputation of the infected breast).

Attending Good Hope Hospital to receive the test results was a day I will never forget. We sat in the waiting area of the oncology department surrounded by people that were either undergoing cancer treatment or on the start of that journey having received a diagnosis. We were called in to a consultation room where the consultant greeted us along with a breast cancer nurse. Em and I sat side by side and waited politely for the consultant to share the results with us. I soon learnt that often, if a nurse is present, it usually meant bad news. That was certainly our experience. I moved in closer to Emma and we clasped our hands together, holding on to each other. We leaned in towards the consultant to not miss a word and looked at him intently hoping for the best. I knew that it wasn't going to be what we wanted to hear, and I was aware that life was about to change. He started by introducing himself and then looked at the papers in front of him and said that it wasn't good news. He looked down and said that he was sorry as Emma had breast cancer and that it was stage 4 and aggressive. We held our breath and I blurted out: 'How serious is it on a scale of one to ten?'. He replied: 'Ten'. I looked at Emma and our eyes filled up and we both sobbed and held each other. It was as if we were in the room alone, nothing else mattered. We thought of nothing else apart from what we had just been told.

Everything slowed down as we contemplated the future, the girls, what will be and will not be. The treatment regime, the limitations, the pain, the loss.

Emma would start her chemotherapy treatment following the mastectomy. She would eventually have both breasts removed and would receive at least four different types of chemotherapy as well as radiotherapy.

We got home having received the dreadful diagnosis and sat the girls down in our front room and Emma explained to the girls that she was a bit poorly but that there was treatment to help her get better. Hannah, being the eldest and most direct in her approach, asked if it was cancer and we confirmed that it was.

We painted a hopeful picture, but I sensed, even at this early stage, that I was eventually going to lose Emma.

I don't know how much of the situation registered with the girls. Lydia was 16 and studying for her GCSEs, Hannah was 18 and making her way in the world. Connie was seven, looking up to the response of her older sisters. It was horribly sad, and I couldn't stop my mind running away to the place of life without Emma. That night we went to bed emotionally exhausted. We sobbed again but said very little because I feared exposing my thoughts to Emma, because she needed me to be strong for her and the girls.

The reality though, was that I was in bits. I started to reflect on my relationship with Emma. Had I been the best husband I could have been? The answer was no. Was I the cause of Emma's illness? Did my selfishness, moodiness and anger trigger the cancer? I started to have all these thoughts flood into my head. I took all this emotion to Jesus and sat down and asked him what the plan was? We didn't get angry about the cancer, and we didn't blame God. We saw him as our answer through this, whatever the outcome.

After the initial shock and realisation of the situation a calm and a hush came over Emma and me. It was God's peace, and it was tangible, like an inner strength that wasn't of human origin.

Emma had her surgery and was laid up in bed at home. She felt a sense of loss losing that part of her body but was pragmatic in another sense that it had to be done to save her life. I remember the days being warm and sunny and the light in our bedroom was comforting and hopeful. I would walk the dog early in Newhall Valley and pick some meadow flowers for Emma and place them in a vase in our bedroom. Emma liked the simple things and we both began to strip away the unnecessary and simplify our approach to life.

We did far more reflecting and talking about the things that mattered. Our relationship with the Lord as a couple improved and we often came before him together looking to him for strength and a replenishment of his peace. The gifts God gives us are totally fit for purpose and the fruits He grows in us benefit us and those around us. Joy would soon visit our home despite our circumstances. We were reminded that the joy of the Lord is our strength. This wasn't happiness, which is based on circumstances. This was his joy that he gave us. It's deeper than happiness and eternal, not based on circumstances.

I found it hard to take in that Emma was poorly and that our lives were going to change forever. But life had to go on. I was an Inspector in the police and had to perform when at work. I was a father, so the girls still had needs and I was responsible for their nurture and upbringing. Emma wasn't going to be as active as she was before and would have a more complex routine with treatment and hospital appointments.

My dad and my brothers and sisters were grieving the loss of mum, but I wasn't in touch with how that felt. I'd boxed it off and was dealing with the current threat to Emma's health. I didn't feel anything of my mum's passing, I was numb and chose not to think about it. Mum would understand and would tell me to look after my wife. Despite being numb about mum, I cried every day in private about our current situation. I wanted to fix it, but I couldn't. I asked God to transfer the cancer to me and spare Emma. The girls needed her more than me. I was a good man but not a very good father of girls. I was aware that I was becoming even more short tempered, and the girls felt the brunt of my stress.

I didn't want to let anyone down so when it came to work, I wore a mask that I thought protected me from exposing my brokenness and vulnerability. Inside it was like the pressure of a volcano growing, with an eruption being inevitable at some point.

Despite my faith I still felt flat and low, and waves of doom swept over me when I thought of the future. It wasn't like the peace that passes all understanding was with me indefinitely. That peace that God gives can be stolen if you give permission for it to be by the world, the flesh or the devil.

My negative thoughts ran away with me and took me to that dark place of death and loneliness. I wasn't keeping my eyes fixed on Jesus whose peace guards our hearts and minds in him. I found that I had to cling on to his promises in the Bible.

This is where believing and standing on the word of God was going to carry us through. I trusted that God stood by His word, and I could depend on it. I felt like we were on a sailing boat approaching a storm. The black clouds were looming, and the breeze was getting up.
Throughout my life physical exercise has helped me get through difficult times. If I needed to clear my mind or felt particularly stressed, I would get my trainers on and run.

Emma would always suggest to me to get out and run or go for a ride if she saw the signs in me that I was struggling. I figured if I stayed close to The Lord and kept fit that would help me to help us. I was very aware that I was the only well parent now and a lot depended on me.

Church was very good and supplied us with meals that were kindly left on our doorstep. We were so grateful for our local family and friends, who did a lot for us practically. Although very kind, this level of help may not have been sustainable for a long period of time so I took on the role of cook and everything else. It would have been very easy for me to slip into an attitude of self-pity, but there wasn't room for a pity party. The balance of keeping everything as normal as possible for the girls was almost impossible. How could you hide the ravaging effects of treatment and surgery on Emma's body?

We weren't sure whether Emma would lose her hair with the first round of chemo, but it was likely. I wanted to protect the girls from it all but I couldn't. I so badly wanted to scream and lose it. I didn't want to be what I had to be. I wanted someone to comfort me, I wanted someone to share my tears, but then I got feelings of guilt because I wasn't the poorly one. How dare I feel like this when Emma had cancer. So, because of this self-condemnation I kept quiet, and the volcano continued to simmer.

One morning Emma came into the bedroom from the shower, and I could clearly see that the majority of her hair had gone. I got up and hugged her telling her it will be alright, but inside I was screaming. I needed the hug more than her, but my heart sank for Emma because this was the stark reality of cancer treatment. I went to the bathroom and could see a large amount of Emma's hair in the bath. When the girls came home, they were amazingly resilient and joked with Emma and talked about the great wigs that were available as well as funky, colourful headscarves. Next to the mastectomy this was the next visible sign that Emma had cancer. Although the girls were upbeat on the outside, I believed they were thinking of their mum.

Connie was so much younger than Hannah and Lydia and had an amazing amount of resilience, probably because she didn't fully appreciate everything that was going on and I was glad that she was living life in another world at times. This was a world that I longed to visit, to be comforted and have a lightness of life attitude. Connie remarked that Emma's shed hair looked like a dead cat! We laughed and then discussed whether it would grow back a different colour or perhaps thick and curly. Emma had thin hair, even before her illness so she would welcome thick curly, even grey thick curly!

Wisdom/Reflection
- *God is in control, and He knows*
- *Don't let the shock of bad news steal your peace*
- *Get on your knees before you get on your phone*
- *Try to resist going into 'task' mode and taking over*
- *Let other people walk the journey of suffering with you*
- *Take care of your loved one and take care of yourself*
- *Lean in and let The Comforter comfort you*
- *Protect your families boundaries from curious people/friends that mean well*

Me with mum & dad and my siblings. Mum was coping with cancer at the time. Sadly she passed not long after this time together.

The riots
– Summer 2011

August 2011, riots spread across parts of the UK, apparently triggered by an incident that occurred in London where armed police officers shot an alleged unarmed black man. Things moved really quickly and most officers in West Midlands Police were mobilised to regain law and order on the streets of the West Midlands.

This was to be the most significant riot that affected a number of cities since the 1980s. Back then police officers would have been ill-equipped, using dustbin lids as shields with inadequate personal protective equipment, (ppe). We were equipped with well-designed public order kit that could withstand a lot of abuse, including fire damage. As a force we had a certain number of officers that were public order trained. The training was an annual requirement and even more frequent for our Operational Support Units, who were the specialists at dealing with public order incidents amongst other things.

I enjoyed public order training because it was something a little different, involving a degree of physical strength and tactics. We trained at RAF Cosford where there was a mock town contained within one of the hangars. Once you entered the hangar to practice formations and tactics, everything was in play. Those that were waiting their turn to practice doubled up as an angry mob that taunted us and threw wooden bricks at the Police Support Units (PSU).

We also had to stand still in a line whilst instructors threw petrol bombs at our feet. This was to give us confidence in our kit and to prove that it was fireproof, up to a point. One year when we were testing our kit against fire, a small plump policewoman standing in line next to me made a whimpering noise and then slowly collapsed to the floor, I imagined in fear of the fire. This was confirmed after we dragged her away and she came round.

Having turned up for work expecting to be doing my day job, I was immediately informed that I need to get my public order kit and report to

Tally Ho, which is a police facility that was to be the coordination point for command and resources. I, along with a number of other officers, made our way to Tally Ho, with a bit of a glint in our eye at the prospect of a bit of action. As an Inspector I was responsible for a Police Support Unit that comprised three sergeants, that each had a serial of seven officers. So, 21 constables and three sergeants, three police vans and little old me. I reported to the command suite and was informed that I was to deploy to West Bromwich and take the High Street back.

By this time the rioting had been going on for some time. In fact, as we were travelling to Tally Ho, we heard an officer scream over the radio that Steel House Lane Police Station was under attack and the order to defend it at all costs! Police cars left abandoned and on fire, shops with gaping holes in their windows. It was a surreal time. I felt in control and silently quite excited. I liked leading in chaos; it brought out the best in me. I could make decisions quickly and safely. My main priority was to get all my people home safely. That said we were going to take back West Brom High Street and there could only be one winner, and it wasn't going to be the rioters.
As our three vans trundled towards West Brom, I asked the sergeant that had local knowledge of the area to lead us in. At this stage we were all dressed in Code 1, which is full riot gear with shields. I was to rendezvous with the outgoing PSU Commander who I knew well as a friend. As we neared the High Street, I could see my counterpart standing in the street waving his hands about and shouting. I told my vans to wait here whilst I liaised with Coops, the other PSU Commander. As I approached him, I smiled and my body language was relaxed to put him at ease and let him know that I was glad to see him. As he turned to face me something wasn't right.

His eyes were wide, and he was jabbering in inaudible tones. I put my hand on his shoulder and asked him to repeat what he was saying. Granted, with the visor down on his helmet it would normally be a challenge to communicate, and there was a lot of street noise. Coops was struggling to communicate, and I think he'd had enough and was most likely glad that we had arrived to relieve him and his troops. I think he and his officers had been there some time and had taken a hammering, so his reaction was understandable. He was a very able inspector and well respected too.

I returned to my van having briefed my sergeants on the plan of attack. We would use the vans to take as much ground as possible and would only deploy from them when we had to. With all our kit on including shields. We were no match in terms of speed, compared to the Nike-wearing hooded thugs.

We mounted up and I gave a knowing look to my sergeants as I closed my door. It wasn't a certainty that we would all return home unharmed. This was a dangerous situation that none of us had ever faced before. Most of my constables had ten years or less service but were all sound characters and up for what was about to come. I motioned to my driver to push on towards the High Street and we would advance in a slow line evenly spaced across the pedestrianised area. Everybody was on high alert and there was silence in the van. All eyes were on the streets outside, scanning for threats.

From my right I heard a crash and splintering sound and we all instinctively locked on to where the noise came from. My driver Gary looked at me for a brief second open-mouthed as the windscreen splintered on the impact of a brick that had been thrown by a rioter. The reality of the situation was now clear. There were people out there that wanted to hurt us. We could see rioters in front of us around 25 metres away, so we continued to drive towards them pushing them on.

I could see around 50 hostiles, most wearing face coverings and clearly excitable. We could see that shops had been looted and there were numerous alarms sounding. My mind was racing as I evaluated and considered when we should get out of the vans and form a cordon, which is a line formation to create a natural barrier. Our vans pushing forward must have intimidated the crowd as there was now at least 50 metres between us, so I decided to get the troops out of the van. They slickly formed a cordon, and we stood observing the crowd. There could only be one winner and it wasn't going to be them. There seemed to be a moment of indecision in the crowd then they turned towards us and started to approach us shouting and chanting. My training kicked in and I gave the obligatory warning to the crowd over the loud hailer which I had slung over my shoulder.

I had given a lawful instruction to disperse and then ordered the whole PSU to draw batons. The crowd slowed down and were curious to see what the police were doing. They could clearly see now that our batons were drawn and visible. They had the warning and now could see we meant business. I gave the order to advance, and as we did the crowd started to fall back.

As we advanced, I could see a burning police car that had been abandoned I presumed. The crowd were making for a subway and were taunting us. We had retaken the High Street and that was our objective. I sensed that we would have got into some difficulties if we had pursued them, pretty much like being ambushed. We held our ground and, now that we had secured the High Street, the Fire Service arrived and started putting out the fires that were giving off an acrid smoke from the burning tyres and bins that were positioned to act as a barricades.
We stayed on the High Street for around a couple of hours and then we were released to patrol the general area ready to be deployed to the next trouble spot.

We had been patrolling for around 30 minutes and it was now dark. My mind was on high alert as there were groups of youths skulking around everywhere. It was as if there was a spirit of chaos rampaging through the streets. The atmosphere was tense and we were constantly scanning for threat and danger. I could hear over my radio that there were flashpoints all over the West Midland region.

I looked left and could see a very large crowd of at least 100 people, all men, running around a small group. We were too far away so I couldn't see immediately what the small group was doing. I asked Gary my driver to make towards the disturbance. I sensed that this was going to present us with some problem so called on the radio to request the helicopter to make to our location to start filming to gather any potential evidence.

AO1 was otherwise engaged with another incident, and I was informed that it would be committed for some time. Resources across the West Midlands were stretched and there would be no knights in shining armour or the cavalry available to come and help us out. My orders to my unit were to avoid making arrests because there would be no replacements and we would be left vulnerable. It was all about dispersal and tactical communications, in other words trying to influence people rather than control them because the reality was that we were very vulnerable and, to a certain extent, alone.

We pulled up close to the gathering crowd and I could see that several men were pounding another man, who was laid in the foetal position on the ground, with sticks. Another man was shouting and allowing his dog to bite the man on the ground. On seeing us approach them, the men with the sticks and the dog melted into the crowd and so did a couple of others that were brandishing what looked like long ceremonial swords that glistened in the available light. The darkness presented another risk, in terms of visibility, along with impaired hearing due to wearing our public order helmets, that had constant chatter coming through the earpiece.

If this crowd decided to take us on, we would lose. I was frantically trying to evaluate what was going on and quickly deduced that the injured man lying motionless on the floor was black and all the aggressors were Sikhs.

Most of my dealings with the Sikh community were very respectful. They are a people I admire and are honourable. So, what was going on? I approached an elderly Sikh gentleman as I thought he could be one of the elders from the temple that was close to the incident. One of my sergeants was protecting the injured male on the ground and had arranged for an ambulance to make the scene. I could see that one serial of officers had formed a defensive circle around the injured man as tensions were very high and some were still trying to get at him.

The power balance between us the police and the crowd was on a knife edge. If we became too commandeering the balance could flip and the crowd could turn on us. I asked the elderly gentleman what was happening and before he started to speak several younger Sikh men interrupted and asked me what me and my officers were doing here. There was a look in their eye that was bordering defiant, and I had to be far more diplomatic than I would have liked. Bottom line is that a man had been seriously assaulted and was the focus of this crowd's attention. Something needed to be done but the situation was complicated. There were no witnesses, and we didn't have the resources to manage such a large incident alone.

My priority now was to get the injured man to hospital and to establish what had occurred and whether by any chance we could locate any witnesses with a view to making arrests later. The injured man may be able to provide evidence but, at that moment, he was unconscious, and we did not know how serious his injuries were.

It transpired that, at another location not far from where we were, three Asian males had been run over by African Caribbean men in cars as they were allegedly making off after looting premises. Although it wasn't said, it seemed like this attack was retribution for what had happened earlier where three men were tragically killed.

Thankfully, the crowd started to disperse as the ambulance took the injured man away, although some remained to guard their temple as they believed that there could be further trouble and potential attacks on the building. I never found out how seriously injured the man on the ground was and to my knowledge there were no perpetrators brought to justice for the attack.

The final deployment of that night would be to guard a building that had a significant high-value cargo stored within it. Somehow this became known to someone as they had attempted to gain access with a heavy-duty forklift truck that was left abandoned with the forks still embedded into the building. We parked up close to the premises and officers were posted around it to prevent any further intrusion. That was Day One of the 2011 riots and what a day it was. It was a real test for the police and other emergency services. It's fair to say we were spread quite thin on the ground and had to borrow personnel carriers from other forces.

Interestingly, the next day we were mainly deployed as reassurance patrols. Quite early on we came across a large crowd of Asian males that were congregating on the street. They flagged us down and started hurling abuse at us saying we were racist and didn't do anything for the three men that were mown down and tragically died the night before. We stopped the van and my sergeant Nicki got out with several officers. Little did the crowd know that Nicki was the sergeant at the scene who tried to save the lives of the three by administering first aid with her officers. Whilst doing so they had to fend off some of the crowd who were anti police. I could see that Nicki was trying to pacify the crowd particularly the most vocal chap, who seemed to be the spokesman.

I was incensed by the situation because clearly, he wouldn't be hurling accusations if he was in possession of the facts. I got out of the van and made my way to the spokesman and introduced myself then explained about what Nicki and her officers had done at the scene of the tragedy. The man's brain took a few seconds to compute what I had just told him and whilst doing so his jaw dropped and the crowd sensed that something significant had been said as they hushed and when the man finally responded to his credit, he said he wasn't aware of that and thanked us for trying to save his brothers. So often the police get bad press but when you look at the detail and the facts, there's often a different story to be told. Not always, but a lot of the time. What a mad week that was but one that put our training and resolve into practice.

Wisdom/Reflection
- Things aren't always as they seem. Get the facts
- The power is often in the pause
- Look after your people and they will look after you
- Lead with courage and wisdom and all will be well
- Go at the pace of the slowest person
- Be ruthless with your enemy and take ground where you can. But remember love always wins!

28.

Chemo and all that Jazz

Back home I'm not even sure the girls knew what dad was dealing with. Emma was a great firewall that told the girls what they needed to know and, despite what she was going through with adjusting to living with cancer, she was a real trooper who I saw a different side to. She graciously endured the recovery from the mastectomy and the relentless chemo and radiotherapy. I hadn't thought about my family over the last week as my mind was on the job in hand and I was always acutely aware that my decision-making would literally affect the lives of both my officers and the public. The nagging persistent concern was around Emma's health. I so wanted her to be well and for this all to be a bad dream. But it wasn't and, in earthly terms, I could lose my wife and we weren't even 50 yet. I wanted to retire and for us to travel and grow old together, enjoying watching our girls have families of their own. To dote on and love our grandchildren, watching them grow and make their way in life.

Chemo appointments at Good Hope Hospital were a regular feature in our routine now. To begin with I accompanied Emma, but it took all my resolve as I found the whole experience to be emotionally draining and depressing. Although it's a place where patients are having treatment to make them better, I felt a heaviness there almost of resignation. The nurses and other hospital staff were great and were very positive and friendly, but even still there was this underlying feeling of fear and hopelessness.

This may have just been my perspective, but nonetheless it's how I felt which made me feel guilty as perhaps I should have put my feelings aside for Emma's sake. But I was learning that the role of carer is sacrificial but all too often carers neglect their own needs because they should be caring rather than thinking about themselves. I slowly learned that this approach is unwise and as a carer it can be a long road which can erode your needs which can cultivate bitterness and resentment if the carer becomes exhausted both emotionally and physically.

Emma could see that I was struggling sitting amongst people that looked very poorly, attached to machines that were pumping poison into their veins in an attempt to kill cancer cells. She insisted that I dropped her off at the ward and then collected her when the treatment was complete. Emma was so cheery and used the chemo appointments as an opportunity to chat with other patients to get to know them and their story. Emma saw it as a necessary process to lengthen her life so she could enjoy as much time with her family as possible.

Emma was always well turned out with perfect makeup and colour-coordinated clothing, although saying that, I always used to laugh when she smiled and had lipstick on her top front teeth. It was a family joke to see if mum had wiped the lipstick off her teeth before going out. The chemo and the medication had an impact on her body, and she would often get upset at how she looked and felt. This was heartbreaking to see as it's not as if we could exercise together as the treatment wiped Emma out, in terms of energy levels. I just wanted to take it all away and God knows on several occasions I'd plead with God to transfer everything that Emma was suffering to me. This was an emotional response, and I knew that this was Emma's cross to bear.

I needed my mum to be here to support us, but that wasn't going to happen as she was gone and there was no one to step into her shoes. I had a sadness in my heart that intensified as every day went by because I knew that time was getting closer to Emma leaving us.

One evening I sat on a deckchair in the garden by myself, just thinking about life and it started to rain, quickly turning into a torrential downpour. It seemed to come from nowhere. I didn't get up but just sat there getting soaked, and I didn't care, nothing mattered anymore. I cried uncontrollably and it was a great sense of relief because I was trying to hold everything together. Kevin Borg was seen as this strong man of faith that had it all together and was respected in the church and community. This mask was about to fall as I started to struggle to hold things together.

I found that my threshold to stress was much lower now because I was having to juggle so many competing demands with this overarching feeling of sadness. This couldn't be contained and would soon spill into my work life too. My friends at work were very supportive but because my mask fitted well, they didn't know to what extent I was suffering.

Tipping Point

It all came to a head one evening when I was the Duty Inspector for the Birmingham North area. A disorder broke out in the town centre. I monitored from the control room hearing officers' updates on the radio. I also had two very capable sergeants at the scene. It became clear that my officers were dealing with a situation that was escalating. I put on my brown leather gloves and made towards the scene to offer my support. Most of the time I would let the sergeants sort things out because sometimes the last thing they need is a meddling Inspector. It's so important not to smother your staff and let them work things out. We knew each other well and I knew that they knew that I was monitoring and available. There comes a point where ultimately, I'm responsible and seeing the Gaffer turn up at the right time can inspire and motivate.

On arrival at the scene, I could see that there was a large crowd that the majority of the officers were trying to control. A fight had broken out and the designated officers had drawn their Tasers. This could have painful implications for the offenders.

As I observed and assessed what was going on three offenders broke away from the main crowd and approached me. I could see that they were intoxicated or in laymen's terms, drunk. I tried to communicate with them, encouraging them to leave the area and to get into a taxi. They sneered at me, and I could see that my advice was unwanted. They were in a menacing mood and circled me eyeing up my protective equipment on my belt. I sensed that this wasn't going top go well. I could feel my patience thinning and that low stress threshold was about to be breached. But right now, they were the enemy that weren't seeing sense and were starting to irritate me. This could only go one way and they were nearly at the end of my negotiation limits. They started to get closer to me pointing to my baton and CS spray. There had been occasions where officers had been assaulted and their equipment stolen. This wasn't going to be an option for them.

I appealed to their better nature on several occasions, but they weren't obliging. This could have given them the impression that I was weak as I was trying to resolve the situation peacefully. There's a proverb in the Bible that says better to take a city by peace than by force. But now the time for peace was over. I took hold of the tallest, lankiest of the three and started to pull him to the ground. The other two made towards me to help their pal. By this time, I told him that he was under arrest for a public order offence. He was struggling and if the other two had intervened I would have been in trouble.

With impeccable timing I heard a shout from the officers dealing with the crowd shout, 'Gaffer!'. Before I knew it Monkey, (not his real name!) had joined me and helped to bring the offender to the ground. The other two tried to disperse but other officers had detained them and brought them to the ground as they struggled. I got up from the ground once my offender had been cuffed and it's fair to say that I was angry because they had been given every opportunity, but now instead we would have to deal with drunken idiots that would take several of my officers off patrol, which meant the remaining officers would have to cover a busy Saturday night with fewer resources.

I looked down at the offender who was whining because the cuffs were hurting him. As I moved away, I moved him out of the way with my foot, because he was blocking my exit. Ideally, I should have moved him properly, but the red mist was still clearing at that time. All of the incident was captured on CCTV and later I would be investigated for my actions.

Over the next 12 months I would have consultations with solicitors and Federation representatives, to ensure that I had the right advice and support. This could result in criminal charges for assault and police discipline procedures at the very least. Everybody at the station knew that I was under investigation, and to the rank and file they were very supportive as they saw me as a Gaffer that got stuck in. That said, my behaviour was unacceptable, and I should have known better as a senior officer. The truth was I shouldn't have been on frontline duties. My head wasn't right, but I was determined to soldier on to my own demise. Now I was in a situation where I had a poorly wife, I may lose my job and my mental health.

Work was very supportive and knew me and my character. I wasn't a bully and had served the public faithfully throughout my career caring passionately for the vulnerable and seeking justice. Work was an escape from the demands of home life. The girls were developing and finding their way in life. They deserved a better dad at this stage of their life. I was preoccupied with Emma's health and with the ongoing investigation at work. I was also responsible for a department of investigators and all the opportunities and challenges that brought. My staff were golden and supported me during Emma's illness. In all my years of leading people, this bunch endeared my heart the most. It seemed that my vulnerability brought out the best in them. It's a balance though, as my vulnerability was in my circumstances not in my ability and they respected that.

My sergeants and I set a culture of trust and friendship. Very few took advantage of this approach, and we were better for it. Within the police there seemed to be some confusion around leadership; there were those that were in the command-and-control camp. They were the boss and that was that. Staff weren't empowered and creativity was in short supply. It was a far more transactional way of leading, that in my opinion was unnecessary.

It was almost as if this type of leader believed the answers had to come from them and only they were capable of making good decisions. As a sergeant I was like this because my only example of leadership was from my time in the army. I soon learnt that it wasn't really fit for purpose in civilian life. That said there were characteristics that did serve me well in terms of perseverance and a high threshold to adversity. As a leader you don't want to be taken advantage of and it's true that if you're seen as approachable and nice, some will take advantage of that. Because of this some leaders don't take the risk of empowering and trusting staff. My view and experience is that it's worth the risk.

I had a good routine at work, cycling to work and then running the department working office hours with weekends off. I believe that this was a gift from God as it would have made life far more difficult if I was working shifts over the other side of the city. If Emma needed me I was a couple of miles away so this gave her peace of mind.

As the girls grew older, rightly so, they became more opinionated and at times pushed the boundaries and with my lowered threshold to stress sometimes they would see the worst in me. My experience with my own father was that when he was speaking, I would stay quiet and listen and there wasn't the option to disagree. What he said was final and, woe betide me, if I deviated from his instruction. Looking back, I knew where I stood and I respected my dad for that. Did it empower me at that stage of my development? No, it didn't, but I personally believe that when you're young you need direction and too much choice is confusing and unhelpful.

In school, the girls were taught to question in order to understand. This wasn't always welcome when I was asking them to complete a chore like putting their clothes away. It wasn't open for discussion and having asked on three separate occasions the fourth was a raised voice possibly even a shout in frustration that they hadn't complied. My eldest daughter called me a control freak, which I would probably agree with because as a parent you have to have a degree of control that lessens as our children become more independent. I used to feel awful when it got to the stage of confrontation, particularly with Hannah as I was acutely aware that I was supposed to be a good example of a man, particularly a man that followed Jesus.

It was the defiance and the sometimes arrogance that they knew best in a given situation. Most of mine and Emma's conversations lying in bed prior to going to sleep were about the girls and their development. We cared passionately about them and helping them to find their purpose. Emma knew how frustrated I used to get, and she was the ointment on my wound. I found parenting teenagers extremely challenging and concede that I probably wasn't the best father of three girls. They were deeply loved by me, and I was immensely proud of them all, but when we sparked it was horrible and I often said things that were hurtful, probably because I was hurt. Hurting people hurt people. My relationship with the girls was always in my prayers as I wanted to get on with them and be that dad that my girls would love, adore and respect. How on earth would I get on if Emma was to die. Emma was the fragrance in our family and without it I feared I would lose the balance and hurt the girls even more.

The girls didn't appreciate what Emma and I were going through and perhaps they didn't need to. But I know I wasn't at my best and at times found them incredibly selfish, but I guess I probably was at their age too. We see life through a different lens when we're young with very few responsibilities. I needed someone to talk to and, thankfully, I found that through a counsellor that West Midlands Police provided for me. This was a great outlet for me because I could voice exactly how I felt without the fear of upsetting anyone. I enjoyed the sessions but oddly dreaded them at the same time because it meant I had to think and voice how I was feeling. That said, it helped me to order my thoughts and take on the advice from my counsellor.

Emma remained on one particular chemotherapy treatment for some time, and it suited her, causing minimal side effects but at one oncology appointment we discovered that it was reducing in effectiveness, as the tumour markers in Emma's blood elevated. This meant trying to find an alternative chemo treatment that could continue to be effective. This was always a risk because if the body didn't respond then it could cause all sorts of problems. Thankfully, our oncologist was very knowledgeable and was familiar with the most up-to-date treatments.

Emma was ultra-sensitive, perhaps paranoid about any irregularities in her body, and rightly so, as she had become so attuned to the slightest variation in how she felt. I could sense that Emma was concerned about a pain that she felt in her chest area and so we played safe and booked an appointment to get it checked at the Breast Cancer Clinic. We spoke with the nurse, and she tried to reassure us that it was probably scar tissue issues rather than anything sinister. She intended to reassure us and send us on our way, but I insisted that Emma be scanned, and a full check be conducted as we got a bad feeling about this latest development. The nurse tried again to reassure us, and I bluntly requested to see our consultant. It was an awkward moment but, although the nurse was friendly and well meaning, we weren't happy with the level of care at that moment. She left the room to speak to the consultant and returned saying that the consultant had agreed to all the tests and scans that we had asked for.

Soon after we returned to the breast clinic to receive the results of the recent tests where we discovered that the pain that Emma was feeling was indeed a secondary cancer site. We were devastated but numb. For four years Emma had endured various treatments and medication that gave her a reasonable quality of life, which we were grateful for but now this was next level. Although I was ever the optimist, the police conditioned me into being a realist too. Bad things happen to good people, and the world keeps turning and people get on with their lives. Wrongly, I wanted to know timescales and what I needed to do to prepare myself and the girls. Why did I always feel that I needed a plan? What was my plan B going to be? There was no plan, never mind plan B. I started to zero everything in to just focusing on the present. It was like my hard drive was full and anything else would just spill over into emotion and frustration.

I started to exercise more, taking on several charity bike rides to raise money for breast Friends who supported us immensely as a local charity helping Breast Cancer sufferers. They provided us with a cleaner and somebody that took away our ironing and returned it crease free.

Wisdom/Reflection
- *Being angry in front of your children will impact on their emotional health. They won't forget*
- *Loss or the threat of loss will make you over critical and over sensitive*
- *Consult with a trusted source when making important decisions in a time of heightened stress*
- *Be honest with God about how you are feeling and take strength and hope from reading and inhabiting the promises in scripture*
- *The devil will take advantage of your situation and ultimately wants to kill, steal and destroy*
- *Remember the fundamentals – eat well, exercise, time alone, sleep and laugh when you can*
- *Sounds strange but take time to sing every day. If you're a Christian, then sing songs of praise and thanksgiving*

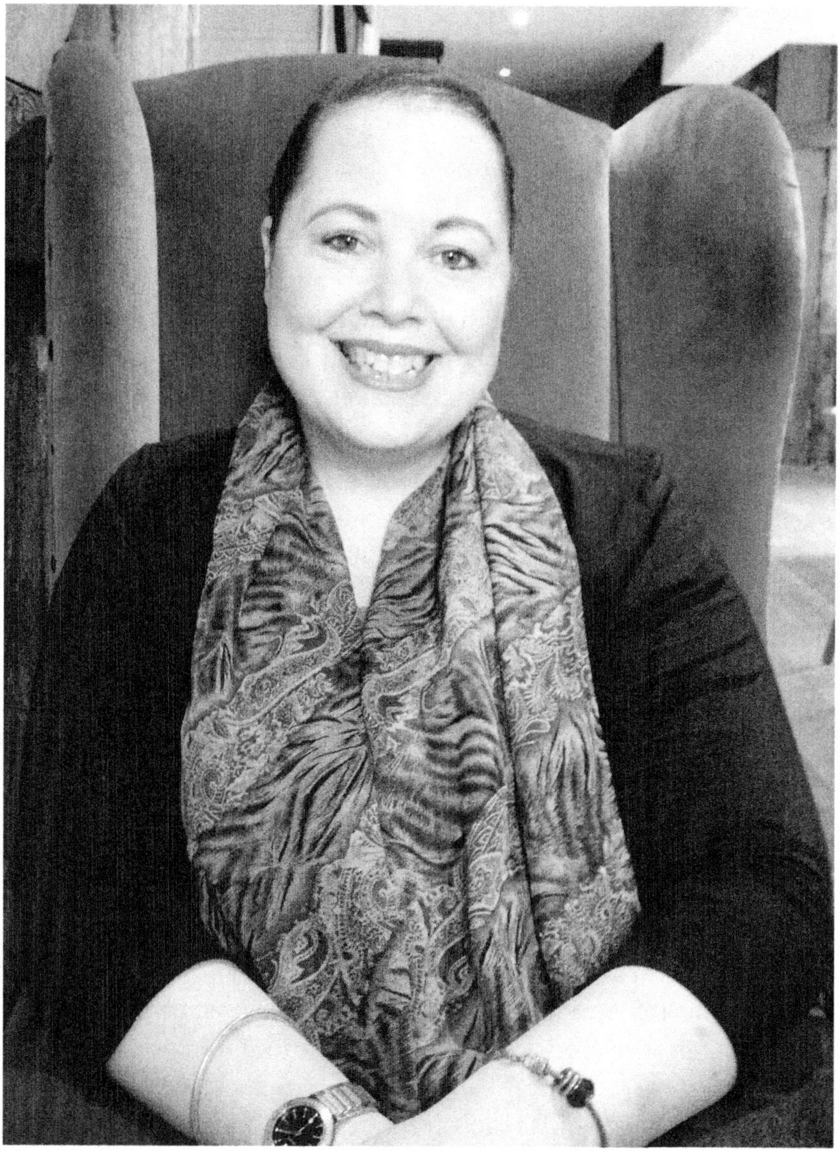

29.
Love, Hope and Charity

Our good friends Carl and Yvonne were on a similar journey, as Yvonne had been diagnosed with breast cancer around the same time as Emma. Carl was a mountain biking buddy and me, him and some others used to meet up to ride. We decided to ride the coast-to-coast ride off-road on mountain bikes. This was a tough challenge as invariably off-road riding is more arduous and technical than road riding. I will never forget having to carry our bikes on our back up Black Sail Pass, in the Lake District.

I had the Satmap navigation unit as it was my job to get us to the right places at the right time. Being the navigator was quite stressful as, if I got it wrong, it meant more riding with limited daylight. At the top of one mountain, I sensed a real feeling of God's awesomeness in creation. The view was spectacular, and as we stood silent taking the view in, I sensed a special moment so I asked the guys whether they minded saying a prayer to give thanks for such a beautiful view and for God keeping us safe so far. Not everyone in the team were believers so it was very gracious of them to agree.

After I had prayed, I found myself getting quite emotional so put my head down and started to walk up the trail. The others were silent and followed suit. By now I was blubbering and crying uncontrollably trying to increase the distance between me and the next rider as I didn't want them to hear or see me in this state. Why I was so emotional, I could only put down to it being the presence of God. He met us on the mountain.

When we arrived at the hostel accommodation that night, I felt led to share how being on top of the mountain had affected me emotionally. To my surprise, Carl responded by sharing that he too was in tears with emotion. Scott then looked up and shared that he was brought to tears too. Carl would later attend an Alpha course and, as a result, decided to follow Jesus too. There were a number of navigation faux pas, one was when I took us across a field that eventually meant we had to wade across a river to get back on track. The other was when we were at the top of a mountain and the mist was thick and it was very cold, so we didn't want to be stationary for too long as very quickly the sweat on our bodies would freeze and getting hypothermia became a risk and reality.

The pressure was on me because we weren't on track, this was partly due to the signal being intermittent to the navigation unit. I had a paper map as a backup, but the SatMap was so convenient, so I persevered with it. I could feel the mood changing because the guys were getting cold. Carl and I said we'd explore to see if the right trail was nearby.

Visibility was poor and even just being ten metres away meant the guys couldn't see us. This was a bit scary because we were on our own in inclement weather. We descended about ten metres, and I stood looking down at the SatMap. I then looked up to heaven and prayed, Please Lord guide us back to the path. We were desperate and as I looked back down at the SatMap, we had a signal and as the mist started to clear as we stood there, the trail appeared about two footsteps away! We called the others down to our position and we were on our way again. We all completed the challenge safely, finishing at St Bees on the east coast. As a team, we built a memory to last a lifetime as well as raising lots of money for local cancer charities.

Another memorable ride was Barmouth to Great Yarmouth which amounted to riding 300 miles in under 24 hours. A team of us, who I class as brothers, committed to training and riding the challenge together under the tremendous banner of the Boldmere Bullets, our local cycling club. We raised over £30,000 and it became quite a community event. The purpose of the ride was to raise funds for our local breast cancer charity called Breast Friends.

Thankfully, we had a very supportive support team, who were responsible for the smoothness of the operation, without whom we would have struggled greatly. It wasn't about just being fit enough to complete the 300 miles, it was about understanding energy management and being efficient with it. Knowing how and when to feed your body so that you don't go into deficit and 'bonk' which in cycling terms means running out of energy because you've let the tank run dry, either by lack of fluids or food.

All the riders were strong and experienced but only one of us had ridden this sort of distance before. The focus of the ride was Emma as I hatched the idea from a need of having to do something. I couldn't fix Emma's cancer, but I could raise money for a charity that was helping us as a family. We had a lot of support from businesses including my brother Martin's company MTCSS. We also had a sports nutrition company provide us with energy products that were gratefully received. One of the products they supplied was an energy gel with a massive dose of caffeine included. Caffeine is probably the only legal stimulant that aids concentration and lessens fatigue and pain. We were keen to try them out and on one of our big training rides (200 miles) we tried them out. We ate as we were riding, storing the gels and energy bars in our jersey rear pockets. As we were riding, I heard one of the guys make a sound like a steam train sounding its hooter. Everyone wondered what had caused the outburst and it soon became apparent that the caffeine gels were the cause of the reaction. Apparently, on tearing the opening tab in order to swallow the contents the sensation felt initially like swallowing a mouthful of Calor Gas before the gel slid down into your mouth. The sensation made each rider look like they were chewing a wasp as they struggled to swallow the thick gel whilst riding. We all experienced the delights of the Calor Gas gel, as they were known for the rest of the ride. That said, they did the trick and did indeed keep us awake, often for longer than we would have liked!

On the day of the ride, everything went like clockwork. The whole membership of the club turned out to see us off, and even included motorbike outriders as we did a tour of Sutton Coldfield town centre. Then we loaded the bikes up and made for Barmouth in Wales.

We were up early to make the most of every second of available daylight, in order to minimise the amount of time we would be riding in the dark. Impressively, the Mayor of Barmouth was up early too to see us off, which we were very grateful for. All riders were very disciplined and as per our training we kept our heart rate in zone 2, which means its reasonably low intensity and would encourage our bodies to burn fat before sugar, which is far more efficient meaning we had glycogen reserves for hills and more challenging sections of the route. The key was to drip feed your body with energy so that it never went into deficit.

The halfway point was Sutton Coldfield, where a local community-minded hotel, called Moor Hall, fed and watered the team. This was where over a hundred people, mainly family and friends, congregated to cheer us on. A whole section of this luxurious hotel had been set aside for us with a buffet laid on that was fit for a king ... or queen. It also served as a convenient point to rearrange any kit or bike issues that had developed having ridden from Wales for a number of hours.

I had a raging toothache and, as we were nearing the stop at Moor Hall, I called a friend who was a dentist and asked if there was anything he could do to help. He met me at Moor Hall and ushered me to the back seat of his car where he opened a case and took out a syringe, packed with some type of pain killer. He looked at me, as only a doctor or dentist could, and told me that this was highly irregular and not in line with regulations. I thanked him very much and gave him a grateful nod and then asked him to get on with it as I was in a lot of pain! I was so grateful for him taking this pragmatic approach. I would have visited him in prison if it had come to that.

Throughout the whole ride I think we only had a couple of mechanical problems, one of which was a puncture. It was now in the early hours of the morning and everyone was feeling the fatigue despite having consumed and probably overdosed on the caffeine Calor Gas gels. As we waited for the support team to fix the puncture, I needed a pee so just did it where I stood. After relieving myself I was joined by Si Barry who decided to lie down on the pavement where I had just urinated. I was too tired to warn him as he lay on his back in my pee. At this stage of the ride, it didn't really matter, but it did make us chuckle after the ride when I told him.

We finished the ride within the 24 hours arriving in Great Yarmouth to the cheer of some friends and family, as well as the Lord Mayor and his entourage. As we rode across the main seafront road in a line it was quite emotional as all the training and planning had paid off. It reminded me of the 5Ps that my days in the army had hammered into me. Preparation and

Planning Prevents Piss Poor Performance!

Bacon and sausage baps were laid on by the Lord Mayor and were gratefully received, although we couldn't stomach too much food as we had constantly been topping ourselves up. The journey back to Sutton Coldfield was one of a short period of euphoria followed by snoring and grunting, with the constant toxic farting from Gibbo, as he seemed to be the biggest consumer of the Calor Gas gels.

Wisdom/Reflection
- *Focus on channelling your energy into doing something that will benefit others and give you a goal as well*
- *Doing something positive with others helps your mindset and stimulates the wellbeing chemicals in your body*
- *Give others the opportunity to support you in a way that they feel comfortable. It encourages community*
- *Be gracious in receiving from others. There will be plenty of opportunity for you to give. This is your season of receiving*
- *Don't look at the whole challenge, break it down into manageable steps*

Coast to Coast Monster Mountain Bike challenge to raise funds

Team 300 - Great Yarmouth cycle challenge in under 24 hours

30.
The moment of Truth

The police investigation into my disciplinary case was coming to a conclusion. It had been a rollercoaster of a time with my emotions and no doubt this had impacted on the family. Either way I just wanted it to be over, but I was saddened that I had let myself down so close to the end of my career. I really wasn't sure what the outcome was going to be.

Thankfully, I had the best Federation rep I could hope for. Steve was so supportive and knowledgeable and was a family friend too that knew our situation with Emma's health. I couldn't imagine me having a criminal record for assault. This would affect my future and my family's future. I felt ashamed and disappointed with myself.

Despite being a Christian, there were consequences for my actions and why should I be treated any different? Wrong is wrong. A lady at church who knew our situation casually prophesied and told me in the middle of another conversation that I would be ok, but I would be punished. She then changed the subject, and I took away what she said to me. It seemed like a God thing and was quite odd at the time. It was if God slipped into our conversation with his message and then slipped out again.

I deserved to be punished but I was hoping not too harshly and counting on my exemplary record of conduct before this incident. I had met with Steve my Fed rep on several occasions and he checked on how I was feeling and updated me with the latest developments of my case. Steve was, in the main, optimistic but as we got closer to my hearing, I noticed he was concerned about the outcome, mainly because the evidence consisted of CCTV and the testimony of the complainant. I had accepted that this could be a bad outcome for me, but I had told God about how I felt and had entrusted my future to Him.

I got to the stage where I just didn't care anymore, because I couldn't control the situation and the outcome was unknown. I did have thoughts though about what I would do for a job to earn an income? Who would want to employ me if I had a criminal record? I still had fleeting thoughts of suicide when I was at my lowest, but I couldn't do it, not because of the thought of death, it was more about how could I take my life that God had given me. How could I take my life when Emma was fighting for hers? What about the impact on the girls, my friends and extended family? I always think about the people who find you once you're gone. It would leave a dark mark on the soul of everyone that was close to me. Despite this rational thinking there were times when those voices screamed: 'Do it!'. It was frightening how real they were, but as soon as I whispered to myself: 'Jesus help!' the voices immediately stopped.

I felt that my true north, in terms of where my life was heading was interrupted, even corrupted. It was as if my character was being unpicked. My relationship with my eldest daughter Hannah was fragile. She was growing up and seeing all her dad's imperfections, making her mind up that I wasn't very nice. I was so up and down that they would sometimes be on tenterhooks wondering what mood dad was going to be in when he got home from work.

I can remember sitting down at the dinner table having said grace before we ate as a family and then the slightest comment that I felt was out of place, caused me to slam my fist down on the table and raise my voice. I know that this frightened the girls, and I so didn't want to scar their minds and hearts with this aggressive memory. And there were others and it's a time in my life that deeply saddened me because I knew that my behaviour had a negative impact on them. This would compound how I felt about myself and I would feel a strong sense of failure.

I was supposed to be a role model of how a man should be, particularly a man that was trying to imitate his God, with the example of how Jesus told us to live. This just added another layer of guilt, and the truth is that I loathed myself. Thankfully, Emma never gave up on me and was my comfort and my support, that always had a smile. She saw the best in me and loved me deeply, despite my behaviour towards her and the girls.

The day came when I had to attend Lloyd House, Police Headquarters. My solicitor met me in the interview room, where we had our pre-interview chat.

I was going to be interviewed by officers from the Professional Standards Department. They deal with all complaints against Police. A Detective Chief Inspector and a Detective Constable would be interviewing me. We went over the facts of the case and then waited for the interviewing officers to arrive. I was remarkably calm, because for me it was about telling the truth and leaving the rest to God. Lying was never an option for me. My dad taught me that honesty was always the best policy, and my Heavenly Father taught me that he wouldn't bless me outside of the truth.

The interviewing officers arrived and introduced themselves. They sat opposite me and my solicitor. They opened their blue books preparing to make notes and prepared to record the interview. So, this was it. My life could change in the next hour.

My solicitor leaned forward before the formal interview started and asked the interviewing officers when the offence had occurred. I thought this was odd as he had all the papers that contained the facts. I stayed quiet and let him do his thing. The officers shuffled their papers to find the information and confirmed that the offence occurred in April. My solicitor nodded his head thoughtfully and then rested back in his chair, looking at the interviewing officers, he informed them that the offence of common assault had a limitation of proceedings of six months. It was now November; the six months had expired. The interviewing officers looked at each other and you could feel the awkwardness as they checked their papers and then left the room to consult.

I looked at my solicitor and he told me that if this was the case then I would not face any criminal charges. The likelihood was that I would still be punished according to the police disciplinary regulations. The interviewing officers returned confirming that the criminal charges would be dropped but I would still be interviewed due to my misconduct. The interview was quite straight-forward and they thanked me for my honesty. Why did my case get unnoticed and expire in terms of criminal conduct? I don't know. The reality of the situation was that they had a very large caseload and some things got missed. Some believed that the job was looking after me. That in my experience wasn't the case as the department was scrutinised heavily by various regulatory bodies and that course of action would have got somebody the sack. It seemed that I was under God's mercy and Michelle's word was indeed accurate. I would be punished and received a written warning for my actions.

Wisdom/Reflection
- *You are human, you are going to make mistakes*
- *Tell the truth and be accountable for your actions, it will pay off in the end*
- *Humble yourself when you're in the wrong, try and put it right, then move on*
- *Fear God more than people. What you do now will impact you in eternity*

31.
On the Home Straight
– Retirement

My time was drawing near to retirement and my time at work was sporadic as Emma's health started to deteriorate. I was so grateful to my bosses that understood and empathised with my situation. They provided me with a counsellor that I visited on a weekly basis. This helped me offload without burdening Emma and the girls.

I think I became easier to live with following the outcome of my case. The relief was tangible in my body, and I felt a weight lifted off my soul. My main focus was Emma and making her life as comfortable as possible. I knew my time with Emma was ticking by and I felt an urgency in my spirit to say everything that needed to be said and for me to hug her and hold her as much as I could. Because the day would come when she would be gone and I would never be able to hold her again or have a conversation. Emma was my mentor in many ways and looked at things differently which often helped me learn about myself, particularly the way I behaved sometimes. She would sometimes say: 'Kev, God's going to have to show you because you're not listening to me!'. That approach was very effective because invariably I would see her point of view and agree, unfortunately though, it was usually a couple of days later. Emma was very patient with me, but it was as if God had given her special insight into how to get the best out of me. She was happy to let me lead the family most of the time and was the epitome of humility. She always had a smile that was genuine and disarming. I'm convinced that Emma was put on this earth to help mould me into the person that God wanted me to be.

As the girls got older Emma was the perfect confidant for them as well as a realistic role model that had good practical advice for being a woman with a Christian faith in today's world.

Emma had a great sense of humour and invariably the conversation would turn to toilet humour which the girls loved, and we would all end up howling either about passing wind or very large poos. The 'F' word was banned in our home, and we were quite strict with slang. The F word being fart. It made it even funnier when they said the word and then ran up the stairs to avoid my rebuke.

From the outside looking at our Christian lifestyle may have seemed a little over the top for some, even some of our church friends. But we knew that the way we were following was the narrow way and not many take it. Being a man that has worked under orders for the majority of my working life, I applied the same principle to how we lived out biblical truths. It's not everyone's cup of tea, I accept, but I figured that if I was in then I wanted to do my best to follow wholeheartedly where I could, with His guidance and strength.

As the girls got older, I think that their experience of the world was a stark contrast to how me and Emma practiced our faith. We tried to apply biblical truths to everyday life, but there was no way round it being the least popular way to live in a progressive society, where the focus was on your truth, not THE truth. As I write this, I know it sounds conceited and arrogant, but this is the truth that we believe. Jesus said that He was the way, the truth and the life and that no one came to the Father except through him. I love Jesus' straight talking. There's no mix up in what he says, no ambiguity as I see it. Emma and I had seen God work in amazing, miraculous ways at times. We'd witnessed miraculous healings. We'd seen people delivered from evil spirits. We'd witnessed people giving their lives over to Christ for the first time, experiencing His love, peace and forgiveness. God had often guided us through His word and through people that had prophetic words for us that guided, encouraged and on occasion warned us. Emma used to get pictures and have dreams that had prophetic meaning. She would often speak into people's lives with words of knowledge that only God could have provided. Emma was an unashamed Jesus follower that had a very warm way of relating her faith, woven into who she was, making it palatable for those that listened.

So despite all of our challenges and troubles, we trusted in Jesus. After all, if he was who he said he was, who else was there to trust?

I was known at work for being a Christian and I always tried to relate my faith to those around me by my behaviour before my words. My people knew I cared about them, and I was known for my mantra 'to do the right thing'. What would you want to happen for your loved ones? It was known as the loved one's test. This helped my people to pause and think, rather than go through a process that would be correct but not necessarily the right thing at the right time.

Towards the end of my career in the Police I felt that I had found my sweet spot, in terms of leadership.

Wisdom was my greatest asset when leading a large department. Little did I know when I asked the Lord for wisdom all those years ago that it would be my main stay in life. I learnt to ask questions rather than jump in with a decision. Gathering all the available information and experts available to help me make the right decision. That said, there were times when dynamic decisions needed to be made and I made them. There's a time to be consultative and there are times where, as the leader, you make the call. My experience was that you needed to strike a balance. I watched some leaders try to be all things to everyone, trying to remain as popular as possible which sometimes skewed their decision-making ability.

Getting too familiar with members of staff often compromises leaders when tough decisions need to be made affecting that person. Familiarity can breed contempt. I always kept an air of mystery, not revealing everything about myself. I had levels of trust, and some had more of my trust than others. Conversely, I have watched leaders try to lead, lacking empathy and self-serving. The police was famous for promotion chasers, that would be seconded to departments to gain the necessary experience to then move on to their next promotion board. Ticking boxes for the promotion application form became a preoccupation for some. Despite climbing the ranks, they didn't have a connection with their people, but I honestly think they were blind to that and only had their prize in sight.

I used to make sure that every morning I had what I called micro conversations with staff. It usually involved me putting the kettle on and making everybody a brew, BUT I only did this on average once a month. Too much of a good thing from the Gaffer can be a bad thing, for me!

There were 70 investigators, thankfully, not all of them took me up on the offer and invariably one of them would come and help me to score some brownie points. My sergeants would be treated to a coffee away from the office, for a check-in. Not necessarily about work but more about us, taking time to build our relationship, which built trust and friendship. I genuinely cared about my people, and I think I balanced the needs of the organisation and the individual quite well. I could be ruthless and would deal with bad behaviour promptly, but as a very experienced HR manager once advised me; get ruthless with the issue and supportive of the person.

The building of trust and relationships paid dividends as Emma's illness progressed. The need for me to have time off was becoming more frequent, but true to form my department put into practice one of our values; to work to the same standard whether the Boss was there or not. I was immensely proud of how my people performed. They cared and it showed, both for each other and the public. I was particularly moved and honoured by my sergeants who not only kept the ship moving but steered it in the right direction too. To this day we remain friends, and we meet regularly to discuss the demise of policing over a beer.

Hannah and Lydia, our two eldest girls, were starting to distil as young adults what mattered to them in life. Both had a heart to tackle injustice. Lydia from an early age used to role play having her own orphanage. She used to draw pictures of what it would look like and how she would look after the children. Lydia would go on to lead a project that she initiated called the Carey Project. She and two others travelled over to Greece to help in the tented refugee camps, serving the migrants that had risked their lives crossing the sea in crowded dinghies. They ministered to the people through dance, art, and drama. Significant memories were made. Lydia later went on to caring for Dementia patients, where she learnt how to be the hands and feet of Jesus in difficult circumstances. Currently, she works with a church organisation, serving the homeless. My little Lark flew high and was realising her purpose.

Hannah had a tough time during her time at sixth form. A horrible time of being bullied that upset Emma and I greatly. It's a real dilemma knowing what to leave your children to resolve and when to step in. Hannah is an achiever and didn't want to allow the way she was being treated sway her off her plan. The bullying intensified and became extremely nasty, so I stepped in and spoke with the school. The outcome was that Hannah left and her experience would later be used for the power of good to create Cherished, an organisation that would support girls around the city of Birmingham and beyond.

As a registered charity, the work of Cherished has received national attention and received numerous awards. Hannah's work has progressed now to support boys too. Both girls have become women that have put their faith into action. Emma and I watched with adoration as they took risks and made themselves vulnerable moving forward despite difficulties and challenges.

Hannah was soon to become a mother, giving birth to our first grandchild, Abel James Simnett. Emma and I were there shortly after the birth and we felt an incredible surge of thankfulness and joy as our daughter held her little boy. We would get to spend time with Abel and delight in his beautiful smile and gurgling. I was so grateful that Emma got to see her first grandchild and spend precious moments with him, whilst she could.

Both Lydia and Hannah provided a sure-footed foundation for their little sister Connie, who looked up to them. Connie and I would venture out into Birmingham City Centre at 04:00 hours early on Christmas Day. Connie wanted her own story to tell so I provided it by taking Christmas gifts to those sleeping on the streets. I think it was a real eye opener for Connie, as well as being quite scary for her. That's where she saw the vulnerability of the homeless who were very grateful for our Christmas visit, where we left them small gifts to open.

I had exposed the girls to the realities of life very early on. I wanted them to get a glimpse of the extent pf the problem. This would light a fire within them that would never go out. A fierce fire to fight injustice but also to bring the love of Jesus in that situation, to transform and bring renewal. So, there's the practical doing but also a reliance on the supernatural, which is where the healing of the soul takes place. When hearts change so does the landscape.

Over time our visits to the Oncology Department became more intense as we looked for alternative chemo treatments once the current one had run its course and become ineffective. I felt that our time with Emma was slipping away, and I often had a panic inside, but had learnt to mask it well. It was difficult for the oncologist because we were attending full of emotions of hope, fear, anxiety, irritation to name but a few. We appreciated that they had many patients to see each week and we were one of many.

On occasions our oncologist was quite matter of fact despite the news not being good. I was particularly stressed because I sensed this was going to be a negative appointment in terms of the challenges we were about to face. As she gave us our options there was very little eye contact, and it was as if I wasn't in the room. I get the fact that Emma was the patient, but we were both on this journey. After shuffling her papers, I leaned forward and said to her that this was my one and only wife and I needed everything to be done to help her. It was an emotional outburst and well meant but probably not helpful. That said she could see my well-meant intentions and an extra measure of diligence was added from that appointment onwards.

A lot of people struggle with difficult conversations. I don't. They are a great opportunity for things to change and for learning to be gleaned by both parties. The key is to be in control of your emotions and to concentrate on the facts. So many I coach and observe don't ask enough questions. In doing so they would gather insights that might change their view or adjust their approach.

Many will avoid the issue and hope it goes away yet still harbour the bad feeling. They think this is a viable solution, but my experience is that people leak (not literally) their true feelings. They are written in their eyes and their non-verbal communication. It's all about timing and delivery; when to make the approach, in the right environment and then visualising how you would like the interaction to go. What questions will you ask? How will you set the tone without making the other person feel defensive or inferior? Sometimes the intensity on our face can be intimidating, and we may not even be aware of it.

I often look in the mirror to practice facial expressions. The truth is sometimes we need to lighten up and smile a bit more. Mirroring behaviour so as the other person is gesturing to broker agreement, we might nod encouragingly in a way that intimates that you're looking for agreement too. Really listening and hearing what they are saying is critical because if people feel heard they are more likely to trust you. All of this takes practice, and you have to inhabit it. Despite being trained and coaching this stuff, I struggle to live it with those closest to me and that's the case with a lot of people. This is because those closest to us know how to press our buttons that are going to trigger the responses we're not proud of.

Wisdom/Reflection

- *Not all distractions are beneficial we naturally avoid pain*
- *Pain lets us know we're alive and is a necessary part of our human experience*
- *Knowing your eternal destination is a comfort but the panic of losing someone will always be present*
- *Transition to a new phase of life can be daunting. Having a plan helps especially when you've committed it to The Lord. He promises to direct our steps*
- *The journey leading to end-of-life care will try to rack you with fear, sadness and hopelessness. This is where the rubber hits the road with your faith and you've got to hold tight and trust*

Ceremony when I received my long service good conduct medal - both of our Dads and Connie

Me feeling strong on the bike - UCI Gran Fondo TOC

32.
The new normal family life

With the girls, my easiest trigger to pull was when I didn't feel listened to and disrespected through disobedience. It brought the worst out in me, and I often struggled to apologise because my rationale was that none of this would have happened, if you had done what you were asked to do the first time, not the fourth.

Discipline nowadays is seen as abuse by many, and it is a fine line I accept. Coming from a default of being a loving father that would do anything for his children balances those times when the discipline has been swift. There were times when I acted out of my anger that sometimes spilled over into smacking. This I regret and as I got older and more enlightened in alternative ways to approach stressful family situations, these flare ups were less frequent. Connie's upbringing was very different to Lydia and Hannah's. They came as a pair and Em and I practiced on them. But it was also about the time of life. When we had Connie, financially we were better off because I had progressed in the police and generally, we had grown as people and adjusted our approach from where we had not got it quite right with Lydia and Hannah.

During the last few months of Emma's illness, the girls responded differently. Lydia who some would view as the most delicate and gentle of the three, really stepped up to facing the challenge of her mum being poorly head on. She helped me care for Emma and made time to collect memories. Connie spent a lot of her time in her room, virtually talking to friends, creating things to look forward to. I think this was avoidance behaviour, which was totally understandable. Hannah was navigating married life and being a parent, having given birth to her first son Abel James. Hannah found it difficult to watch the deterioration of her mum and I don't remember her being around that much but that was understandable.

I continued to get a lot of miles in on the bike and my relationship with Jesus was in a season of him wanting me to be still as he led me into still green pastures. It was almost as if he was saying rest because you're going to need it. Quietly in my souls I considered myself to have been given the gift of wisdom after asking for it all those years ago. Little did I know how my future actions would seem everything but wise.

I had simplified my life and cut out anything that was too complicated. That included people who routinely had a negative mindset. In normal circumstances, I would be happy to accommodate most situations but where I was at and where we were as a family, I couldn't take on any extra baggage. I tried to avoid people because I didn't want to give an update on how things were. I know that some people were well-meaning and were praying for us as a family, but there were some that were just being nosey.

My resilience levels were low, and I noticed that my threshold to routine challenges had lowered. I shied away from anything that would draw on my energy levels both emotionally and physically. I started to think more of the future in practical terms; would I continue to live in our family home when Emma was gone? Would I marry again? How would I support the girls? Would I be well enough to continue working? What would the funeral arrangements look like? Who could help with all the admin that has to be addressed when someone dies? These were all issues that would become a reality sooner than I thought.

The turning point in Emma's health started at the end of May 2018. Lydia had literally returned from a time in Atlanta, U.S. It was as if Emma was waiting for her to return before she started to deteriorate. That night at 02:00 hours we received a call from Good Hope Hospital, asking Emma to attend the hospital asap as recent tests had shown that she had blood clots in her lungs, and it could be fatal.

I looked over at Emma whilst she was taking in the information on the phone and through squinted eyes wondered why this couldn't wait until a more decent hour. Presumably someone was checking through test results through the night. Well, if it was life-threatening then, of course, we would go. Emma was given some medication and she was discharged within a couple of hours. The visit to the hospital seemed to add another layer of sadness as this new development squeezed more sand out of the hourglass and would be the beginning of the end.

Emma was still cheery and tried to function as normally as possible, to be a supportive mother and wife, but her energy levels were depleted, and she often needed to rest. When Emma rested, I went out on my bike and beasted myself to expend some energy and take my sadness out on the hills. But I found that my physical resolve was affected by how I was feeling emotionally.

My determination seemed to have been eroded and I didn't have the fight in me I used to have. Another symptom of my long-term stress was that exercise wasn't giving me the high it used to. I'm sure there's a scientific reason for this, and often I would return from a ride feeling as sad as when I started the ride.

I was conscious that I had to be there for the girls, but I soon realised that I had to be there for me too. I was struggling to carry everyone's weight and the reality of it was I probably didn't have to carry it, but my expectations of myself were that I had to hold things together in the family because soon Emma would be gone. I so wanted to get this part of the journey right as it would determine how the next leg of the journey would pan out.

These were special times, and I wanted to make sure that Christ was in the centre of this dark situation, so my faith would grow, as well as positively impact on those around me. We started calling people to prayer. Groups of friends started to come together to pray for us as a family but particularly Emma's health. The level of support we received was amazing and it was mainly church folk that created meal rotas to ensure we were fed and watered. It was just one less thing to think about as Emma's physical challenges grew.

As a family we felt the power of prayer. That didn't mean that everything was sweetness and light and we still had waves of anxiety and sadness but there was an underpinning of peace; that we were being lifted and surrounded by the prayers of the saints. Jesus prayed in the Garden of Gethsemane. Someone later told me that if you suffer without calling on Jesus to help you the suffering can last a very long time, like trying to navigate through a minefield. But with Jesus it's a lot shorter because he knows the best way through. Despite everyone's challenges in life the world keeps turning and we all manage our troubles often in isolation.

Life goes on and despite Emma being in the last season of her life, people still laughed and cried. People still got married and divorced. Babies were born and some people faded away and died. It was surreal and I often felt how insensitive the world was for not knowing our situation and feeling it like us. The reality is that everyone has a different take on a situation and why should they know what we were going through? I didn't know what they were going through. This whole situation made me over sensitive and over critical of others.

I was quite often grouchy because I had this dark cloud following me. It was like death was lingering but I refused to be engulfed by this cloud of hopelessness. In the Bible it says, oh death where is your sting, oh grave where is your victory. The words in the Bible and the promises God made were my main source of strength. Just like all those years ago when God gave me Psalm 91 before going off to war, here I was again fighting another battle, holding fast to these ancient words that were hope and power filled.

I found that things in the world were constantly changing and shifting, sometimes for my benefit and sometimes not. But, thankfully, God is the same yesterday, today and forever. He never changes so he couldn't love me any more and he couldn't love me any less and I held onto this. I had a lot of time in my mind and heart on my own. Only Jesus could join me there, whether it was two in the morning or whether I was in the middle of a forest in Wales on my mountain bike. He's omnipresent (everywhere), omniscient (all knowing). He knew exactly how I felt and because he made me, he knew exactly what I needed. The pain and anguish weren't going to be taken away. It's part of the human experience and I had to remember that all things work for the good of those who love him and are called according to his purpose. That was me so I hung onto that.

I remembered that God said he wouldn't put me through more than I could bear. The most difficult aspect about being a Christian man was learning to trust God, someone I hadn't seen physically and had only heard once audibly. Even though I had his written word it was still tough because my rational mind would intellectualise with logic rather than faith. Particularly when things were going well my self-sufficiency button would be pressed as I took hold of the reins and asked God to ride in the back.

Then, in the challenging times, I would feel that there were other people worse off than me, and my situation was down to me, so I had to fix it. This perception was distorted and did not display the Father's character. So, my true north was the Bible where I could rely on the truth of who God is and his commitment to me. It took me a long time to grasp that my performance was secondary to my reliance on the provision that Jesus made by dying for me. When we partner with the Holy Spirit, we do things together, but he supplies the power and direction. We provide the trust and obedience.

I've found that God answers in yes, no and wait and he does this when I prayerfully read his word, something relevant pops out at me and in faith I take that as direction from the Holy Spirit. The backstop is if peace doesn't accompany that direction, then I usually stop and retrace my footsteps back to the point where I thought I gained the direction.
Wait is often hard for me to abide by and on many occasions, I haven't waited and have pressed on only to have a lack of peace and for things to not turn out the way they should have, and that usually meant time and/or money wasted.

We were on the fourth type of chemo and, unfortunately, it wasn't as effective as we had hoped. Emma's tumour markers in her blood were rising and Emma was becoming more fatigued. The oncologist informed us that the cancer had spread to her ovaries and bones.

Connie was avoiding any acceptance of how poorly Emma was and that was totally understandable. She spent a lot of time in her room talking to friends on social media. This didn't sit right with me, but I was so taken up with looking after Emma I couldn't focus on Connie as I would have liked.

Emma was upstairs and, as she came downstairs, she blacked out and fell, landing awkwardly at the bottom of the stairs. I was in the front room and heard Emma fall, so I jumped up and ran to her aid. I could see Emma lying on the floor and as I watched a pool of blood formed around her head. Connie must have heard Emma fall as when I looked up, I saw the fear and horror on Connie's face as she saw her mum in such a helpless position bleeding. She looked wide-eyed and then just turned around and ran back into her room. I wanted to comfort her and reassure her, but I had to help Emma. She was unusually calm and just lay on the floor looking up at me. I think she was conscious that she didn't want to move in case she had broken a bone. Despite having seen many badly injured and dead bodies, this really hit me, and I had to draw on all my strength to not burst into tears. This was one of those occasions where I just wanted to scream in desperation because I didn't know how much more of this I could take.

I called an ambulance and thankfully it arrived promptly. Emma hadn't sustained any serious injuries, but she did have a two-inch gash to the back of her head which they managed to superglue up.

Wisdom/Reflection
- *Prolonged stress is going to adversely affect the way you react and behave, particularly towards those closest to you*
- *Approaching the loss of a loved one you are going to experience waves of sadness. Heartfelt prayer and worship were my antidote*
- *Now is when you need to take God at His word so read it and remind Him of His promises to you*
- *It's ok to be very sad and cry. It's ok to scream. It's ok to sit out in the pouring rain without a jacket. You will feel detached and life will seem surreal*
- *Take control of your thought life or it will take control of you*
- *You will naturally look to escape from your feelings, through prescription drugs, alcohol and other things. None of the above are a lasting healthy solution*
- *Surround yourself with Godly people that get you and are willing to climb this mountain with you. Stay in touch with them and meet face to face whenever possible*
- *Don't try and manage everything alone. Delegate graciously and sleep when you can. You are exhausted, or will be if you go it alone*

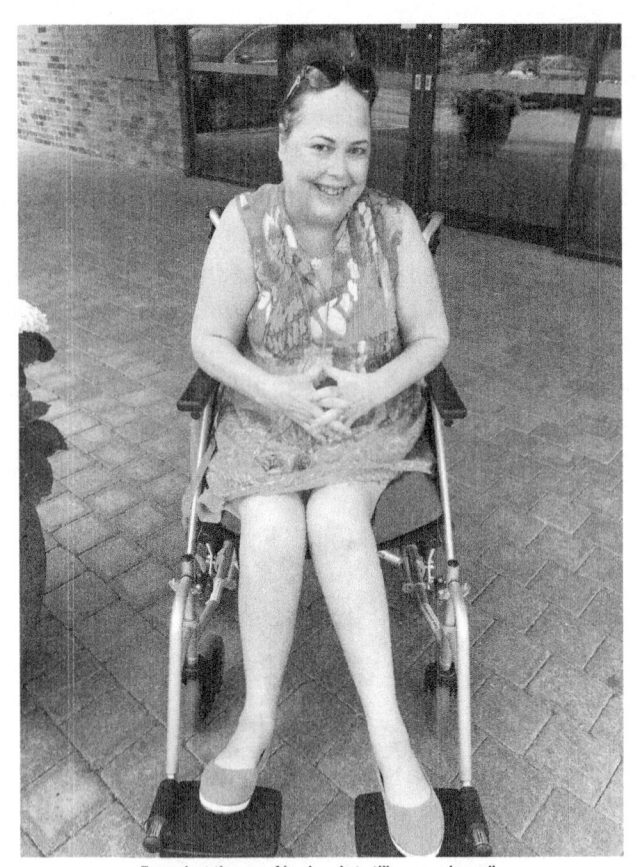

Emma lost the use of her legs but still managed a smile

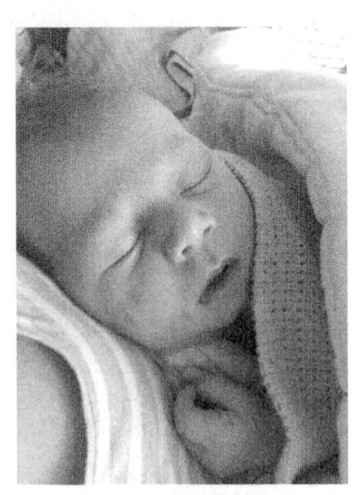

Our first grandson - Abel James

33.
Losing my Precious Emma

At our next oncology appointment, we would discover that they feared that the cancer had spread to the lining of the brain. This would explain the blackout that Emma experienced earlier.

Due to the likelihood of Emma having seizures, it was agreed that she would be admitted to the local St Giles Hospice in Whittington for them to observe her and assess her to get a better understanding of her pain management needs. This was a significant shift for us as a family. Emma's presence was no longer in our home and psychologically my mindset was that the hospice is where people go to die, and most don't get to leave.

This is in no way meant to reflect negatively on what the wonderful staff at the hospice do, as my view was partly based in ignorance. Being at the hospice, although being a very sad time, provided me with a time of respite and allowed them to really focus on Emma to get her medication right, considering the more recent diagnosis.

I didn't think the stress could get any more intense, but it had ramped up to a new level, as we entered the hospice stage. We visited Emma every day and there was a significant decline in her health. She now had to be supported by a wheelchair as she found it hard to walk, in terms of leg strength and energy levels. Emma didn't appear to be quite with it and at times seemed to be in another place. It was distressing to see, and I could see that it had dawned on the girls that we were in the final stages of caring for Emma.

I was frequently tearful and now my life had focused right in to just caring for Emma. My routine had simplified even more than before. I wasn't maintaining friendships and work was intermittent and I felt that I had lost that connection despite work being super supportive.

In some respects, I no longer felt like a husband but identified more with being Emma's carer, because most of my tasks were about functional, practical tasks. The intimacy of just hugging and being close, or a kiss didn't happen as much. Not because Emma didn't want to, it just seemed that the cancer created a gap in our behaviour. I perhaps was reluctant to get too close because I knew I was going to lose her so was trying to protect myself. With all the medication and fatigue, the times we did hug and get close were very special but also very emotional and painful.

On my way to the hospice, I found myself crying uncontrollably and, on several occasions, I found myself screaming at the top of my voice to try and almost get the pain and sadness out of me. I didn't want to live without Emma and, as a natural protector, I wanted to take her pain and her death sentence. God knows how many times I begged him to take me and leave Emma with the girls.

The bible says that His ways aren't our ways, and His thoughts aren't our thoughts. I didn't understand the whys, but I was in unknown territory, and I just knew that I had to go with this and continually take my pain to him. He was my strong place and kept me in a place where I could manage, but only just. I remember reading that you don't always have to understand to be obedient. This is counterculture but God seems to do things differently.

He tells us in the book of Proverbs not to lean on our own understanding but to acknowledge Him in all our ways.so that's what I would do. If I had to go through losing my wife then I wasn't going to waste the experience and wanted to glean every bit of understanding God more in this and for Emma's passing to be a blessing to many in some sort of way, and that was down to God. So, co-cooperating with God was my way forward. I didn't feel any special heavenly presence but then do you necessarily get that when you're in a storm? Even with Jesus in the boat with the disciples, the storm still raged until Jesus said stop. I didn't know when the stop would come so my focus was in the present but that didn't come easily either as my mind would wander ahead of the present so it was a constant struggle to return to the now.

At this stage I found it difficult to mask my emotions and feelings from the girls. Hannah was married so not living at home, but Lydia and Connie were subjected to my mood swings and low state. I found myself welling up and breaking down more often in front of them. Initially, I apologised and tried to get a grip but as time went on it became the norm and regretfully, they saw the raw dad more often than not. Most of their lives they had witnessed a dad that could fix things and was a problem solver, ever the optimist as well as a realist. Now they saw a broken man with many failings, floundering.

Friends and family were taking the opportunity to visit Emma in the hospice, and I had to manage that process carefully as Emma had limited energy. I felt very protective as some people were unaware of her needs and sometimes it was more about their needs. I found that everyone had something to say, I'm sure for the right reasons, but we valued the quiet and sometimes just resting and relaxing in the moment rather than having to fill every second with noise.

The darkest day in the hospice was when me and the girls witnessed Emma having her first seizure. I was on the edge as it was and could see that Emma was a bit vacant in her eyes and expression. There was a nurse in the room sorting out her medication when I saw Emma's head fall back and the life seemed to leave her body as her eyes rolled into the back of her head and her mouth remained open. She slid down the chair she was sitting in, and I really thought she had died. A doctor was in the room within seconds and nurses were on hand too. I lost it and burst into tears uncontrollably. I didn't know where to put myself and ran out of the room onto a patio area where I lay face down on the ground. I just wanted to hide and for the ground to swallow me up. I couldn't get any lower as I pressed my head into the ground sobbing. The girls ran out to me and held me and comforted me. I was a mess, and I wasn't there for them. I tried to run away, escape. That's unlike me because ordinarily I would stand and face anything.

The nurses came out to me and said Emma was ok now and that she had had a seizure. I went back into the room after wiping my eyes and composing myself. She was sat up and asked me what had happened. She could see that I was upset and encouraged me to go over to her and she gave me a warm hug and reassured me with gentle words that soothed me. Once things had settled down the consultant called me out of the room and informed me that Emma didn't have long left and it would probably end with a seizure. These words had an echo and it felt surreal as for the first time someone had told me that death was imminent. I kept this information to myself as I couldn't see how the girls would benefit from hearing such devastating news.

When Emma had stabilised over the next couple of days we took her to the Dog Pub in Whittington, which was just a short walk from the hospice. Emma could no longer walk so I wheeled her down in a wheelchair. It was a time of normality where we enjoyed being with Emma, and it felt like we were gathered as a whole family again. But the reality and sadness returned as we took Emma back to the hospice.

Each day I visited Emma I noticed empty beds appearing as sadly patients passed away. I was keen to get Emma back home, despite the hospice doing a great job, we just needed a homely feel with all our life around us.

A few days later Emma was discharged and returned home. We had made the dining room into a cosy place for Emma to live. She looked out onto the garden and the weather was warm and light. These last days were precious. We would go to sleep together but I was up a lot in the night helping Emma go to the toilet and get comfortable. To begin with I could manage lifting her into the wheelchair or onto the commode, but I soon found that it was becoming a more difficult task as my back started to take the brunt of the constant lifting, particularly during the night when I was tired and not as alert. Our bed became uncomfortable for Emma too so we talked about seeing whether we could get a hospital bed that would make Emma comfortable avoiding her developing bed sores and had the ability to sit her up via a remote control.

The local community nurses started to visit to check on Emma and this was well received as a family as Emma had become frailer and more confused. The carers were a Godsend as they washed Emma and made her comfortable. Although it was an incredible privilege caring for Emma, I now understand how being a carer can take its toll on the carer, both physically and emotionally. At one point because the caring for Emma was so intense, I realised that I hadn't showered or brushed my teeth for three days. I was so consumed with getting the medication right and co-ordinating visits and carers that I had neglected myself. I wouldn't believe it myself, but it happened.

One morning Emma awoke and told me that everything was dark, and she couldn't see. The cancer on the brain had interrupted the signals to the eyes and now Emma's sight was gone. Emma was very calm and had a humble acceptance that she was now blind. In addition to losing her sight, the seizures started to increase in frequency. Each time she had one it brought a fear with it because this could be her last moments and they were so traumatic I didn't want Emma to leave that way.

I imagined her slipping away with all of us there saying our goodbyes. I was advised that every time Emma had a seizure, I was to call an ambulance. I wasn't quite sure what the purpose of their attendance would be because Emma had decided she did not want to be resuscitated and I agreed with her decision. Initially, I complied and called the ambulance on the emergency number, but we soon found their arrival caused its own level of stress and the girls in particular found it very stressful. It sounds terrible but we decided that we would allow Emma to have a seizure and allow her to naturally come round or not. Difficult decisions had to be made and this was one of them. It was torturous watching Emma have a seizure and we found it deeply distressing.

Emma was hooked up to a morphine drip now and had regular daily visits from nurses and carers. I sensed that our time was short now, so Emma and I had our final conversations and one of those was late in the evening, which was unusual because she was usually asleep by now. She was looking up at the ceiling and she smiled and said: 'No regrets Kev'. I replied, 'No regrets Em', and I wept. It's like a wave of forgiveness was released over me and any wrongs were swept away by Emma's love for me. We knew that Jesus was giving us a good ending.

For those of you reading that, for whatever reason, don't believe as we do, it may be hard to relate to some of the experiences I'm describing where God shows up and touches us with His presence. It's like a feeling inside that connects with you and somehow you get a feeling that everything is going to be ok. The puzzle is that most of the time it's not predictable of when he's going to show up. But when he does the timing is perfect and we trust that He knows what we need, where and when. Nothing seems to be a breeze even when you're following the one that is all powerful and knows all things and holds all things together. I could still feel the intensity of the pain in our circumstances, but we were not overcome, we were not bitter, we were not angry. We knew that this would be breaking the father's heart too, but suffering and death was part of the human experience, but from where he's looking it's just the beginning of a wonderful life, for those that have chosen to accept him and his invitation to follow him in this life.

For many though this is the end and that's why the finality causes so much pain for many who don't feel or have the reassurance of God's promises. My humanness related to some of those feelings of finality because, although I knew Emma was going to be with Jesus, I still wanted her here with me. I knew I'd never hear her laugh again or have a conversation with her about the girls. I would be alone humanly speaking, separated from the one I chose to do life with. Emma told me that night that she was looking forward to being with Jesus and was excited to seeing what heaven was like and to see her mum. There was no doubt for her where she was going and she told me that although her sight had gone, she could see so clearly.

On September 7, 2018, Emma was in and out of consciousness and our close friends came to visit that evening. I went to the chippy and bought us fish and chips, that we ate whilst sitting around Emma's bed. Her eyes were closed, and she looked beautiful and at peace, no pain and she was breathing regularly.

Peter, Sue, Nigel and Angie recalled stories from our friendship, and we sang some songs too. As Emma had prophesied a few months earlier the four people that she said would be around her bed were there that evening. The day before we had a visit from our pastor, and he sat with me and Lydia and asked us if God could do one thing for us what would it be? I looked at Lydia and then responded by saying that we wanted God to take Emma and release her from her pain and suffering. Lydia nodded in agreement and our pastor prayed.
As we sat around the bed, there was a pause in our conversation and Peter

stood up and with purpose said: 'We all need to go now and leave Kev and Emma alone'. Nig and Angie looked at each other and there was a moment of awkwardness, because it came out of the blue, but to Nig and Angie's credit they could sense this was a God thing and Peter had been moved by the Holy Spirit to act. All four of them promptly left after we had a group hug.

I sat down close to Emma and Bertie; our black Lab came to my side and lay down. The house was quiet, and I sensed something was about to happen, and it did. I watched Emma's breathing slow as I became transfixed with watching her chest rise and fall. Her breathing was quiet and the time for her chest to rise and fall started to take longer, until at 20:58 hours her breathing stopped. I couldn't believe it, I kept watching her chest expecting it to rise again.

This was it; my precious Emma had passed away. I held her hand and thanked her for being my wife and life partner. I placed her hand back on the bed and I closed my eyes to try and take in the moment and find God in it. As I set by her side with my eyes closed, I had a rush of warmth pass through my body. I kept my eyes closed as I sensed that Jesus was in the room. I started to pray in tongues and just savoured the feelings that were washing through my body. I was aware that a blanket of tiredness had wrapped itself around me. I'm sure that part of this was linked to the sense of relief that Emma was free and so were we in a different way. I opened my eyes and made my way to the double bed that was in the room where I normally slept.

I was ready to fall asleep but first I must let the girls know. I dreaded the day that this would become a reality; and now it was here. Lydia and Hannah were in Derby and Connie was at a church youth group party. I called Lydia and Hannah first and they were distraught and started to make their way home immediately. I waited for them to arrive before I called Connie, so that they could help me comfort Connie and each other. Lydia's boyfriend and Hannah's husband were present too.

After I had called them, I lay down and fell straight to sleep only to be awoken by me hearing the front door open. The girls stood in the hallway, and I went out to them. I started to cry as did they and we hugged. There was such a feeling of sadness and heartbreak as we held each other. I asked them if they wanted to see their mum for the last time and initially Hannah didn't want to, but I reassured her that Emma looked peaceful and as if she were asleep. Both Hannah and Lydia went to be with Emma and were clearly impacted by the fact that she had gone. We all sat in the living room next door to where Emma lay.

The girls agreed that Connie now needed to be called. It was a difficult call because I didn't want to share what had happened on the phone, so I just said she needed to come home now. She didn't ask any questions and was dropped off by one of the leaders a short time later. I met Connie at the door and took her through to be with her sisters. Connie is the eternal optimist and kept a quizzical smile on her face but no doubt she could sense that something wasn't right. At that moment she would never have known that her mum had died and was in the next room lying where she last saw her. As she entered the front room the girls held her, and Hannah prepared her by saying that she had some sad news to share with her, but everything was going to be ok because we had each other.
Lydia came alongside Hannah and Connie was embraced by her sisters. I was so glad I had the girls, and this is where they came into their own. As their dad I needed them so much and was so proud of their response. Connie paused and then started to sob in disbelief, saying has mum really gone? Connie didn't go in to be with Emma and we supported her in her choice. She wanted to remember her mum as she last saw her.

I don't think there's a right or wrong approach to this particular issue as we all have a different response at the time. The rest of the night into the morning was very painful as there were certain administrative tasks that had to be completed by me as well as being with the girls in between. No one went to bed, we all stayed together in the front room dazed and numb as we attempted to rest but the reality was, we were lying on the sofas just staring into the darkness trying to make sense of our new reality. So many thoughts racing in my mind, of the funeral and how would we cope, registering the death, cancelling joint policies, bank accounts and bills. Why was I thinking of these things at this time when I should have been focusing on the now?

My thoughts were disturbed by the doorbell, as the GP arrived to examine Emma and certify her death. I was there throughout and silently gazed at Emma as the GP checked her heart and other vital signs. When he had finished, he paid his condolences and left. Next was the Funeral Director to come and collect Emma's body. The girls remained in the front room on my advice as I knew this was going to be traumatic. The woman that I treasured and called my wife was about to leave our family home never to return. It was so final to know the next time I would be with Emma would be at the funeral prior to the cremation.

Two men arrived early in the morning and paid their respects to me as I opened the front door to them. I knew what they had to do because I had been present at many collections of deceased relatives throughout my career in the police. The black body bag seemed so clinical and impersonal for a loved one to be placed in. I stayed out of the room whilst they prepared to take Emma away. I couldn't bear seeing them zip the bag up. I had to hold things together because the girls were very delicate, and I didn't want to use up all my emotional energy on witnessing the unpleasant task that these two very polite men had to do. After they had taken Emma's body to their vehicle, they came back to tell me that Emma would be kept at the Walmley office, that was literally a minute from our home.

I felt so empty and overwhelmed. I felt that I had to be so many things to so many people. My priority now was the girls, but I was clueless on what to do next. There was nothing to fix now, from being Emma's carer to not being her carer in itself left a massive void. It had provided me with routine and stopped me from thinking too much because I was always busy taking Emma to appointments or helping her get around or preparing medication. This whole routine had now stopped.

In a sense, I was relieved because it was over, the day that we knew was coming had come and gone. Our prayer the day before had been answered and one strand of the emotional torment had ended but another sorrowful chord had replaced it. My grieving process although had already started before Emma passing, it had now changed in intensity as I contemplated the thought of not ever having another conversation with her or laughing about silly things. Getting excited about going on holiday or talking and getting excited about the girls' future.

The girls wanted to do something as it seemed unbearable to stay at home. It was too close to the events of the previous evening. We decided to go for a walk, so we agreed to go to Dovedale on a walk over Thorpe Cloud and across the stepping stones on the river Dove below. We would finish our walk at the Isaac Walton pub for some lunch. Looking back, it seems surreal that we were walking within 24 hours of losing Emma. I would discover that a lot of decisions and thought processes would appear odd or untimely when I reflected years later, but at the time it seemed right and sometimes what is right at the time is hard to understand later.

The day of the funeral was soon upon us, and the girls and I had agreed what part we would play in the proceedings. I have a very sketchy recollection of who attended as there were so many people. There was well over 500 people at the church celebration of Emma's life, including the Lord Mayor no less. It was a surreal time that just carried us. The ceremony and other arrangements guided us through the day. Emma wanted white cars so white cars she had. As I scanned the crematorium and the church, I could see lots of familiar faces from different seasons of our life.

I was now a widower, a man no longer a husband., Still a father but one that had lost his balance, his consistency, his fragrance in the wind. I felt a surge of panic and sadness flood through my body as I put my hand on Emma's coffin prior to it disappearing behind the curtain in the crematorium. Emma loved The Carpenters, so we played their song 'Sing' that was a particular favourite of hers. Emma's body would be no more, and this was my final moments of being in her presence. Despite knowing and believing that she was now in the presence of Jesus, in heaven, my humanness didn't want her body to go. It's all I had left but as I touched her coffin for the last time, I said one final goodbye.

Life after Emma's funeral was very quiet in terms of people staying in touch and checking in with us. We needed to be alone, but we needed someone to sit by us. I wanted to forget but I wanted to remember. I felt so lonely and all of us were occupying our own space in our own place of pain and loss. I was constantly checking up on the girls, despite feeling like I had had my arms and legs torn off. I did it out of love and care, but I also felt that I had a duty to pull everyone together and be the strong one.

Not long after Emma's life celebration I felt incredibly lonely I so needed someone to hold my hand. I needed a hug and words of reassurance and affection. I tried to hide these feelings from my girls as I felt guilty because Emma had not long been gone. I knew how this could look from the outside and I was conscious that people were observing how I would cope, well it felt like that anyway. Spiritually I was clinging to Jesus as I was in unchartered territory. Having my girls close was comforting but I craved someone that could look into my eyes and tell me things were going to be ok. I didn't have anyone now that could be that for me. If my mum was alive perhaps she would have supported me and been that person that could have offered me comfort. I felt led to enter a period of 40 days of lament through my grief. I had to be intentional about this setting time aside to think about how I was feeling and drawing off power and healing from the words in the bible, particularly the psalms and proverbs.

I would sit in my snug that leads off from my bedroom and would sit in my cosy chair waiting for God to apply his healing balm to my heart. I didn't have many words; all eloquent prayers were absent. It was as if there was just a faint beacon signal emitting from my soul, expecting God to pick up my signal and see to my need. Although I knew that The Lord was in the middle of the pain, surprisingly the pain was still present, and it was as if I needed to feel the loss and grief and in it, I would depend on his provision.

On one occasion not long after Emma had gone, I was meditating waiting for the Holy Spirit to show up and I heard Emma whisper my name. It was tangible and real. The voice broke into the silence. Was it real? I don't know, but it shocked me, and I remember being motionless to not disturb the moment and to be alert to if anything happened. I don't crave to hear from Emma because my theology is that she's with Jesus and there's no better place to be. I would rather hear from God than Emma. A few people offered words of comfort in the days after Emma passing, saying that she was still with me and walking beside me, guiding me. Not true and although they were well meaning my beliefs were different. When you're gone, you're gone. So, what did I hear? It sounded like Emma, but was it wishful thinking, I don't think so as I didn't expect to hear from her. Hearing what I heard made me smile and look up saying thank you Lord for letting me hear her voice one last time. I never heard anything again.

Although I tried to support the girls I felt wholly inadequate, because the truth was I could hardly manage myself, let alone care for others. I felt extremely guilty about this because I was supposed to be a father that they could come to for comfort and reassurance.

I wanted to meet someone and already my mind was considering how that would happen. How could I think like this so soon after Emma passing? I knew that my girls would disapprove and I found myself being secretive about my feelings and it wasn't the sort of thing I wanted to discuss with them anyway. Naturally I'm a fixer and wanted to fix my problem of needing to be held, loved and comforted. I too wanted to continue being a husband to someone. Being a Christian man; casual relationships weren't an option. I would only be with a woman that was a Christian as our values would be aligned. So, the women that would fit that criteria would be a small pool to fish in. But even thinking this way made me feel disloyal to Emma and I also felt quite desperate and the right thing to do would be to let the grieving process takes its time. In the meantime, to just focus on the girls and heal together as a family. That's not how it happened. The times ahead would be challenging and the most important thing to me, my girls would become casualties of my behaviour. How would life after Emma unravel?

What would my new life look like remarried? Would I manage the complexities of my girls needs and my own? How long would all this take? This part of my journey would be as painful in different ways and will be told as a sequel to this book, to encourage and guide those that choose to embark on that risky journey of love again.

Wisdom/Reflection
- *Jesus is real and eternity belongs to Him. Seek him whilst He may be found*
- *Death is a reality that demands life at the appointed time, but it does not master the follower of Christ*
- *Knowing the eternal destiny of those that have passed is a great comfort*

and promise to those still living
- *Loneliness encourages impatience and pain avoidance. With a loved one gone you will long to be loved. Give it time*
- *You will want to remember but you will want to forget*
- *You will want to be with people but you will want to be alone*
- *Be careful to not let self-pity over your threshold when you're grieving*
- *Sit in your grief and make time to feel it, but anchor your time inviting Jesus to sit with you in your loss*
- *Call on all of heaven's resources to equip you to continue the journey*
- *Invite wisdom to your table as she will serve you well with the decisions you will need to make*
- *Don't try and second guess your children's grief cycle because they are all running a different clock. Be present and let them dictate the pace and activity*
- *Stay connected to your church family and let your grief grow that beautiful fruit that many of us are called to cultivate for the nourishment of ourselves and others*

Emma's Ride a week after Emma had passed. A celebration and tribute to her life from the running and cycling community

Hannah, Lydia and Connie after Em had passed

Trying to do life the best we can with the addition of my first grandson Abel

A personal note to my family present and future.

To my girls, their children and their children's children – You may have the opportunity to read this when I'm alive my precious ones. No doubt some of you may pick this up when I have passed.

Remember this; I thought of you often, even those of you that haven't been born yet. I am confident that despite me not being here, The Lord will bless you, my family line because I trust in his promises. In addition to my hope, I know that you have your own faith journey and experience of God's goodness. BUT you must choose to partner with The Holy Spirit and the rate of your transformation will depend on how much time you put in being in His presence.

You will have days of sunshine, where everything feels good, and you're excited about life. Enjoy these times and savour the moment. There will be dark and rainy days when you feel the whole world is against you and you feel misunderstood. Your trust may have been broken or you may feel that you've been betrayed. You may feel alone and abandoned. It's ok, because I have felt like this, and I can tell you that it will pass. A righteous person has many troubles, but the Lord delivers them from them all. When these times come, reflect on whether you are close to God and either way thank him. Gratitude develops a more hopeful outlook and is the seedbed where The Holy Spirit gets to work to work out your purpose.

Pray whenever you can so that it's a conversation with God. Don't worry if you don't feel you're getting anything back. He will show up and he will answer you. Remember he cares so much for you even if you feel far away and numb. You are always on his mind.
Hopefully, you will still have his written word in time to come. This is your compass, your true north. All of the treasures of God's promises are contained within. The power to change situations is breathed into the words that were declared long ago. Without his word your faith will lack foundation and grounding. Without the flow and relationship with the Holy Spirit you will lack the power and action that proves his word. Proverbs 3 is a scripture I constantly referred to and lived my life by. I would encourage you to, too.

Always find something to laugh at and always look for the good in a situation. Cry with those that cry and laugh with those that laugh.

Look after your body. Exercise and find a discipline that you are naturally good at and enjoy. I loved cycling and working out in the gym. Don't get fixated with fitness and remember that your nutrition is just as important. If it becomes your main focus then you have the balance wrong. Walking the dog may be the only fitness you need with a good diet. BUT never let your desire to be fit, strong and looking good, take precedent over your spiritual routine that will make your soul shine, and is eternal.

Listen carefully to what's being said and hear what isn't being said. Value people and you will always find favour.

Give when no one is watching and always make time for just you and The Father to have heart moments where you are the child, and He is your father. Even if you're all grown up, approach him as His son or daughter.

Be fierce with sin. It is your enemy. Be compassionate with the sinner, and those that offend you. Forgive as you have been forgiven. If you don't, this can create unexplainable barriers and blockages in your life.

And finally, love as much as you can and if you're struggling to love ask the Holy Spirit to pour the Father's love into your heart that will enable you to draw on his love to love. Remember love always wins. One day we will meet and those that knew me may pass on stories about me. I tried to live as a man after God's own heart, but I wasn't always good, caring and gentle. But, towards the end of my life, I learnt and experienced the beautiful grace of God that freed me and softened me.

I pray that the heritage and fervour for Jesus remains in my family line and that you play your part in this wonderful story. You are from a line of prophets so prophesy and declare in power what God has anointed you to do.

Proverbs 3

My child, never forget the things I have taught you.
Store my commands in your heart.
2. If you do this, you will live many years,
and your life will be satisfying.
3. Never let loyalty and kindness leave you!
Tie them around your neck as a reminder.
Write them deep within your heart.
4. Then you will find favour with both God and people,
and you will earn a good reputation.
5. Trust in the Lord with all your heart;
do not depend on your own understanding.
6. Seek his will in all you do,
and he will show you which path to take.
7. Don't be impressed with your own wisdom.
Instead, fear the Lord and turn away from evil.
8. Then you will have healing for your body
and strength for your bones.
9. Honor the Lord with your wealth
and with the best part of everything you produce.
10. Then he will fill your barns with grain,
and your vats will overflow with good wine.
11. My child, don't reject the Lord's discipline,
and don't be upset when he corrects you.
12. For the Lord corrects those he loves,
just as a father corrects a child in whom he delights.